PARENT and CHILD

PARENT and CHILD

Studies in Family Behavior

BY

JAMES H. S. BOSSARD

UNIVERSITY OF PENNSYLVANIA PRESS
PHILADELPHIA

7089
Library of Congress Catalog Card Number: 53 - 9551
Manufactured in the United States of America

To

William T. Carter

and

William Carter Dickerman

in appreciation of their understanding of the requirements of social research

Foreword

FOR a number of years I have been exploring the situations, chiefly in the family, which seem to me to be of basic importance in calling forth the behavior patterns of its members. These explorations have resulted in a series of research studies, the more recent of which are presented in this volume.

A word might be said about the research philosophy underlying these studies. While they were planned with great care, the technique of their execution was subordinated always to the main objective of gaining new insight. It is my firm conviction that research in the field of human behavior often makes the researcher and his methodology too conspicuous, like a suit of loud clothes. Good research technique should place student and technique in the background. To be well dressed means to be dressed inconspicuously, so that the clothes call attention to the person rather than to the clothes. The same applies to research. Good research technique accentuates the problem, not the procedures of its study.

There are various acknowledgments that must be made in regard to this volume. For permission to reproduce parts which had been published previously, I am indebted to the *American Sociological Review, Social Forces, Child Development*, and the *Journal of Abnormal and Social Psychology*. Dr. Eleanor S. Boll and Mrs. Winogene Pratt Sanger, sometime research associates of the Carter Foundation, have contributed much to selected projects reported on in this volume, and have appeared with me as joint authors in some of the material previously published. Finally, this volume owes much to the active support I have received from the Carter family, and it seems proper to dedicate it to two of its members.

JAMES H. S. BOSSARD

Wynnebourn, in Wynnewood, Pa.

Contents

CHAPTER I

Proprieties in the Study of Mankind

The proper study of mankind is man.—ALEXANDER POPE

PEOPLE are the most interesting thing in the world. They tend also to be the most difficult and troublesome. Getting along with them is, for nearly all of us, our most engrossing problem. To meet it successfully is one of the keys to a happy life; to do so readily, it is necessary to understand people—and ourselves.

If the reader cannot accept these statements completely, agreement with them will be sufficiently close, it is hoped, to retain his interest in a book which seeks to contribute to an understanding of human behavior, and particularly in this opening chapter, which is devoted to proprieties in the study of mankind. More specifically, this chapter deals: first, with certain very fundamental difficulties in the study of human behavior; second, in somewhat negative vein, with some prevalent diversions; and third, more constructively, with some obvious proprieties.

TWO FUNDAMENTAL DIFFICULTIES

There are two fundamental and well-nigh universal difficulties which impede progress in the study of behavior. One of these is a certain paradoxical contrast in human nature. This shows itself in a variety of ways. We want to be loved, yet we put obstacles in the way of those who want to love us: this is the perversity of the human heart. We want to resolve the miracle of the relationship between God and man, but we depart constantly from the path of our will to believe: this is the agony of the human soul. We want to understand people, yet we place every obstacle in the path of the inquiring spirit: this is the paradox of the human mind. We seek to develop insights into the problems of life and human living together, but we avoid the costs of organized research: this is the obstinacy of the social tradition. Perhaps Ovid said all this in fewer words when he wrote in his *Metamorphoses* VII: 20-1: *Video meliora proboque, deteriora sequor.* It is the challenge of human behavior that we approve the better but choose to follow the worse.

A second fundamental difficulty is man's attitude toward himself and others. Because he thinks of himself with unseeing pride and of others with condescension or depreciation, it is much more pleasant to rationalize human behavior than to analyze it scientifically. Rationalization is the king of mental sports. Freud and other members of his guild have shown the universality of it as a human habit, and no less a scholar than the late James Harvey Robinson dismissed the major part of what "had passed for social science, political economy, politics, and ethics" as "mainly rationalizing." "This conclusion," he added, "may be ranked by students of a hundred years hence as one of the several great discoveries of our age. . . . As a historical student, I am personally fully reconciled to this newer view."[1]

One comes to the conclusion, albeit reluctantly, that man is not disposed by nature to look at himself objectively. Certainly man is the last thing that man has studied scientifically. The history of science begins with the study of the stars and the far-distant worlds, the story of its development is that of a gradual approach to the study of man and his everyday life. But even here, when he comes to view

[1] *The Mind in the Making.* New York: Harper and Brothers, 1921, pp. 47-48.

himself objectively, he begins with the factors that are most remote. Thus, for example, he studies the theories of marriage more assiduously than the requisites for happy family living. Moreover, he finds the requirements in this self-study a heavy and unpleasant discipline, so that he tends to stray quickly and often, usually to the avoidance of reality and in the direction of wishful thinking. It is more pleasant to live in a world of make-believe, to rationalize the realities of our own selves into the fantasies of Egoland.

There are, however, factors which are influencing modern man to a more realistic approach to himself and his fellows. He lives a life interrelated with a great many other persons, and the greater the density and mobility of population, the greater the degree and scope of interrelatedness. Being forced to deal increasingly and at close range with other persons, he is forced to face the realities of human nature. Then, too, his treatment of other problems is increasingly scientific, and the successes he gains as a result feed his vanity and enthuse him with a sense of his ability to reconstruct life to his own liking. Thus he comes, in spite of himself, to think of mankind with increasing objectivity; thus arises the contemporary interest in the study of human behavior which he hopes will enable him, like another God, to create life within the image of his own desires.

TWO SCIENTIFIC DIVERSIONS

A straight line may be the shortest distance between two points, but man seldom takes it as he moves toward his goals. The history of human effort is one of many diversions from the main objectives, some amusing, some tragic, some trifling, and others yielding unexpected returns. Man's effort to understand his own behavior is no exception; its story is one of many diversions. Two of these are of especial current interest.

The Search for Short Cuts. The first is the search for short-cut explanations of behavior, the effort to identify some one or a few particular traits, or to devise some simple method, on the basis of which the entire personality and its expected behavior could be interpreted or predicted. The search for short cuts is, to be sure, an old and common human interest; it is only when it manifests itself in the field of science, where the emphasis is so much upon comprehensive and thoroughgoing procedures, that it strikes one as a trifle out of place. What becomes still more odd is when these approaches are magnified into the pretense that they are the scientific study of behavior. In this respect, the old regular army sergeant who insisted that all he needed to know about a recruit was to see how "his ears sat on his head" is at one with some of our most recent "scientific" cults.

One of the more naïve of the short-cut diversions was the emphasis a generation ago upon the intelligence rating of the individual. As early as 1908, Dr. Henry Goddard, then with the Vineland Training School for the Feebleminded, brought the Binet scale of testing children from Paris, and utilized it in the classification of inmates of the school. Later on, in perfected and modified forms, these tests were applied to large numbers of school children and, with the development of group tests, to almost two million men in the armed forces of World War I. Great enthusiasm for these intelligence tests developed, with the widespread belief that the giving of a standardized test enabled a properly qualified "expert" so well to rate a person as to place him in his proper occupational, scholastic, and social niche. Soon, at the height of their usage, one qualified as an "expert" by passing a brief summer-school course at some academic institution. Unfortunately many persons were so assigned, often with an air of omniscience and finality, to their great handicap in subsequent time. The fact that the whole personality make-up of the individual had to be considered was established ultimately, but only after a good deal of resistance by the devotees of the short-cut cult.

In the years since, there have been various other short cuts to flash, meteor-like, across the range of one's observation. One of the most recent of these has been the ink-blot technique, otherwise known as the Rorschach Test. This was developed by Dr. Hermann Rorschach, a Swiss psychiatrist, to facilitate the discovery of emotional and mental difficulties. Although published in 1921, his work was not translated into English, so that his technique acquired no vogue until within the past fifteen years. Confined at first to use with children, it has more recently been used to diagnose adult personality traits and problems. Its procedure, in essence, is that of the interpretation, for diagnostic purposes, of reactions of persons to a series of ink blots, and there is much to be said for the opinion that it is not a test at all, but a "psychodiagnostic instrument of the play-technique type."[2] Nevertheless there has been an abounding confidence in its simple use for diagnostic and prognostic purposes. Two examples must suffice.

The People of Alor[3] appeared several years ago as a highly suggestive study of the people of a Netherlands East Indies island. The major body of the volume is an ethnographic account of the Alorese culture. Using this material as a basis of prediction, autobiographies of eight Alorese men and women and thirty-seven Rorschach Tests are then presented as a check of the predictions. The analysis of the latter is particularly intriguing. Dr. Emil Oberholzer devoted fifty-two pages to their discussion. After admitting the lack of a statistical basis for scoring, and the absence of

[2] P. E. Vernon, "The Significance of the Rorschach Test," *The British Journal of Medical Psychology*, 15:200 (1935).

[3] Cora Du Bois, *The People of Alor*. Minneapolis: University of Minnesota Press, 1944.

norms or standards, the conclusion is presented that they can be used cross-culturally (p. 589). Some forty-six pages are devoted to conclusions, including the following: "The Alorese must be lacking in individual personal contact, living beside one another but not with one another" (p. 600). "Lack of responsiveness is as much a part of their being and existence as their egocentricity" (p. 601). "Neurotics, therefore, are undoubtedly not a common phenomenon among the Alorese" (p. 601). "The Alorese are not of a theoretical turn of mind. They are as little given to synthesis, to constructive thinking, to synopsis and correlation, as they are given to problematizing, contemplating, and meditating" (p. 633). The author concludes modestly that any contributions he has made are a tribute to the excellence of the Rorschach records (p. 640). In commenting upon this work, Kardiner later writes: "The value of the Rorschach Test in establishing basic personality was first demonstrated by Emil Oberholzer in connection with the research on Alorese culture."[4]

A pretentious combination of the psychoanalytic method and the Rorschach Test is found in a recent study of the American Negro by Kardiner and Ovesey in the volume just cited. Published under the title of *The Mark of Oppression*, this volume devotes 387 pages to the impact of specific and identifiable pressures upon Negro personality. The psychological aspects of slavery and emancipation are considered in detail, as are also the pressures of the caste system. The basis for this discussion consists of the histories of twenty-five Negroes obtained by the psychoanalytic-interview method and Rorschach Test responses for twenty-four of the twenty-five subjects analyzed. The Rorschach interpretations, presented by Dr. William Goldfarb, were made blind, i.e., he knew only the age, sex, and racial origin

[4] Abram Kardiner and Lionel Ovesey, *The Mark of Oppression*. New York: W. W. Norton Co., 1951, p. 331.

of the subjects. Inferences made are to the effect that "the bulk of their emotional strivings are organized along lines of aggression" (p. 323). "One sees manifest expression of conflict (shock) denial and rejection reaction" (p. 323). "Shading shock (to colored cards) is seen in 100 per cent of the test records. The inference drawn is that these subjects are characterized by intense, pervasive anxiety" (p. 325). "In the individual test interpretations, a compelling, keen desire for status is interpreted in 54 per cent of the group" (p. 326). "Finally in 46 per cent of the cases (7 of 13 males and 4 of 11 females) sexual conflict is conspicuous" (p. 326). Although the chapter ends with a summary of the shortcomings of the Rorschach Test, it begins with the claim that it "is probably the best psychological test for the delineation of character structure."

One hastens to say that this reference to short-cut methods is not meant to depreciate the importance of intelligence or personality tests. Both tests referred to, and others, may be of value. The point emphasized here is their identification, either directly or with more subtle smugness, as the one important test, that here, at long last, is the key to omniscient insight. Perhaps the best way to summarize our own viewpoint is to recall a very old student of personality differences who once said: "Yes, by all means, give all the tests you have, carefully record the results, then tear the record into small bits, and continue with your study." Nor can one resist the opportunity to object to the characterization of large populations on the basis of a handful of cases. One recalls here the old nursery rhyme:

Three wise men from Gotham
Went to sea in a bowl.
If the bowl had been stronger
My tale would have been longer.

The Preoccupation with Methodology. The second scientific diversion of recent years has been the preoccupation with methodology. It may be necessary at this point to reiterate the word "preoccupation" because the basic importance of method cannot be denied. Science, after all, is method, and a rigid insistence upon its soundness is essential in the study of behavior as it is in any scientific procedure. With this acknowledgment to common sense and orthodoxy, two forms of undue concern with methodology may be noted.

One obtains in the use of the case method, by which is meant here the study of the behavior of the individual person. Our objection is chiefly to that small group of students who insist that only the most intricate and subtle psychoanalytic procedure, and interpretation, can reveal the real nature and origin of behavior. The attitude can be illustrated by the story of the two analysts, each walking with his wife. They met accidentally in the park. "Hello," said the first analyst. "I wonder," growled the second one, in a startled aside to his wife, "just what he meant by that?" In other words, white is never white, and black is never black, two facts to be established by merely looking at them. White is really a figment of a neurotic imagination, the result of having been lost as a child in a cotton field, and black only seems so because of a bad case of fright at midnight in a forest in a dream when very young. Furthermore, no interpretation, however fanciful, dare be rejected, because to do so is to be resistant, thereby but proving the soundness of the interpretation. Heads I win, tails you lose.

The other undue concern with method involves certain overly zealous statisticians. Here one finds academic exhibitionism at its best, and worst. Even though the total number of cases is but twenty-seven, let us say for example, with but one or two cases in separate categories, every conceivable statistical technique is applied, sometimes proving, sometimes disproving, the obvious. By way of contrast, one cannot do better here than to quote the words of an outstanding statistician in his presidential address to the members of the American Statistical Association. "There are many problems in economics and sociology or the public health," said Dr. Edwin B. Wilson,

> which are as yet very much in the . . . position where we need not so much some kind of mathematics or some particular statistical technique as a general survey of a wide range of facts, many of them qualitative rather than quantitative, which may serve as a basis for some decision. . . . If choice must be made between familiarity with his subject and familiarity with mathematics, I should unhesitatingly prefer the former. Mathematics is a queer horse and all too easily runs away with its rider; and then there is a satisfaction in trying its various gaits in all sorts of roads that many a rider has gone off in almost the opposite direction from the path he should have followed in his pursuit of the solution to some scientific problem; he may have ridden right over his solution to some purely fantastic goal. . . . In my youth, I acquired an unusually good acquaintance with mathematics. And if in my present studies I use but little of the vast amount I once learned, it is not because I do not like the exercise of using it but because I prefer tools more appropriate to my job even though not so refined—one gets ahead faster.[5]

Nor can one resist the temptation to cite the sage observation of another student who has made such signal contributions to the understanding of behavior. "Taken in themselves," wrote W. I. Thomas, "statistics are nothing more than symptoms of unknown causal processes."[5a]

One hastens to add that the foregoing comments must not be interpreted to imply any depreciation of the quantitative method in science. Assuredly it does have many values. It places a premium upon tangible and quantitative data, and encourages the student to conceive of social facts as much as possible in such forms. There are, of course, dangers in this too, discernible in two directions. One is the exaggera-

[5] Edwin B. Wilson, "Mathematics and Statistics," *Journal of the American Statistical Society,* March 1930, pp. 5-6.

[5a] William I. Thomas, *The Unadjusted Girl.* Boston: Little, Brown and Co., 1923, p. 244.

tion of this tendency, i.e., an overzealousness in squeezing social facts into countable form; and second, the development of an attitude of superciliousness toward facts and investigations which do not permit expression in these forms.

The quantitative method has value, too, in the verification of hunches, i.e., of specific hypotheses, and some sociologists seem to conceive of social research in terms of the statistical verification of hypotheses. This ignores the very obvious fact that a prior and very important part of research in any given area involves the formation of hypotheses.

In regard to methodology, then, my viewpoint is this, that methodology, to be of maximum helpfulness, must conform to two requirements. One of these is a proper balance of, and respect for, the various methods which the scientist may employ. The quantitative is one of these methods, but not the only one. The second requirement is an emphasis upon methodology as an incident, and not an end, in research. It is my observation that research in the field of human behavior often makes the researcher and his methodology too conspicuous, like a suit of loud clothes. Good research technique should place student and technique very much in the background. To be well dressed means to be dressed inconspicuously, so that the clothes call attention to the person rather than the clothes. The same applies to research. Good research technique accentuates the problem, not the procedures of its study.

Perhaps most unfortunate of all is the combination of the short cut and the statistical procedures in the study of behavior. Instances of this kind tend to conform to the following pattern. Some one particular trait of behavior is selected, like picking one's teeth with a pin. One selects, then, a hundred teeth pickers and compares them with a control group who see their dentist twice a year and have no teeth-picking habits. One then looks up the grades in school of both groups. The first group do well in mathematics but score low in chemistry; the second group do poorly in mathematics but do unusually well in chemistry. Conclusion—Don't Pick Your Teeth if You Want to Be a Chemist. With good publicity, one tooth-paste company and a leading chemical company then jump into the gap, setting up a pretentious research project in education for chemistry.

PROPRIETIES IN THE STUDY OF BEHAVIOR

Individual Behavior Is Learned. Behavior is inborn, developing inevitably as do brown eyes or black hair, or it is acquired, like the ability to skate or read Sanskrit. Contemporary scholarship rejects the idea that behavior as such is inherited: the alternative, then, must be that it is acquired.

The conclusion that all behavior is learned behavior runs through a great many specialized studies about human beings. Consider, for example, some of the outstanding studies of delinquent behavior of the past generation. Healy and Bronner, writing more than a quarter of a century ago, pointed out that:

> The moral spirit of a community is easily reflected in the conduct of its children. Where such general spirit is poor there is a very ready imitation of the predatory tendencies of public officials and of other adults who are allowed to persist in evil doing. The knowledge of graft in connection with a city hall, of laxity or venality in a public prosecutor's office, of loose administration of justice in a court (and one of the shrewdest policemen we have ever known has assured us the last point is of vast importance) are all influences that determine trends toward delinquency and crime. One may note this directly exhibited in individual and group lawlessness, and even in youthful self-justification in mis-

doing. Where community spirit in such matters is better, certainly delinquencies are commensurately milder.[6]

The late Edwin H. Sutherland stated the view clearly in his interpretation of white-collar criminality:

> The hypothesis which is here suggested as a substitute for the conventional theories is that white-collar criminality, just as other systematic criminality, is learned; that it is learned in direct or indirect association with those who already practice the behavior; and that those who learn this criminal behavior are segregated from frequent and intimate contacts with law-abiding behavior. Whether a person becomes a criminal or not is determined largely by the comparative frequency and intimacy of his contacts with the two types of behavior. This may be called the process of differential association. It is a genetic explanation both of white-collar criminality and lower class criminality. Those who become white-collar criminals generally start their careers in good neighborhoods and good homes, graduate from colleges with some idealism, and with little selection on their part, get into particular business situations in which criminality is practically a folkway and are inducted into that system of behavior just as into any other folkway. The lower class criminals generally start their careers in deteriorated neighborhoods and families, find delinquents at hand from whom they acquire the attitudes toward, and techniques of, crime through association with delinquents and in partial segregation from law-abiding people. The essentials of the process are the same for the two classes of criminals. This is not entirely a process of assimilation, for inventions are frequently made, perhaps more frequently in white-collar crime than in lower class crime. The inventive geniuses for the lower class criminals are generally professional criminals, while the inventive geniuses for many kinds of white-collar crime are generally lawyers.[7]

Or there is the judgment of the Gluecks:

> *We are thus led to the conclusion that it is not primarily or fundamentally either chance or the fear of punishment, but rather the presence or absence of certain traits and characteristics in the*

[6] William Healy and Augusta F. Bronner, *Delinquents and Criminals.* New York: The Macmillan Co., 1926, p. 191.

[7] Edwin H. Sutherland, "White-Collar Criminality," *American Sociological Review,* February 1940, pp. 10-11.

constitution and early environment of the different offenders, which determines their respective responses to the different forms of treatment and determines, also, what such offenders will ultimately become and what will become of them. Those who behaved well, either during or after treatment, were, as a class, more favorably endowed by Nature and circumstanced by Nurture than were those who did not respond well.[8]

Culture Is Learned Social Behavior. Similar are the conclusions of the anthropologists. Two ideas are basic to their interpretations. One is that "culture *is* behavior—learned ranges of responses common to a group of human beings," is the way one of them puts it.[9] Second is the emphasis that culture is learned. It is what people have learned about the problems of living; an accumulation of their experiences, evaluations, and insights. As such it is superorganic and super-individual. While participated in and produced by individuals, it is social and cumulative, comprehensive yet pervasive. Much, perhaps most of it, becomes regularized in the form of habits. Culture, then, as Ralph Linton and others have pointed out, is a set of habits, an arbitrary but selected set of patterns of action and thought.

Into this existing culture or complex of social experience, the individual is born. As he grows up, he is inducted into this culture. Thus the new-born infant becomes an East Side New York American boy, a Tahitian lad, a Japanese youth, or a Russian boy, dependent upon the culture into which he is inducted. This is the process of socialization or personality formation, which is essentially the process of learning the culture. Kluckhohn, in popularizing anthropology for laymen, puts it this way: "Like rats learning to run a maze that has food at its exit, children grad-

[8] Sheldon and Eleanor Glueck, *Criminal Careers in Retrospect.* New York: The Commonwealth Fund, 1943, p. 285.

[9] John L. Gillin and John Philip Gillin, *An Introduction to Sociology.* New York: The Macmillan Co., 1942, p. 128.

ually familiarize themselves with the well-trodden but often devious intricacies of the cultural network."[10]

Personality Formation a Learning Process. But learning does not take place in a vacuum. We learn from other people, and what we learn has meaning in terms of our relations with other people. This leads to the sociologists' emphasis upon personality formation, not only as the result of cultural conditioning, but also of group life. Behavior patterns grow out of social interaction, they result from the interplay of person with person. Behavior and personality are social concepts and social products: they result from social contacts. The main groups in which these contacts occur are, of course, the family, the play and other peer groups, and then later in life the neighborhood, the community, and the larger society.

Experience as the Schoolmaster. How do we learn? This is the next question that presents itself. And the answer is obvious. We learn from experience. All current theories of behavior agree that it is the product of experience. "The first and last schoolmaster of life is living,"[11] wrote Thornton Wilder. Group behavior, as reflected in the folkways, mores, and values, is the product of group experience; and individual behavior is the result of individual experience, within the complex of the existing group patterns.

The meaning of all this for the study of behavior at once becomes clear. To study the behavior of a person, one must study his experience or life history. Behavior is a historical product, an accumulation of responses resulting from the life history of the individual. The simplest, yet the most exclusive and pervasive, definition of personality is to say that it is what a person is to start with, plus what he has gone through. It is this phrase, *what he has gone through,*

[10] Clyde Kluckhohn, *Mirror for Man.* New York: McGraw-Hill Book Co., 1949, p. 205.

[11] Thornton Wilder, *The Ides of March.* New York: Harper and Brothers, 1948, p. 35.

which is the clue to the proper study of mankind. Just as we study the intellectual history of a people to understand their contemporary ideas, so the only adequate way to understand a person is to learn how he got that way. Behavior and personality are never finalities: they are processes.

Social Learning a Continuing Process. One specific implication of the foregoing deserves special consideration, and that is its bearing upon the question of the time period when personality is "fixed." It has been popular in certain circles in the past to assume that behavior patterns are formed for the most part in the first few years of the child's life. The first six or seven years have usually been identified as the all-important ones.

The results of this belief have been unfortunate in many instances. Some parents, accepting this view, have concluded that, since their children had reached the end of the seventh year without untoward symptoms, their responsibility to the next generation's behavior had been discharged. Others decided that, since the early years of their children's lives had presented certain behavior problems, the situation for the future was for them rather hopeless. Still other parents, in their great fears that they traumatize their children during these years, succeeded only in becoming neurotic themselves.

The concept of behavior and personality as the result of a learning process disposes once and for all of these undue emphases. Since learning is a continuing process, it must be obvious that behavior patterns can attain to no finality at any age or stage of development. One goes on learning all through life. True, the rate of learning, the disposition to do so, the nature of the process, and the kinds of things learned, may vary through the years. If learning were confined to the first few years, then this book would not have been written, and even more obviously, there would be no readers for it. We agree entirely with Brown, when he writes:

> Too much emphasis has been placed upon childhood experiences per se. In reality, subsequent experiences determine the importance of these early activities. . . . The individual is not a product of his childhood but is the result of what adolescence, youth and adulthood do to childhood experiences. Each subsequent period becomes a testing place for the human nature developed in a preceding period.[12]

The Role of Experimental Psychology. Agreement is rather general upon the sequence of ideas thus far presented: it is from here on that disagreement raises its head. Many students of behavior conclude at this point that the next step is to study the laws and processes of learning, as found in the field of experimental psychology. Such attempts have followed the lead chiefly of Miller and Dollard.[13] Murdock, for example, has written: "If culture is learned, it must obey the laws of learning, which the psychologists have by now worked out in considerable detail."[14] Similar is Gillin's conclusion: "If we admit that culture is learned, we must then go to psychology for the basic principles of learning and behavior which have been tested by experimental procedures on man and other animals."[15] But the best-known example of an analysis of socialization through the learning theories of psychology is Whiting's study of the Kwoma.[16]

[12] Lawrence Guy Brown, *Social Pathology.* New York: F. S. Crofts and Co., 1942, p. 11. *See also* Weston LaBarre, "The Age Period of Cultural Fixation," *Mental Hygiene* (New York), April 1949, pp. 209-21; and Earl J. Simburg, "Must Our Children Be Neurotic?" *ibid.*, January 1951, pp. 96-103.

[13] Neal Miller and John Dollard, *Social Learning and Imitation.* New Haven: Yale University Press, 1941.

[14] George P. Murdock, "The Cross-Cultural Survey," *American Sociological Review,* June 1940, p. 264.

[15] John L. Gillin, *The Ways of Men.* New York: Appleton-Century-Crofts, 1948, p. 190.

[16] John Whiting, *Becoming a Kwoma.* New Haven: Yale University Press, 1941.

Interesting and significant as this approach may be, it would seem to fall within the province of experimental psychology. If so, what then is left for other sciences, like sociology? Should they seek to become experimental psychologists? This kind of thing has happened often in the past history of sociology. Its development has been retarded because, throughout its history, its devotees have strayed repeatedly into adjacent but nonsociological fields. One can only hope that this phase of the work will be left to psychologists, and recognized as but an incidental aspect of the main quest for an understanding of why we behave as we do.

The Minutiae of Experience. The hypothesis presented here is that progress in the understanding of human behavior must come chiefly from the completeness of the history of its development. The history of experience and the learning process must be detailed, very detailed. That is just what it has not been, for the most part, and that is why much of the interpretation of behavior, while academically impressive, is pragmatically of lesser value.

James Boswell, that stalwart biographer, recorded the point many years ago. "I told Dr. Johnson," he entered into his diary under date of July 16, 1763, "that I put down all sorts of little incidents in it. 'Sir,' said he, 'there is nothing too little for so little a creature as man. It is by studying little things that we attain the great knowledge of having as little misery and as much happiness as possible.' "[17]

From whom and from what does one learn? Who now can tell? A chance word, a breathless view, a superficial satisfaction, a smarting hurt, a good book, a boresome play, a near accident, a burnt finger—the list is endless. The process of living is a continuing process, which goes on for the most part unconsciously. That is why we miss the boat

[17] Frederick A. Pottle, *Boswell's London Journal.* New York: McGraw-Hill Book Co., 1950, p. 305.

so often in the study of behavior. We are blind to the significance of details in the continuum of experience. It has been a trite saying for many years that it is the little things in life that count: so true that it seems naïve to repeat it; yet we have not yet recognized it in the study of behavior.

A major part of the study of personality formation, then, is the study of the minutiae of living. Life is, from one point of view, a series of detailed experiences, laid end to end. Or, to change the metaphor, personality formation is like the ceaseless wash of waves upon the shore. True, there is an occasional storm, when the waves of experience beat high, so that the whole shoreline may change overnight, but mostly it is a quiet, ceaseless lap of the waters that creates and molds the substance of the shore. It is so in the history of human experience. Some are spectacular and impressive, opening up vast vistas or leaving ugly scars, but personality and character are mostly the result of a slow and usually uneventful accumulation of the minutiae of experience.

The study of the minutiae of living is in large measure a study of the commonplace aspects of everyday life, and it is the role of the commonplace which has been most often overlooked. Because so much of what makes us tick is as common as the air we breathe or the water we drink, we ignore its role and go on to study the exotic and the unusual, and the unfortunate part of this is that these are the studies that are recognized as scholarship, while the patient study of the commonplace is labeled as interesting but not important. This repeats in essence the history of science, where the movements of the heavenly bodies became the focus of serious study long before the behavior of children received a casual attention. I have emphasized elsewhere some of the aspects of everyday living which mold behavior,[18] and it is on the permanent and perennial impor-

[18] James H. S. Bossard, *The Sociology of Child Development.* New York: Harper and Brothers, 1948, chaps. VIII-XII.

tance of the commonplace, detailed minutiae of everyday living as the matrix in which behavior is formed that I am willing to stake any claim to professional status.

To insist that the accumulating minutiae of life's experience have to be known to understand behavior does not mean that its study is dull or drab or devoid of thrill. These minutiae may center about great events or spectacular figures. The details of Washington's surveying expedition, as recorded by Freeman in his life of Washington, are but the daily routine of a budding engineer in an unexplored area, but they give a better understanding of the formation of the character of a great American than a library of generalization. Similarly, a boy's daily contacts with an inspiring teacher may fall under the general heading of trivia, but they may be the explanation of a life of outstanding achievement.

Here are the great unexplored areas for the study of behavior formation—the detailed experiences of childhood visiting, a weekly walk with a stimulating uncle, basketball in the parish house, the contents of childhood books, a series of petty achievements, a succesion of embarrassing experiences, the deeply effective role of shame, the endless talk at mealtime, the acquisition of words, the imitation of gestures, the ways of greeting people, modes of expression, habits of conversation. These are the grist of the mill of life, and they are unmentioned in treatises on behavior or in the discussions of the personality experts.

Sumner has a sense of this slow, down-to-earth accretion of behavior patterns. He states it for the group rather than for the individual:

> The folkways . . . are not creations of human purpose and wit. They are like products of natural forces which men unconsciously set in operation, or they are like the instinctive ways of animals, which are developed out of experience, which reach a final form of maximum adaptation to an interest, which are handed down by tradition and admit of no exception or variation, yet change to

meet new conditions, still within the same limited methods, and without rational reflection or purpose. From this it results that all the life of human beings, in all ages and stages of culture, is primarily controlled by a vast mass of folkways handed down from the earliest existence of the race, having the nature of the ways of other animals, only the top-most layers of which are subject to change and control, and have been somewhat modified by human philosophy, ethics, and religion, or by other acts of intelligent reflection.[19]

Documents for the Study of Behavior. For the study of this process in the life of the individual, the best documents include, as W. I. Thomas pointed out, case studies, life records, psychoanalytic confessions; in fact, anything that represents a continuity in life situations. "We are safe in saying that personal life-records, as complete as possible, constitute the *perfect* type of sociological material."[20] Elsewhere he explains that "the life history is an autobiographic narrative which should be as detailed as possible, and unguided except for inventories of items to assist the subject in a relatively complete anamnesis."[21]

In recent researches conducted under the auspices of the William T. Carter Foundation at the University of Pennsylvania, it has been found fruitful to secure segments of life histories, devoted to or centering around some specific phase of experience. The study of Childhood Visiting, which appears as a chapter later in this volume, was carried through almost entirely on this basis. A large number of younger persons were encouraged to record in detail their recollections of experiences on visits away from home as

[19] William Graham Sumner, *Folkways.* Boston: Ginn and Co., 1906, p. 4.

[20] Edmund H. Volkart, *Social Behavior and Personality.* New York: Social Science Research Council, 1951, p. 147.

[21] *Ibid.*, p. 297. *See also* Louis Gottschalk, Clyde Kluckhohn, and Robert Angell, *The Use of Personal Documents in History, Anthropology and Sociology.* New York: Social Science Research Council, Bulletin 53, 1945; John Dollard, *Criteria for the Life History.* New Haven: Yale University Press, 1935; and S. S. Sargent and M. W. Smith, *Culture and Personality.* New York: The Viking Fund, 1949.

children. These constitute, then, life-history documents related to a specific subject and, when contributed by persons with training and facility in expression, and on subjects relatively free from inhibitions, serve as helpful source material in the study of the experience history of the individual.

Reasons for Ignoring the Obvious. The preceding pages have but stated the obvious, and the undone. Why then has behavior not been studied in this manner? Candor compels us to present four reasons.

1. The role of the publication market. New insights into the understanding of behavior, to be recognized, must be publicized. But publication of research is problematical. The market for scientific publication is not too unlike that of the daily press. In the latter, the vagaries of a married man with a blonde are first-page stuff; the good life he leads with his wife has no news value. In like manner, an interpretation of the development of normal children pales before a book on delinquency. The normal and the obvious find it difficult to compete with the exotic, the bizarre, and the unusual.

2. The folkways and mores of the academic world combine to reward the study of the abnormal, abstract, and the remote. To become a great scholar, one is counseled to study the sex cycle of the tsetse fly in Isrataria. Since no one knows where Isrataria is, and comment of the sex cycle of any kind of fly is academically acceptable, professional recognition for such work is prompt and generous. Should one, unwisely, study the sex life of boys on the university campus, both tenure and rank are imperiled.

3. The lack of historical perspective is obvious in much of contemporary thinking. Someone has said, rather aptly, that the trouble with modern man is that he has not read the minutes of the preceding meeting. This lack is amazing, in view of the implications of the evolutionary approach, in

which so many leaders of thought have been trained. Perhaps the explanation lies in our preoccupation and pride in our technical innovations. Since the people who lived in 1900 did not have Cadillac cars with a rear that looked like two salmon swimming up stream, it is assumed that their understanding of everything must have been wholly inadequate. In fact, the whole trend of the Instrumental Theory which dominates modern thought is to emphasize that which one can become, not what one has been or gone through.

4. The wishful forgetting of ancestry. There is perhaps a larger aspect to the lack of historical perspective, and that is the apparent unwillingness of so many contemporary Americans to think of their own past. One hastens to add at once that this must not be interpreted to mean that such people have criminal records or skeletons of various kinds in their closets which they wish to hide. The reference is rather to the fact that they have risen in the world, that they have raised their status in our open-class society, that they have outgrown their kin and their ancestral hearth. People who are on the up do not want to think of their past; they want to grasp toward their future. Margaret Mead has written of this as the wishful forgetting of ancestry.[22]

The Study of Social Situations. The minutiae of life, which we have been emphasizing, need, however, to be considered in terms of a framework. This is the second and complementary part of the thesis presented in this chapter. In order to assess their real meaning, the detailed data of experience must be considered in relation to each other. This leads to the concept of the situation.

The situation is the combination of circumstances that calls forth behavior. "A situation," we have written elsewhere, "consists of a number of stimuli, external to the organism but acting upon it, organized as a unit and with a

[22] Margaret Mead, *And Keep Your Powder Dry.* New York: William Morrow and Co., 1943.

special relatedness to one another as stimuli of the specific organism involved."[23] The situation presents itself, the individual recalls similar situations, his experiences in dealing with them, and his behavior follows. All behavior is purposive in relation to the situation which calls it forth. It is a solution to the problem or "crisis" which the situation presents, an answer to or definition of the situation, made by the individual on the basis of other situations and previous experience. Situation, evaluation, behavior, experience are so many parts of an endless circle of living, with each part taking its meaning from the circle as a whole.

It is not meant to infer that behavior is the result always of conscious reflection and reasoned judgment: Behavior really stems from three sources, or, putting it another way, operates at three levels. One consists of compulsions, unconscious as a rule and neurotic often, which result from experiences of a forgotten past. This is the area which the psychoanalyst emphasizes and probes. Second are the habits of the person, with neural pathways worn smooth and functioning readily because of long-continued usage. Finally, there is the level of conscious choice, involving judgment, values, inertia, expediency, calculation, risk, and the like. "The crown of life," Wilder reminds us, "is the exercise of choice."[24]

It is one of the contentions of this chapter that social situations can be relatively isolated, described, classified, and evaluated in an orderly, inductive procedure. There are a number of studies which fall within the province of our concept of social situations. Analyses of culture, studies of group structure and functions, background factors in the production of delinquency, are illustrations of this kind. Most of these studies, however, either are general in character or were developed to serve other ends.

[23] Bossard, *op. cit.,* p. 38.
[24] Wilder, *op. cit.,* p. 15.

As an illustration of an inductive analysis of social situations, the reader is referred to a study by Becker and Useem.[25] They present a sociological analysis of the dyad, or pair grouping, pointing out its configurations, characteristics, limitations, division of functions, and prevailing types. There is a distinctively sociological approach to a distinctive kind of social situation, analyzed per se. Such an analysis is helpful, not only in understanding the behavior of the members of the dyad, but also as a situation confronting nonmembers who are brought into contact with it.

Another illustration of the significance of changes in a given situation in the behavior of a child can be found in a case study made by the author and his research associate.[25a] This records in detail the behavioral results of a change in the home situation of a young child over a seven-week period, as noted by two trained observers.

Background Information: Cynthia was seven and a half at the time of this experience. She is an only child of intelligent parents. The father is a graduate of a well-known university, with postgraduate work in two noted American universities. The mother held a responsible and remunerative position for some years previous to her marriage. The father is now engaged in professional work, and the mother, until recently, devoted herself to housework and the rearing of the child. Both parents are well read and of personable appearance.

Cynthia's family has lived in an apartment hotel, in a one-bedroom apartment. Cynthia has lived in this apartment during her entire life. Absences from it have been of short duration. During these years, Cynthia has developed a series of behavior patterns within the apartment and adjusted to its physical features and expanse. The mother summarizes these under five heads. (*a*) While the mother is busy, Cynthia plays with her toys, cuts

25 Howard Becker and Ruth H. Useem, "Sociological Analysis of the Dyad," *American Sociological Review*, February 1942, pp. 13-26.

25a James H. S. Bossard and Winogene Pratt Sanger, "Social Mobility and the Child: A Case Study," *Journal of Abnormal and Social Psychology*, April 1949, pp. 266-72.

out paper dolls, plays house with them, colors crayon books, and reads to her mother. Occasionally she tries to help her mother: she will dust, keep her toys in order, and arrange in orderly fashion her belongings in a chifforobe. (*b*) When the mother is not busy, she and Cynthia go to nearby parks and playgrounds, or other recreational facilities. As soon as they get there, Cynthia tends to forget her mother's existence, eagerly participating in activities, and, at times, wandering away so far and so long that her mother becomes apprehensive. (*c*) She has a close relationship with her mother on these trips. They walk both ways, regardless of distance, and talk in intimate and friendly fashion of Cynthia's experiences. (*d*) Cynthia is obedient at home, observing relatively well the rules of conduct laid down by her mother, such as times to go to bed, to get up, to dress, and to arrange her toys. (*e*) Behavior of Cynthia is rather routinized, especially when she and her mother are alone. The presence of the father may lead to some deviation from this routine, but Cynthia is so attached to her mother that her life is organized about her, and, so long as she knows where her mother is and what she is doing, Cynthia follows the above pattern.

From this routinized life, Cynthia was transplanted suddenly to living in a house. The house is a suburban one, with fourteen rooms and four baths. It is located on an estate of about two acres, handsomely landscaped, and with a planting of some eighty trees. Cynthia had not lived in the house before, and had seen it only on a brief visit when she came to look at a nest of newly hatched robins. When Cynthia came to live at this house, there were only two other occupants, her mother and another woman. This other woman did not participate to an appreciable extent in the living routine of Cynthia and her mother.

Methodological Note: Cynthia's behavior in the new situation was observed for a period of seven weeks. These observations were recorded at the close of each day by two persons. One of these was Cynthia's mother; the other person, living with them, was a professional observer. The mother, knowing Cynthia's routine behavior before coming to live in the new home, devoted herself to noting and recording changes from Cynthia's early routinized behavior. The other observer noted the new patterns without knowledge of the previous routines. Observations were recorded independently, and in considerable detail. The remainder of this article summarizes their observations. Since the change in residence was the only change in Cynthia's setting, save for the inconspicuous presence of the second observer, it is contended that the changes in Cynthia's behavior may be attributed wholly or largely to the change in home setting. The problem posed is this: How did this change in home and scale of living affect Cynthia's customary behavior, as revealed in her activities, talk, and interests? Cynthia apparently had no knowledge of being observed, both adults living in normal relation to her. The mother merely continued her past relation; the other adult was favorably but not actively regarded by Cynthia.

Summary of Observations on Cynthia's Behavior:

1. When Cynthia came to the house, she was given a separate bed in a large room, to share with her mother. This impressed her very much, and almost from the beginning she gave evidence of a strong sense of possession. She insisted on making her own bed. She resented her mother's placing some of her toilet articles on Cynthia's dressing table. She did not want anyone to sit on her bed. A part of this feeling may have been due to the fact that she occupied a bed which had previously been occupied by an older girl whom Cynthia admires very much and who seems rather glamorous to her. She speedily showed signs of identifying herself with this older girl. The idea of a shower bath next to her bedroom impressed her. She told a girl friend that everyone in the house had a bath or shower right next to her bed. She took this girl friend into the house and showed it to her with evident pride. She had also been careful of things in the house. She seems to act as if everything were hers and had to be taken care of constantly.

2. Almost from the first day, Cynthia began to show evidence that she thought the house was something to be lived up to. Always interested in her personal appearance, according to her mother, she now insisted on changing her clothes twice, and more often, daily. She consistently refused to wear the same clothes in the afternoon as she did in the forenoon. When her mother remonstrated with her concerning the speed with which she was using up her clean clothes, Cynthia pointed out that now that she was living in a house it was necessary to do this. Throughout the entire seven-week period, she insisted on looking her best, consistently refused to, or protesting against, wearing her old clothes, and insisting on wearing her new clothes which "were right with the house." On the fourteenth day of her residence in the house, she became interested in combing her own hair. Soon she would

change the hair-do as often as four times in a half day, and on the twenty-sixth day she combed her hair eight times before two o'clock in the afternoon. Combined with the hair changes would be changes in clothes, often four or five times a day, "now that we live in a house." On the thirty-fifth day, she changed her clothing five times and put up her hair seven times. On this day, she also experimented with lipstick and rouge.

On the thirty-sixth day, the mother comments as follows: "Cynthia is having the time of her life. She feels as big as anybody in this house, at being a part of this big place and the people living in it. She has just now walked around and absorbed every bit of this place. With no children about, she has been so busy being an adult that she has spent almost no time being a child. It was not until yesterday that she spent any time roller-skating, and got down for a short time to playing at being a child. Up to now she has just been soaking up this house, trying to live up to it."

On the thirty-eighth day, while busily engaged in trying new hair arrangements and experimenting with lipstick, she confides to her mother that she is having the best time she ever had. This is the best summer she can remember. Yet she had relatively few contacts with children, she has not been read to as is done customarily, and she has not asked for most of the customary things and activities. While Cynthia tells her mother about the summer, the mother notices a smug expression on her face and notes that she seems tremendously pleased with herself.

3. Early during the period under consideration, Cynthia's mind turned to the problems involved in the acquisition of a house in which to live. Beginning with the second week, Cynthia would notice other homes whenever she and her mother went into the city from their suburban home, and ask questions about them. "How much do homes cost?" she would ask her mother time after time. Then she would ask: "How much money do you have, mother?" "How much do you earn, mother?" Finally she offered to give her mother two dollars she had saved and relinquish her rights to her weekly allowance of twenty-five cents to make possible the purchase of a house. Almost daily, for several weeks, Cynthia would turn to her mother, often several times a day, and say: "Don't you like living in this house?"

On the twenty-third day of her stay in the house, Cynthia talked to the owner of the home. Almost at once she began to ask him all kinds of questions. How much did he earn? Why did he get so much money? What did he pay for the house? How much did he want for it if he sold it? Do you have to pay anything to anybody after you buy a house? When the idea of taxes was explained to her, she asked how much the taxes cost on this house. How much is that a month? How much do you earn a month (evidently comparing his with her mother's monthly earnings)? Do you like me? Do you like my mother? Which one of us do you like the more? "You need not be afraid to tell me."

A week later, the owner again came to call, and was invited to have lunch with Cynthia and her mother. While the lunch was in progress, Cynthia asked quite suddenly: "Mother, are you going to change your name soon?" Her mother replied: "Why child, how would I change my name?" To this Cynthia replied, with a nervous little laugh, that she might marry Mr. Blank (the owner of the home).

On the thirty-second day, Cynthia noticed that the linoleum on the kitchen floor was not in keeping with the rest of the kitchen and the house, and she told her mother that it was not as nice as the linoleum in the kitchen in the hotel apartment where she had lived, and she asked her mother if she thought the owner of the house knew that the linoleum needed his attention.

Two days later, Cynthia's father visited her mother and her. Cynthia promptly took her father around, showing him every nook and corner of the house, her room in particular, her bath, the grounds surrounding the house, and the neighborhood area about the home. While doing so, she remarked over and over again that she likes the house and enjoys living there. The following day, Cynthia again asked her mother how much money she had, and renewed her offer to give her her savings of two dollars in order that she might buy the home.

4. Both observers note constantly, throughout the seven-week period, how much Cynthia is constantly "under foot." At her former apartment home, she plays, reads, or knits by herself by the hour. From the first day on, while living in the house, she constantly follows her mother, scarcely permitting her to go out of sight. There is a swing outdoors, a hammock, a croquet set, games of various sorts, a piano to play indoors, various indoor games, a large desk at which to draw and write, and many children's books and games. Cynthia goes to all of these things, but stays with them for scarcely more than a minute. She goes outdoors, swings for perhaps a minute, and comes in to her mother. Next, she goes

to the piano, drums on it for a minute at most, then proceeds to look up her mother. At times she seems to act as though she feared her mother might be lost, at other times she behaves as though she were trying to keep her hand in every activity that went on in the house. On the nineteenth day, both observers refer to her as having become quite a "little itch," talking into everything, not letting older people talk, following everybody everywhere.

This leech-like behavior continues during the entire period of this study. On the thirty-second day, her mother spoke to her, a bit testily, about her being constantly under foot. To this Cynthia replied: "If I don't stay close to you, mother, I don't know where you are. Every time I look for you, you are in a different place." When Cynthia does not tag after her mother, she does so after the other adult observer. This habit of keeping close to adults, noted repeatedly by both observers, is referred to by the mother as being in marked contrast to her behavior previously. In her former apartment home, Cynthia is active with only a slight and occasional sign of awareness of her mother's presence.

Several times, during the seven-week period, Cynthia and her mother came into town to the office where the mother is employed when not on vacation. Here, in the crowded city, Cynthia walks four city blocks away from the office, through unexplored territory, even entering a store and asking the proprietor about the cost of a Mickey Mouse watch in the window. In other words, timidity and a holding close to adults in the quiet of a suburban estate; boldness and adventure for the apartment-reared child on the streets of a crowded, noisy city.

Toward the close of the period, the mother comments that, while living in the apartment, Cynthia seemed to feel safe and assured because the mother's whereabouts were relatively fixed; in the large house, her mother moves about, and this creates a feeling of insecurity and uncertainty in Cynthia. The mother now thinks that Cynthia's being constantly "under foot" is the result of her need to keep in touch with "the home base," as it were, amidst surroundings that suddenly are quite different in size and complexity. (During the seven-week period, Cynthia and her mother made a hurried two-day trip to the former apartment home. During the time there, Cynthia promptly returned to her old pattern of keeping occupied in the apartment without coming near or paying any attention to her mother.)

5. Cynthia gives evidence constantly of being impressed by the

lack of people in her new surroundings. Her former hotel-apartment home was in the down-town section of a large city, in the heart of the down-town hotel residential area. Here Cynthia is accustomed to seeing many people, and at all times. Transferred to the quietness of a suburb, she says, "The pavements are so empty." She says that she likes to see people walking on the pavement, and it is lonesome when there aren't a lot of people hurrying around on the pavement. Nevertheless, during the entire seven-week period, she has not once asked to be taken anywhere, even with two favorite cousins living less than a mile away. This is in marked contrast with her behavior previously, when she teased her mother constantly to be taken to places, especially where there are recreational facilities.

6. In contrast to the foregoing, and perhaps by way of answer to it, is the rate of conversational flow from Cynthia since living in the house. Cynthia verbalizes readily, according to the mother, at all times, mostly the childish prattle characteristic of her age. During the period herein reported on, this rate has been greatly increased. Both observers agree that she has talked incessantly, to anyone "on sight," ranging from mother to cleaning woman, laundress, and gardener. Much of this conversational flow has been disjointed, a jumping from one thing to another, as though overstimulated. As time went on, this talkativeness developed to the point where she would start sentences, without knowing in the slightest what she was going to say, as though she wanted to hold the floor, conversationally speaking, until she could think of something to say. Curiously enough, when taken into the office and the crowded city, Cynthia would leave her mother, stop talking even when sitting with her mother in the office, or slip outside and wile away an hour in perfect quietness on the busy city street. On returning to the quietness of her suburban home, Cynthia's volubility was at once resumed.

Changes in residence and scale of living, suddenly thrust upon a child, and with few other changes in living circumstances, were followed by six discernible changes in behavior, as noted constantly in the daily notes of two participant observers. These are as follows: (1) Marked increase in sense of possession and responsibility for things possessed. (2) Change in scale of personal behavior to conform to the new living conditions. (3) Preoccupation with means of acquiring a similar setting, even to the point of suggesting that the mother do so through a new marriage.

(4) Feelings of insecurity and uncertainty to the point of fear of being lost, or of losing the mother. (5) Feelings of isolation because of lack of constant contact, yet "hugging" the new isolation. (6) Marked increase in verbalization.

SUMMARY

This chapter has attempted to emphasize selected proprieties in the study of behavior. It is in no way intended as a theory of behavior or behavior study. The outline for such study has been presented in other publications.[26] The purpose has been rather to emphasize the following facts.

1. Two fundamental difficulties in the study of human behavior are (a) certain paradoxical contrasts in human nature, and (b) man's tendency to rationalize behavior, particularly his own.
2. Two scientific diversions may impede progress in the understanding of behavior: (a) the search for short-cut explanations, and (b) the preoccupation with methodology.
3. Proprieties in the study of behavior include the following: (a) individual behavior is learned; (b) culture is learned behavior; (c) personality formation is a learning process; (d) experience is the schoolmaster of life; (e) experimental psychology can study its procedure; (f) the minutiae of life need to be emphasized; (g) the chief sources for their study are life-history documents; (h) the minutiae of life operate in terms of, and as responses to, social situations; and (i) social situations can be studied objectively.

[26] *Cf.* Bossard, *op. cit.* Also, James H. S. Bossard and Eleanor S. Boll, *Ritual in Family Living.* Philadelphia: University of Pennsylvania Press, 1950, chap. 10.

CHAPTER II

The Family as a Group

Man is social, even in his egotism.—SANTAYANA

THE group concept is fundamental in sociological thinking. This is inevitable because people, particularly in contemporary society, do not live isolated lives, in vacuo. Moreover, group life is indispensable for human development. It socializes the individual, and it is through the medium of the group that the impact of culture is stamped upon the individual. The role of group life in general, and of any group in particular, varies from one culture to another, and from one stage of individual development to another, but such variations are but differences of degree in an importance that is both pervasive and fundamental.

The role of the group is particularly great in the child period of life. The child begins life with a total dependence upon the group, customarily the family group, and the lessening of his dependence upon this first group, as the years go by, is but part of a larger process whereby he transfers his allegiance to, and dependence on, other groups. Freedom from the family group is paid for or exchanged by dependence upon other groups.

The elaboration of this concept of the family as a group, and a project in group living, is the substance of this chapter. Its aim is to emphasize, by way of correction and revision of past omissions, this concept of the family as a group. Although the importance of the group as a determinant in the development of the personality is generally recognized, specific studies of groups as such have been confined largely to play groups, peer groups, the clique, the gang, and the like. When students have turned to the first group of which the individual is a member, that group is studied as *the family*, and not as a group. As a result, the family has not been studied sufficiently within the group frame of reference; research studies in the family have been slow in recognizing that the generic problems and processes of group life are pertinent leads for inquiry in their particular area. The point emphasized here obviously is one of degree: the insistence is that more consideration be given to the family as a species of the group genus. It is to a consideration of the child's first family experiences as group experiences that most of this chapter is devoted.

THE CHILD'S FIRST GROUP EXPERIENCES

To avoid confusion in the present discussion, it is necessary to clarify our usage of the group concept. To do so, one may with propriety begin with Small's definition: "The term 'group' serves as a convenient sociological designation for any number of people, larger or smaller, between whom such relations are discovered that they must be thought of together."[1] But this obviously is inadequate, for it permits the inclusion of almost any aggregation that has a unity for the time being. Von Wiese comes more to the heart of the matter when he writes that "those interhuman plurality patterns are termed groups which are of such relatively long duration and relative solidarity that the persons therein affiliated come to be regarded as a relatively homogeneous unit."[2] To this latter statement we would add only one idea, namely, that the members also so regard themselves. In other words, it is the essence of our usage that a group means two or more people who bear an explicit psychological relationship to each other, of such duration and solidarity, that those participating, and those

1 Albion W. Small, *General Sociology*. Chicago: University of Chicago Press, 1905, p. 495.

2 Howard Becker and Leopold von Wiese, *Systematic Sociology*. New York: John Wiley and Sons, 1932, p. 489.

perceiving it, are aware in some degree of the relationship. Its basis is the continuing sharing of a common unifying experience.

In considering the family as the child's first group, one is prone to assume that all the members of the family constitute the child's family group. Actually this is not true, and especially not for the young child, if the term "group" is interpreted to mean anything more than the sharing of a common abode. Viewed from the standpoint of the child and the true essence of the group relationship, his growth in group experience, even within the family, is slow, selective, and at times never comes to embrace the entire family personnel. Two case histories are summarized for their bearing upon the last-stated phrase.

Christine was three years old when a relative of the mother came to live with the family, with the understanding that she would aid the mother in Christine's care. To the advent of the newcomer, Christine made no comment, nor any other signs of approval or disapproval. Soon, however, it was noticeable that Christine, although obedient and co-operating with the new "cousin" in the discharge of necessary duties, ignored her completely in all other ways. When spoken to by her cousin, she would answer; otherwise she would play an entire afternoon in her presence, but in apparent complete oblivion of it. Seven weeks later, the cousin withdrew from the household. When asked if she had found Christine disobedient or difficult to manage, she replied that she had been a model child. Obviously, Christine had treated her with complete indifference or contempt. Seven months later, Christine seemed to have no recollection of her cousin whatsoever.

John was the seventh child in a family of twelve. The fourth child was a daughter, named Lillian. At the age of thirty-four, John is writing out an analytical history of his family life. In doing so, he mentions all his brothers and sisters save Lillian. When this omission is called to his attention, he replies that he scarcely knows her, that as a child he ignored her, that they scarcely spoke to each other as they grew up, and that from the time she left the parental roof he has not seen her or communicated with her. He is not sure that he would know her if he met her now.

Cases like these suggest that, so far as the inner unity of the child's group life is concerned, not all members of the household or kinship circle are members of his family group.

THE PAIR OR TWO-PERSON GROUP

In many families, especially in the contemporary small immediate forms, the child's group experience begins with the dyad, or two-person group. This consists most frequently of mother and child. A number of factors combine to make this the almost exclusive group form for the young child. There is the biological bond or sense of physical identity between the two. There is the physical contact during the suckling period. There is the care by the mother during the period of physical helplessness and uncertainty. These factors are reinforced by cultural pressures—the moral, religious, and artistic emphases upon the ideal of motherhood; and the religious influence of the Virgin cult. In short, all the social forces of custom, manners, and morals bind mother and child in our culture. Society cooperates with nature, it has been said, to repeat the happy conditions in the womb.

This dyadic or generation pair group is the first group factor in the development of personality. We agree wholly with von Wiese when he writes:

> The study of specific types of groups is best begun with the smallest, namely, dyadic groups or pairs. . . . If any thorough understanding of a given person is to be achieved, one of the most necessary items of information must be the dyadic relations affecting him. Moreover, if the development of larger plurality patterns such as clubs, sects, families and business enterprises is to be correctly apprehended, close attention must be paid to the dyadic groups which have or might have formed during the period covered.[3]

This first dyadic group is so important, not only because it constitutes the first group experience of the child, but

[3] Becker and von Wiese, *op. cit.*, pp. 508-10.

also because it gives expression to the most intimate relationships that can be found. Again we quote von Wiese to point out that

> the two most deeply rooted forces of approach and association, namely, love and friendship, find in the pair pattern the form of union best adapted to them. Love and friendship can never exert their full binding force outside the pair; their very nature makes for intimacy, and this intimacy diminishes when the number of participants to which it must be extended increases.[4]

It is not to be assumed that this intimate and pervasive dyadic relationship exists to any marked extent in the early life of all children. Familiarity with the facts of family life reveals that this is not true. But its omission may be the key to much of the emotional striving which such an individual subsequently exhibits. Omissions of this kind are ordinarily found among the children in large families, and it would seem to be of related significance that such children tend to make most satisfactory marriages, i.e., they find the satisfactory dyadic group relationship in maturity and in marriage rather than in early childhood. The Burgess-Cottrell study of success and failure in marriage clearly reveals this, as well as that the only child and the last child, who find a satisfactory dyadic relationship in early childhood, seem to be less likely to do so in the maturer challenge of matrimony.[5]

THE EMERGENCE OF THE TRIANGLE SITUATION

When a third person comes into close relation with a dyad, something in the nature of a crisis arises. This fact is not given sufficient weight by the average observer who, if he considers the matter at all, sees only the more conspicuous *triangle* disturbances of marriage and friendship.

[4] Becker and von Wiese, *op. cit.*, p. 512.

[5] Ernest W. Burgess and Leonard S. Cottrell, *Predicting Success or Failure in Marriage*. New York: Prentice-Hall, Inc., 1939, chap. VII.

Actually within the family, and so far as the child's early experiences are concerned, the father or another sibling creates the first triangle situation. Either or both come as disturbers of the child's first dyadic relationship.

Two aspects of the coming of a third party to a mother-child dyad are of paramount importance, so far as the child is concerned. One of these is the reaction of the mother when the third party is another sibling; the second is the treatment of the mother by the father when he is the third party.

The reaction of the mother to another sibling is a perennial problem for all children in families where there is more than one child, but it naturally is most serious for the oldest child. For such a child, the coming of the second child constitutes a major psychic shock. Its specific seriousness depends upon a number of situational factors. One of these is the stage of the dyad relationship when the new child comes. How long has the relationship continued? What is the age of the child member? Related to this is the age differential between the siblings. If this is narrow, a close emotional tie may develop between the siblings, and the dyad becomes a sibling pair. Another factor is the number of times the psychic shock is repeated. Oldest children in large families speak of a certain emotional numbness that comes with the repeated birth of younger children. But perhaps the most important factor, as far as the child member of the dyad is concerned, is the attitude of the mother, since she is the dominant member of the pair.

The mother-child dyad may continue after the birth of younger children, under certain circumstances. One important such circumstance is the sex of the newcomer. If the newcomer is of the same sex as the child member of the dyad, then the newcomer may be recognized as a threat; if of the opposite sex, the result may be different. Here, again, the attitude of the mother is of the greatest significance. In this connection, the following excerpt from a case in the study of the large family system (Chapter VI) is interesting.

> Being the only daughter for twelve years (she had four younger brothers and the only other female in the household) I continued to be very close to mother. I thought that she was perfect—in speech, in dress, in looks, in ability, as a mother, as a wife, as a leader in the community. As I grew older, these early impressions became deeper. She never wavered in my eyes but became more and more of an ideal to follow. . . . She is the best-organized person and the most excellent manager I have ever met.

The situation is quite different when the father approaches the mother-child dyad. What the child is chiefly aware of is how the father treats the mother. Common parlance of everyday family life reveals constantly this emphasis. As one passes from family to family, one seldom hears reference to how mother treats father, but invariably what father does to and for mother. Now it is the father that is in the dominant role, and the inevitable price is to turn the spotlight on *his* behavior. Other circumstances reinforce this process of putting the father on trial. How does he fit into the family life? He is away from home a great deal. When he is at home, he may be called upon to be the administrator of family justice and punishment. When he is away, they may be administered in his name. In addition, mother, kinfolk, and guests may build up the stereotype of the stern father, or the errant husband, or the inadequate provider, which comes quickly to be sensed by the child member of the dyad.

In everyday family life, one finds all kinds of situations in which the attitude of the mother or the behavior of the father keeps the latter from being admitted to the we-feeling of the dyad. The cases of Margaret and Daisy reveal the mother as manipulator of the situation; that of Milton, the bungling of a father.

Margaret is a Christian woman, married to a Jew. The union has not been a happy one, and she was particularly unwilling to bear him a child. Nevertheless, she felt strong maternal urgings, and these finally found expression in the opportunity which her brother's escapade provided. This brother became the father of a child born out of wedlock. Although unwilling to marry the mother of the child, this brother accepted responsibility for the child. It was at this point that his sister offered to adopt the baby, thus satisfying her longing for a child, without the necessity of "mixing her blood" with her husband. From the very beginning, Margaret did everything to "freeze" the adopted father out of the relationship, and with such success that by the time the child was nine years of age he gave every evidence of resentment against his supposed father.

Daisy has a deep-seated animosity against her husband, and father of her only child. From the very beginning of the child's life, Daisy has been consistently adroit in placing the father in an unattractive role before his son. He is made to do everything for the baby which makes him cry. Later on, she saves every bit of discipline and the handling of any unpleasant situation for the father. When Daisy does discipline her son, or brings pressure of any kind to bear upon him, she plays the role of being made to do so by the father, because he is a stern man and she is afraid of him. The result of this has been to drive mother and child together, into a sort of secret understanding, as fellow conspirators and victims of the father's sternness. A strong "we-feeling" exists in the mother-child dyad, with the father having the status of alien.

Milton has created much the same type of situation by his attitude toward the mother of his son and by his general ineptness in parent-child relations. Milton, the product of a highly over-solicitous mother, expects his wife to assume all of the family responsibilities and household cares, as well as to attend to his personal affairs. Although she tries to do so faithfully, he criticizes her constantly, and often quite unreasonably. He does this repeatedly in front of their son, now nine years old. At times, he reinforces his criticisms with physical violence. He is also critical of the mother's methods of rearing the son, which are aimed at developing a sense of responsibility in the boy. To give point to his disagreement with the mother, he interrupts the mother's handling of situations, often with acts of extreme indulgence. Once, for example, when the mother was bringing some pressure upon the son to meet a school demand, the father interrupted the procedure, took the boy down the street and purchased a new bicycle for him. The net result seems to be a lack of respect and affection for the father, and a marked concern for the safety of the mother. The son tries not to leave the mother alone with the father; when he does so, he seeks assurance from the mother that she will not be afraid.

The organization of relationships within the triad is exceedingly difficult. A normal type of triad is rare, if one conceives of it as based upon the complete equality of all three members. "What is really normal," writes von Wiese, "is that two of the members are more intimate with each other than they are with the third, and that A affects B differently from the way in which he affects C. Again, it sometimes occurs that one of the group is the leader and the other two are followers; more frequently, however, two members become allies, as it were, and . . . relegate the third to an inferior rank."[6] While it is true that the structure of the triad changes frequently, showing new alignments, it is invariably upon a two-to-one basis. In other words, the triadic pattern has a tendency to exclude one of the three participants through pair combination, or so to influence him that his isolation is in some measure voluntary. The history of triumvirates of all kinds gives some empirical indication of the accuracy of the above pronouncement.[7]

Thinking in terms of child development, one cannot but speculate upon the fundamental importance of the triad in the child's early family experience. One specific phase of this is the father-mother-child triad. Which of the three is habitually the odd one? Is the father-mother dyad the intimate combination, or is the mother-child the one? Who is

[6] Becker and von Wiese, *op. cit.*, p. 525.
[7] Becker and von Wiese, *op. cit.*, p. 526.

consistently cast in the role of the odd or underprivileged member of the triad? What patterns of adjustment does the odd one develop? If it is the child, are these patterns as they develop within the family transferred later on to other triadic situations? Are some persons invariably the odd member in life's triads? When patterns of antagonism rather than of acceptance develop, what forms do they take? May these become consistent and harden into personality traits?

What are the various adjustments to the problems of relationship within the triad for the odd or underprivileged one? Six possible answers are apparent. One, already identified, is to accept the subordinate position. If long continued, this pattern shades into the attitudes and traits of the indispensable assistant type of person, always content with the tertiary role. Second, there may result a struggle for power. The odd member may seek to dominate the pair. The father member of a family triad often seeks to do this, in order to control or break up the pair. Or the effort may take the form of acquiring prestige, so that both members of the dyad may recognize the superiority of the odd member, thus become the ideal or model for the pair. Again, the third person may seek to weaken the dyad by making fun of it, or belittling one of the pair. This frequently happens in family life. Fifth, there is recourse to competition, where the odd one seeks to lure or wean one of the dyad away from the other. This competitive bidding for the allegiance of the third member again is very frequent in family life, and particularly so between father and mother for the allegiance of the child. Finally, the odd member may seek to strengthen his position by forming an alliance outside the triad. Finding a new partner means that the triad becomes a double pair. Two dyads have now been formed.

THE IDEA OF FAMILY UNITY

Another major phase of the child's earlier group experience comes with his awareness of the existence of groups larger than the dyad or triad, and a comparison of his group with other larger groups. Here the child becomes conscious of his family or play group or gang in contrast to other families, play groups, and gangs. Quite frequently one sees this first in the child's growing awareness of his family as a unity. This comes usually somewhere between the seventh and the tenth year. It may express itself in various ways in comments of comparison of his home with those of other families, or in questions about the father's income. "How much do you earn a year, Daddy?" "How much does Mr. Brown make?" "What did the Singers pay for their home?" "What did we pay?" In one instance, it was found that these family comparisons, made by the children, centered upon the different times when the head of the family left for work in the morning. It is suggested that the child's discovery of his family as a unity, his reaching out to "feel" this unity, his experiences in achieving it, and his comparisons of his family unity with that of other children, constitute a basic factor in his personality development.

Evelyn is an only child. She is seven and a half years old, well featured, with high scholastic aptitude, and referred to by her teachers as highly teachable. From her school, church, and other social contacts, she recently has become aware of the idea of family unity, both in terms of her own and that of other families. But her own family does not function to any great extent as a unit. The father tends to be weak and erratic, and rationalizes his own defects by constantly criticizing and depreciating the mother. He frequently calls the mother a fool in front of the child. The mother admits that she does not love the father, but manages to show a good deal of restraint in her relations with her husband. She tends to go her own way to a considerable extent, organizing her life in ways that ignore the father and, to a limited extent, the child.

The effects of this lack of family unity upon Evelyn seem to manifest themselves in the following ways. First, she grasps at anything in her own home which points in the direction of family unity. She fairly revels in a family dinner when, for example, her parents entertain another family. She seeks constantly to have her father and mother go with her to church or other social event. She does not succeed in this often, but when she does it seems to mean a great deal to her. Again, Evelyn shows a real eagerness to visit in certain homes where a strong family unity exists. She has spent a part of the past summer visiting in a home where such unity prevails, and she has identified herself to a marked degree with one of the daughters in this family. Also, Evelyn shows an interest in peer groups somewhat greater than is common in girls of her age. She is very loyal to the nonfamily groups in whose activities she participates.

THE SIZE OF THE GROUP

Size is a basic factor in group functioning. It determines not only the kinds and varieties of small combinations that are formed, like the dyads and triads we have just discussed, but it affects also many other aspects of its operations and effects upon individual members. A good deal of significant work has been done in recent years in this area. Reference might be made here to the work of Bales,[8]

[8] Robert F. Bales, *Interaction Process Analysis: A Method for the Study of Small Groups.* Cambridge, Mass.: Addison-Wesley Press, 1950; also, "A Set of Categories for the Analysis of Small Group Interaction," *American Sociological Review,* April 1950, and "Channels of Communication in Small Groups," *ibid.,* August 1951.

Goldhamer,[9] Hare,[10] Hemphill,[11] Homans,[12] James,[13] Kephart,[14] Murchison,[15] Simmel,[16] Thelen,[17] as well as to my own.[18]

A great many additional questions await study. Just how, for example, does the internal life of a group change as its size changes? Is it true that each group has an optimal point for the development of its individual members? If so, what is it? What size of family fosters the highest type of family life, other factors remaining relatively equal? (Certain aspects of this will appear in subsequent chapters in this volume.) Similar questions may be raised about the optimal size of classes in our schools and colleges.[19] At what size of university class is the discussion method of instruction most effective? What size of college fraternity promotes most effectively fraternal relations between its members? What size of military unit makes for

[9] Herbert Goldhamer, "Communication and Social Solidarity," notes of a course given in the Department of Sociology, University of Chicago (Society for Social Research, University of Chicago, 1948. Mimeographed.).

[10] Alexander Paul Hare, *A Study of Interaction and Consensus in Different Sized Discussion Groups.* University of Chicago dissertation, 1951.

[11] John K. Hemphill, "Relations Between the Size of the Group and the Behavior of 'Superior' Leaders," *Journal of Social Psychology,* August 1950, pp. 11-22.

[12] George Homans, *The Human Group.* New York: Harcourt, Brace and Co., 1950.

[13] John James, "A Preliminary Study of the Size Determinant in Small Group Interaction," *American Sociological Review,* August 1951, pp. 474-77.

[14] William M. Kephart, "A Quantitative Analysis of Intragroup Relationships," *American Journal of Sociology,* May 1950, pp. 544-49.

[15] Carl Murchison, "The Time Function in the Experimental Formation of Social Hierarchies in Different Sizes in *Gallus Domesticus,*" *Journal of Social Psychology,* February 1936, pp. 3-17.

[16] Georg Simmel, *The Sociology of Georg Simmel,* trans. by Kurt H. Wolf. Glencoe, Ill.: The Free Press, 1950.

[17] Herbert A. Thelen, "Group Dynamics in Instruction: Principle of Least Group Size," *The School Review,* March 1949, pp. 139-48.

[18] Bossard, *The Sociology of Child Development,* pp. 145-49.

[19] Consult here Carl M. Larson, "School Size as a Factor in the Adjustment of High School Seniors," The State College of Washington, Institute of Agricultural Sciences, Washington Agricultural Experiment Stations, Bulletin No. 511, November 1949.

the most effective fighting machine among foot soldiers? What, in other words, is the significance of size of group, per se?

The family, it has been emphasized, is the child's first group experience. To this group his first patterns of response and adjustments are formed. He learns to behave, or misbehave, in a certain sized group. Obviously the child reared in a large family has a group experience that differs in many respects from the one that grows up in a small family. He learns different modes of behavior. Also his affectional patterns will differ. The original mother-child dyad has a lesser development ordinarily both in depth and range of intimacy. Also it is of relatively shorter duration. Is this first group experience and resultant attitudes and behvaior transferred to subsequent groups of which the child is a member? Does the size of the family group in which the child is reared determine the size of the play, school, military, and work group in which he subsequently can make his most effective adjustment? It would be entirely reasonable to suppose so. If so, the significance for this in subsequent guidance work would be very great.

THE COMPOSITION OF THE GROUP

Groups differ from each other, not only on the basis of size, but also in the nature of the elements that compose them. The two most apparent and socially significant of these differences are sex and age. It is in this respect that the family is a unique group. In its normal form it combines both sexes, as well as differing ages. Moreover, it combines them in a continuum of experience, and in the most intimate areas of life. No other group compares with the family in this respect.

But family groups vary significantly from each other in composition. One or the other sex may predominate, and often does. Similarly, the age differentials may be narrow or wide. Examples of deviations of both kinds will appear in Chapter X.

Again it seems reasonable to suppose that the behavior which the individual first learns on the basis of the age and sex composition of his family group is of importance in determining the nature of other groups in which he will or will not make a satisfactory adjustment. The girl who has grown up happily with six brothers, for example, might be very unhappy in a woman's college, or at work in an office exclusively staffed by women.

SUMMARY

Five facts have been emphasized in this chapter:

1. The family is a group, generically speaking. Family life is a project in group living, and growing up is a form of adjustment to group living.

2. The individual's first group experiences are in the family, and it is here that the original patterns of response to group situations are formed.

3. The first of these family group experiences are those of the simple dyad and triad, involving relationships ordinarily first with the mother, and subsequently with father and/or sibling.

4. Later family group experiences are influenced by the size and composition of the family group.

5. Subsequent adjustments to other groups, such as play, school, military, marital, and work groups, are determined by these earliest family group experiences.

CHAPTER III

The Family Background of the Child

God setteth the solitary in families.—PSALM LXVIII:6

ONE of the big problems of the very small child is to orient himself to the idea of family, what it is, whom it includes, and why. This knowledge, and understanding of it, come slowly, for he must learn the parental relationships within the family and, in addition, a whole series of other relationships which may exist within the intimate circle of his household, some of which are of a kinship nature and bear his own name, some of a kinship nature but with a different surname, and still others that are no kin at all but live as members of his family-household group. This is a slow and difficult process because it is a highly complicated one. It begins usually around the fourth year, and he may be well along in years before the full import of all the relationships and distinctions are known to him. Because students of the family, adult and wise though they pretend to be, seem to find it necessary to go through a similar process of discovery, it seems pertinent at this point to raise and discuss the very simple question of who it is that constitutes the child's family background, with prime reference to the molding of his behavior patterns.

THE FAMILY AS A BIOLOGICAL UNIT

Students of the family, and particularly those interested in its role in child behavior, have thought of it primarily in terms of the procreative unit. Who is the child's family? What does his family background consist of? The answer has been simple. It is his father and mother. Somewhat later, his siblings have been admitted to the frame of reference, but still largely in terms of the rivalries and problems they created, and only very recently in recognition of their part in the learning processes by which behavior is formed.

Is this type of family a statistical reality or is it an ideal construct of our wishful thoughts? A glance at some facts is rather revealing. The 16th United States Census figures show the following summaries:

1. About 35 per cent of the people of this country live in households consisting only of father, mother, and child or children.

2. Another 12 per cent live in households consisting of a man and wife, who have not had any children or whose children have grown up and left home.

3. About 27 per cent live in households comprising a family of one of these two types, plus some relatives or roomers who do not of themselves constitute family groups.

4. In excess of 12 per cent live in households containing two groups of relatives, usually two married couples or one married couple and a parent-child group.

5. Approximately another 12 per cent live as groups of individuals maintaining separate households, such as a broken home (consisting of one parent with his or her children), two or more relatives of miscellaneous relationships, and persons living alone or with roomers.

6. Roughly 2 per cent lived, at the time of this enumeration, in military establishments of the United States, or in institutions of one kind or another.

For purposes of this volume, the really significant facts in this connection are the proportion of children who grow up in families of this purely procreative type. This differs from the data that are available ordinarily, which show the number who live in such families at a given time. A great many families, listed at a given moment as of the procreative type, pass through the stage when other persons are living with them. Particularly is this true of families at the time when their children are young.

To throw some light on the quest as stated, I have secured information from a total of four hundred and ten students in a large urban university. One item only was solicited: list all the persons who lived as members of your household prior to your tenth birthday. The results follow:

1. An even one hundred were families which had consisted of parents and children only. This is roughly one out of every four.

2. In thirty cases, or 7 per cent, there had been but one parent or a stepparent, for at least a part of the time.

3. In fifty cases, or 12 per cent, servants, but no other persons, had lived in during that period.

4. In two hundred and thirty cases, or 56 per cent, relatives and/or other persons had lived in the household as members of it. Families, with servants living in, and other persons, have been listed in this category.

It may be pointed out at once that university students represent a selected group, and this is true. There can be little doubt, however, that the number of families with only parents and children living in the household would be larger than in the general population. Unfortunately, too, this sample, while suggestive, is too small to be definitive.

KINFOLK AS A HOUSEHOLD UNIT

Considering kinfolk, one finds, in everyday life, an amazing variety of forms in immediate families with children. During the year that the manuscript of this book has been in preparation, a listing was made of all structural forms of immediate families with children which came to notice. The list follows:

1. Father, mother, and child or children.

2. Father and children, mother dead.
3. Father and children, mother deserted.
4. Father, stepmother, and children, mother dead.
5. Father, stepmother, and children, mother divorced.
6. Father, paternal grandmother, and children.
7. Father, maternal grandmother, and children.
8. Father, his sister, and children.
9. Father, wife's sister, and children.
10. Father, children, and his mistress.
11. Father, children, mother in prison.
12. Father, children, mother in mental institution.
13. Father, children, and woman housekeeper.
14. Father, children, legally separated from mother.
15. Mother, children, father dead.
16. Mother, children, father deserted.
17. Mother, children, father legally separated.
18. Mother, stepfather, children of mother.
19. Mother, stepfather, children of both.
20. Mother, stepfather, "yours, mine, and our children."
21. Mother, maternal grandfather, children.
22. Mother, paternal grandfather, children.
23. Mother, maternal grandmother, children.
24. Mother, brother, and children.
25. Mother, sister, children.
26. Mother, paramour, children.
27. Mother, father in prison, children.
28. Mother, father in institution, children.
29. Mother, father in military service, children.
30. Mother, lodger, children.
31. Mother, boarder, children.
32. Foster father, foster mother, child.
33. Foster parents, adopted child, natural child.
34. Children, oldest brother as parent.
35. Children, oldest sister as parent.

36. Father, mother, children, aunt.
37. Father, mother, children, uncle.
38. Father, mother, children, one grandparent.
39. Father, mother, children, two grandparents.
40. Stepfather, stepmother, child.

The list is not all-inclusive. One can think of other combinations. Suffice it here to point out the many varieties of family units there are if one thinks only of kinfolk living in the household as members of the family. Only slight recognition, usually under the general heading of kinfolk, has been given to these situations. Obviously, each specific combination carries its own significance in child development.

THE INTERACTING UNIT AS A FAMILY

When one leaves the traditional ways of thinking about the family and looks upon it as a household group that molds the behavior of children, it is obvious that one must think not only of the parents, but of all persons who share in the common life of the household. The family that conditions the development of the child is the group that lives together. This means all the persons who interact within the household. We shall speak of this as the interactive family unit. This includes, then, not only the parents, but also any relatives, friends, servants, etc., who are living with the family. In other words, the family background of the child, the family that fashions the behavior of the child, is the household group from which the child learns his behavior patterns. If one thinks of the formation of behavior as a learning process by the child through his group contacts, then it is little short of ridiculous to assume, as has frequently been done, that only the parents are to be considered as the teachers.

General sociological and anthropological theory have long recognized the basic idea involved. Both sciences have emphasized that the family is a social rather than a biological group. Three lines of evidence in support of this viewpoint are usually presented. One is the fact, revealed by the anthropologists, that family groups exist in societies which do not understand the biology of reproduction. Second is the universal rule which permits adoption into the family, a practice which admits the stranger and nonrelative into the full intimacies of the family's common life. Finally, there is the tracing of family descent through either the male or female line, thus ignoring a large number of blood relatives, and indicating again the triumph of social acceptance over biological fact.

THE ROLE OF THE DECEASED

One tends to conclude, at this point, that the foregoing coverage of what the child's family background includes has been complete. But now comes the careful student who points out one omission. No mention has been made of members of the family now deceased. They are gone, to be sure, but no one who knows family life would say that their influence has ceased. Specifically, one hears in many homes statements like these: "What would your Aunt Ellen say if she were alive?" "What do you suppose mother would do?" "You know what Grandfather Jones always said." Snatches like these show how the memory of deceased family members survives, how their remembered attitudes continue to influence behavior patterns. At times, too, it is not so much an attitude that is remembered as a figure that is built up against the horizon of the past. This happens often when a parent died during the infancy of the child. The deceased parent may be made into a paragon of virtues, or, as unfortunately happens at times, as a scapegoat responsible for all the present problems of the family. Readers of Daphne Du Maurier's *Rebecca* will remember how the memory of the first wife intruded into the marriage with the second wife. Obviously the same vivid influence in the development of the child may continue after the death of a parent or other family member.

There is another way in which the family's past influences the development of children, and that is through the heritage that is transmitted from generation to generation. Reference is made to two aspects of this heritage. One has to do with such tangible possessions as pictures and portraits of ancestors, furniture, letters, books, clothing, and the like. One might term these the physical aspects of family continuity.

The retention and role of such possessions have undoubtedly declined in recent decades. Earlier, families lived in houses, and often in the same house for generations, so that such possessions grew both in extent and influence. The story of the Boswell papers is an excellent illustration. The history of these papers runs through five generations, during which time they were kept in attics and in various rooms in the family ancestral home. Only recently, with their purchase by an American, their eventual transfer to the Yale University Library, and their publication in part, are their existence and importance coming to public notice.[1] Ours, today, is an apartment-living and heirloom-destroying generation, and visible reminders of the family's past are found less frequently, although the accuracy of this observation varies considerably from one part of the country to another.

The other aspect of the family's social heritage consists of ideas, values, practices, and traditions which are found to some extent in all families. These are not dependent for storage in attics, nor need they be destroyed when the family moves into an apartment. The Pilgrim Fathers, we might recall, brought very few tangible possessions to the

[1] Frederick A. Pottle, *Boswell's London Journal.* New York: McGraw-Hill Book Co., 1950.

New World, but the whole history of the United States reveals the intangibles that they imported. It is so with many families: their past histories reach into the present, and through the present into the future, not only biologically, but also in terms of their specific family cultural content. According to the late James S. Plant, family tradition begins to play a role in the orientation of the child after the third or fourth year.[2]

THE KINSHIP GROUP AS FAMILY BACKGROUND

In addition to the immediate family or household group, the child hears the word "family" applied to two other groups of persons. One of these groups consists of relatives who have the same name as the child: they are daddy's folks; the other group are mother's people, and their name is different. In addition, each of these groups consists of persons who are blood relatives and people who are relatives through marriage. These two groups, i.e., daddy's and mother's folks, may be much like each other in the way they talk and act and live, or they may be quite unlike each other, even speaking different languages, going to different churches, and living in a quite different manner. They may be friendly, or they may dislike and avoid each other, in varying degrees. Whatever these circumstances, both groups are a part of the child's family background. Not only is the child told that this is so, but he will learn that he is identified with these groups of relatives by other people. For many children, either one or both of these groups of kinfolk become a sort of outlying province of the home. Children leave their own homes to visit in the homes of these kinfolk; often the latter become a kind of second home. Week-ends, holidays, vacations may be spent there. This development of childhood visiting is discussed more

[2] James S. Plant, *The Envelope*. New York: Commonwealth Fund Publications, 1950, p. 15.

fully in a subsequent chapter in this volume. On the other hand, these kinfolk come to visit at the child's home in varying extent, and are received with differing degrees of intimacy and welcome.

This larger circle of kinfolk related to the child is spoken of here as the kinship group. Some students apply the term "extended family" to indicate this larger group. Neither term is wholly satisfactory, nor is this important. The essential fact is that the reality and role of this larger aspect of the child's family background be recognized, for part of the background it certainly is. In fact, the distinction between the immediate or household family and the more extended body of kinfolk is a relatively recent one. For many peoples, and in some cases down to the present time, the term "family" has been applied only to the latter, or more extended, type.

THE RELATIVE IMPORTANCE OF FAMILY MEMBERS

Adult members of families generally tend to conceive of their importance in the development of the child on the basis of nearness of kinship. Particularly is this true of parents. Because they are the child's parents, they rate themselves as the most important, with other kinfolk and members of the family household in the order of biological nearness. Is such rating really correct? Much as adults may hate to admit it, is it not true that they are looking at the child's family background through their own eyes, and egos?

The proposition presented here is that the relative importance of family members in the child's development is not determined solely by degree of kinship, but also, and perhaps even largely so, by the needs of the child and the satisfaction of those needs by the various members of the family group. One of the basic facts about children is that they think of parents and other adults largely in terms of their own needs, for the simple reason that they look at parents and adults through their own eyes and from their own point of view.

These needs, may it be emphasized, are not so much the kind of needs that academic folk identify in their ivory-towered classifications, but very concrete wants that grow out of the specific situations that confront the child. When Mary falls and hurts her knee so that it bleeds, she may need someone to give first aid to the knee, and a bit of comfort to the spirit. The role of the adult to whom she comes, and her rating of that adult, depends on how that need is satisfied. When Jack is lonely and discouraged, he may need merely the silent, understanding presence of someone, and Uncle John may give that. When all the other children have a television set, and Jane wants one too, then father is measured by his response to that need. In other words, children are not born with measuring sticks of family-member importance or with a theoretical framework to evaluate family situations. The child knows only needs that are concrete, specific, and for the most part direct and immediate. They are needs which grow out of experience in living: the extent to which they are met, the ways in which they are met, register the family member's importance in the development of the child. A word of caution must be added, however. This does not mean that surrogate parents can satisfy all the needs of children. There are fundamental longings, of belongingness, for example, that only a parent can give, but there are many other needs that can be met by other persons. We must not sell short the role of nonparent family members.

As this is being written, a New York columnist reports the following incident. It is reported here as not entirely inappropriate to the foregoing discussion.

When, pursuant to arrangement with her ex-husband, Dr. Peter Lindstrom, Ingrid Bergman had a reunion with their young daughter, Pia, in London, the screen star looked forward to the meeting with deep anxiety. She felt that she would have to dispel the countless distortions by cruel detractors, the newspaper reports and gossip repeated by those unaware of its effect upon the child's mind. Much of Pia's future happiness, she realized, depended on her ability to dispel any clouds of doubt and torment. Miss Bergman therefore decided to be utterly frank with her young daughter.

After the first embrace and the preliminary exchanges, Miss Bergman said to Pia: "Now ask me any questions you want. You have heard so many things, and you may want to ask me about them. I'll answer fully and to the best of my ability. Anything you ask." . . . Pia's brow furrowed, and she hesitated, then asked about the one thing which had been troubling her, only one question: "I hear there are many Communists in Italy now. Are you and Mr. Rossellini Communists?" "No, we're not," her mother assured her. Pia beamed, no longer troubled, and then the reunion became a gay one.[3]

THE REFRACTING ROLE OF FAMILY MEMBERS

Another common error in analyzing the part the family plays in molding the behavior patterns of the child is to separate somewhat arbitrarily the family from other groups, and the family life from other aspects of life. The assumption seems to be that the role of the family is confined to its internal life, as though it were isolated from other influences. Actually, this is not true. The family is in many respects more of a transmitting than of a generating station. It is constantly contacting, bringing into the home, assessing, and evaluating the outside world. The home is a sort of crossroads, to which comes constantly the outside world. To change the metaphor, it is the place, according to the tart comment of one mother, where the members of the family drag the dirt of everyday life. But this is only partly correct, because it is also true that the family is the intermediary between the intimate life of its members and the outside world. A few illustrations from life are in order.

[3] Leonard Lyons, *The Philadelphia Inquirer,* January 25, 1952.

1. Mother and Jane go for a walk. They meet a dog. The dog licks Jane's face. Startled, she looks at her mother. Her mother may smile, consider it a joke, and make friends with the dog. Or, she may look disgusted, or act frightened, shout at the dog, and chase it away. Thus is laid the foundation for Jane's attitude toward dogs. Next, they meet another child. The same process is repeated, if not in detail, then in substance. Then they meet Mrs. Lewis. Mother greets Mrs. Lewis, and Jane learns how one greets another person. Later, in answer to Jane's question, mother "interprets" Mrs. Lewis. Still later, mother may "interpret" Mrs. Lewis to father. The two interpretations may be similar, or they may differ, and Jane learns about mother and social conventions.

2. Father and Bill go to the movies. During the program some children nearby are noisy. Father expresses himself about the children, their parents, and the management. Afterwards, father and Bill talk about the plot, actors, girls, Hollywood, Louella Parsons, newspaper columnists, and the nearby parking facilities. Ostensibly, father and Bill have gone to the movies; actually, Bill has been exposed to an interpretation of a dozen phases of contemporary life.

Growing up is like that. The child contacts the outside world, i.e., those phases to which the family members have access and which they select, and "sees" them through the eyes of the parents. Here is a simple process, but its importance is very great, and the ways in which members of the family serve the child in this respect differ greatly. The basic fact is that the family member serves as the eyes, so to speak, of the child. He refracts the idea, event, value, etc., as he passes it on to the child. Some family members refract but slightly, describing clearly, transmitting fairly, and evaluating judiciously. They help the child to see things for himself, to understand them, and form his own evaluations. Many parents are excellent reporters and good teachers; others are biased in their interpretations and highly inept in their teaching. These are among the details which comprise the essence of child development.

THE IMPORTANCE OF UNDERSTANDING THE CHILD'S FAMILY BACKGROUND

There are many reasons why an appreciation of what the child's family background really includes is important. Five of these will be summarized briefly.

1. Progress in an understanding of child behavior depends upon the realization of its detailed complexity. The child's family seldom is a simple matter of parents and sibling, as is shown in the case of William.

William's behavior has puzzled a child-study agency because it confounds the nature and simplicity of his home setting. He is an only child, living with his father and mother. His father is the oldest of eleven children. The paternal grandfather is a veteran of one of our wars, a picturesque figure in many ways. The paternal grandmother is a quiet, mild-mannered, soft-spoken woman. Of their eleven children, five work for William's father, who is a successful industrialist. William's mother is one of nine children. Her father is an incessant reader, pipe smoker, talker, and arguer; her mother is an attractive, colorful woman, a great entertainer, and loved by all her children and grandchildren. Three of their nine children have worked for William's father, and the youngest of the nine was William's nurse. The two groups of kinfolk have been constantly sniping at each other, with obvious jealousy of the financial success of William's father. As he grew up, William spent a great deal of time with his grandparents, particularly those on the maternal side. William also remembers twelve servants in his home while growing up. What, now, is the family background of William that must be known to understand his behavior? Is it his father and mother, or is it the parents, plus the twenty-two kinfolk, plus the twelve servants?

Many years ago, Herbert Spencer, in his assessment of the difficulties in the way of developing a social science, stressed the inadequacy of trying to force complex facts into a simple mental mold. He likened the procedure to trying to put five fingers into a glove with but room for two.[4]

2. The kinship group, more than the average immediate family, is a sort of world in miniature for the small child, in which he learns many of the facts of life. He learns how people not living in the intimacy of the immediate family treat each other. He sees petty jealousies and open rivalries, revealed in crude nakedness or clothed in conventional niceties; he hears frank talk about absent kinfolk and dissembling with those who are present; he sees unselfish sharing and family helpfulness, at times with scarcely a word of thanks or any expectation of it. How kinfolk treat each other is a school in human behavior for the child, the operation and significance of which are still largely unexplored in the scientific literature.

3. It is in the complexity and naked incisiveness of family relations that children are first introduced to the reality of conflict and tension. Not only are there the relations between the parents and the siblings but, in the majority of families, relations with other persons. There is tension between mother and her mother-in-law who lives with her; between father and his brother-in-law; between father and cousin Jane, who came to visit for a few days some three years ago. Important in this respect are the cultural differences between the two kinship groups. Father's family are Presbyterians, mother's people go to the Roman Catholic church. Father's father owns his own business, mother's father is the janitor in the high school building. Cousin Audrey on mother's side has a coming-out party, cousin Helen on father's side clerks in the five-and-dime store. Here are the situations, the contrasts, from which conflicts, jealousies, and bitterness are first brought home to the child, in the vivid dress of persons he knows and loves.

[4] Herbert Spencer, *The Study of Sociology*. New York and London: D. Appleton and Co., 1873, p. 115.

4. An understanding of this larger web of family relationships throws light upon the controversies that arise over the control and custody of the children in the event of the break-up of the immediate family. The unfortunate fact is that in many such cases the child becomes a pawn between conflicting groups of kinfolk. Often, when satisfactory compromises might be effected between the parents with but little difficulty, individuals or combinations of individuals in the two opposing groups of kinfolk enter the controversy, more for the sake of gaining a victory over each other than because they seek the best interests of the child. This seems to be true particularly when religious or class differences exist between the kinship groups.

5. Finally, there is the very great significance of the child's identification with individuals and kin elements in his family background. Every student of behavior knows how important this conception of one's self, of one's role, is in the development of the personality. One of the sources of this conception of the self comes from the person or persons one identifies himself with. Who is this in the family background? What is his status? What is the nature and degree of the identification? With which side of the house is the child identified? This is a matter that is discussed constantly, and from infancy, in most families. "He is a Smith all right." "Look at that Smith nose." "He walks just like his grandfather Smith. Yes, and he talks like him too." These are common comments to which John Smith is constantly exposed. As a result, he grows up to think of himself as a Smith, like grandfather William Smith. And William Smith was a carpenter. Yes, sir. Always good with his hands. Didn't talk much, just sawed away. But a good worker. Yes, sirree. Didn't take second place to anyone. "A day's work for a day's pay," he always said. And so one of the keys to that Smith boy's behavior is the image of grandfather Smith, the silent, conscientious, hard-working

carpenter. Whether he became a truck driver or a bond salesman, whether he achieved the stereotype or rebelled against it, John Smith's identification with the Smith rather than his mother's side of the house, and with grandfather Smith in particular, was a part of the learning process which produced his behavior patterns.

SUMMARY

1. One of the problems of every child is to learn the web of his family relationships.

2. First, there is the procreative unit: father, mother, child, and other children, if any. In its pure form, this exists in a minority of family backgrounds of American children.

3. The immediate family includes a great variety of combinations of kinfolk.

4. From the standpoint of the child's behavior, the important group is that in which he grows up. This is termed "the interacting family."

5. In addition to the living, there is also the role of the deceased, of family possessions, and traditions.

6. Finally, there is the more extended circle of kinfolk, to whom the term "family" is applied, but who are not members of the household.

7. The relative importance of persons in the child's family background depends, in addition to nearness of kinship, upon the extent to which they satisfy the child's needs.

8. The family is a transmitting as well as a generating station, refracting the world to the child.

9. A knowledge and appreciation of the child's family background give an insight into the complexity of the child's primary conditioning group; it affords a world in miniature to serve as a behavior school for the child; it

shows how the child first learns of the conflicts and tensions; it reveals the sources of controversies involving the child when the family breaks up; and it gives an understanding of the child's conception of himself and his role in life.

CHAPTER IV

The Immediate Family and the Kinship Group*

Fate makes our relatives, choice makes our friends.
—JACQUES DELILLE

THE distinction between the immediate family and the larger kinship group is drawn increasingly in the current literature on the family. This reflects obviously their growing divergence in contemporary life, and accentuates in turn the facts concerning the relationship between the two. Since many of the succeeding chapters summarize research studies bearing on these distinctions, it seems desirable to devote a chapter to this general area of development in the family field.

This chapter consists of two parts. The first one summarizes briefly current conclusions about changes in American family structure, and their significance for child development; the second is a report of a research study on the relationship between the immediate family and the kinship group, as viewed through the eyes of contemporary youth.

I

Four basic changes in family structure receive current emphases in the sociological literature. Considered together, they constitute a revolution in the social back-

* Author's Note—In the research project reported on in this chapter, I have had the assistance of Eleanor S. Boll, present Research Associate of the Carter Foundation. She should be noted as co-author of this chapter.

ground and socialization process of the child. Each of these facts will be presented in summary form.

CHANGES IN FAMILY STRUCTURE

1. *Decline of the Kinship Group as the Family Unit.* For centuries and among many peoples, the term "family" meant a body of kinfolk, usually of considerable size, including several generations as well as lateral relatives to the third and fourth degree of kinship. Heading this group was an elderly ancestor, spoken of in some cultures as the patriarch. Perhaps the best illustration was the historic Chinese family, with its ideal of "five generations under one roof."

This type of family functioned as a unit, and in many aspects of life. The "old man," who was its head, managed the out-of-doors affairs of the group; the mother's function was to rear children, particularly sons, and manage the indoor household activities; the children were expected to be coöperative, dutiful, and respectful. Much stress was laid upon the concept of familism, involving the subordination of the individual to the group. The individual had few rights, per se; the family as a group had primacy above everything else.

Families of this kind obviously were a product of certain conditions of life, wherein the task of supporting the family and the protection of its members necessitated group solidarity and unified group action. With economic progress and more developed forms for the maintenance of social order, these conditions are declining, and this in turn has led to a decline in this type of kinship group family. True, there are scattered areas and peoples among whom it still persists, but throughout Western society it is no longer the prevailing type nor the form held up as the ideal of family life to be achieved.

2. *The Rising Predominance of the Immediate Family.*

Complementary to the decline of this larger kinship or extended type of family is the rising predominance of the immediate family. This is a form of family which is confined to the immediate household unit, and includes only the procreative pair, their children, and such other persons who, for the time being, are living within the household. It is the form found typically in the urbanized centers of population, with their apartments, residential hotels, and small row houses.

Many factors have contrived to bring about this type of family living. Increasing productivity of wealth and its more equitable distribution have made it possible for smaller family units to function on their own. Modern methods of travel and communication have increased the mobility of population, with a resultant greater spatial distribution of kinfolk. Large-scale migration from one country to another has separated many groups of kinfolk by thousands of miles. Social security systems have lessened the dependence of the older, and the responsibility of the younger, members of families to each other. Our current stress upon democracy has accentuated an emphasis upon the individual and his rights to develop irrespective of the group, even of the family group.

More and more, then, does the immediate family constitute the ideal of American family life. Ties with relatives are maintained or not, as the case may be, but the goal is "to each his own," i.e., each procreative pair is to have its own home, rear its own children, and lead its own life.

3. *The Declining Size of the Immediate Family.* Not only is the immediate family becoming the prevailing type of family structure among the American people, but it has been declining in size. Long-term trends in birth rates and data on size of households clearly reveal this. The American family has been standardized for size, clustering about the two- and three-child level. The small-family system has

become the American family system. Further discussion of this follows in the succeeding chapter.

4. *The Changing Nature of Family Dissolution.* Families are broken up in most cases by death or by divorce. In former times, death was the arch offender. In recent decades, two developments have changed this. One has been the decline in the death rate; the other, the rise in the divorce rate. As a result, family dissolution has been the result increasingly of divorce rather than of the death of the spouses. This, too, will be discussed more fully in a subsequent chapter.

Significance for Child Development. The foregoing changes, considered in combination, constitute a major revolution in the social setting of child development, chiefly because they change the whole family background of the child and, as a result, the entire child-rearing process. Many results accrue from this. The size of the group in which the child is reared is changed. The number of persons, both adult and juvenile, to which the child must adjust; the number of persons with whom he can share his emotional life, from whom he can gain feelings of security, and from whom pressures emanate to compel conformity to the accepted code, is changed. These are changes which have been tacitly recognized in the literature on family life and child development, but whose more specific implications have not yet been established by empirical procedures. Most of the succeeding chapters of this volume will attempt to throw light on selected aspects of these changes.

II

Changes of such moment in family structure throw into relief a whole series of specific questions. How are family relatives regarded by contemporary youth? How strong is their feeling of identification with the larger kinship group? What is the overall tone of the relationship between the immediate family and the kinfolk? What problems are created for the immediate family by the coming of relatives, as viewed through the eyes of the younger members of the family?

Part II of this chapter is a report on a research study which throws light on some of these questions. It is based on information obtained from sixty-eight students at an eastern university, who wrote in free-essay style about their families and their relatives. These essays range considerably in length, frankness, and specificity, but they do rather generally convey information bearing upon particular aspects of the relationship between their immediate families and their relatives, as well as indications of the overtones of these relationships. Analyzed and summarized, seven general conclusions stand out which are presented here wholly for the suggestive value they contain.

1. *There is a marked degree of identification with kinfolk as such, regardless of what they are like or how well one has known them previously.* Two aspects of this are particularly noticeable. First are the differences in allusions to relatives and to friends. Although there are many references to friends, there were no suggestions of identification with friends or neighbors at all comparable to those with any or all relatives. This seems significant in that our friends are of our choosing, but we are born to our kin. Close identification, then, was with the people "inflicted" upon the writers. In cases where the relatives were acceptable people, this was a source of satisfaction and ego-inflation. Many wrote of talented relatives who visited and glamorized their very homes with their presence. On the other hand, those who were immoral, peculiar, faddish, infantile, the shabby, the uncouth, and the uneducated: these are sources of deep shame, personally.

A second aspect of this identification with kinfolk is evidenced in the references to their special treatment. No matter whether they were loved or hated, whether they lived next door or across the ocean, they were a part of the family and had special prerogatives as such. This acceptance of special prerogatives worked in two directions. The relatives felt it their right to drop in unexpectedly; to stay as long as they chose; to walk into the kitchen to find themselves something to eat; to rearrange the guest room furnishings; to use the personal belongings of the family members; to make comments upon the clothing, household management, behavior, and discipline of the family.

Operating in the other direction, the family felt compelled, because of kinship, to accept these people and their prerogatives with at least some show of grace. "*Must* we have Aunt Nancy up here?" mother asks. "I'm afraid so, dear," father replies. "You forget I am her only nephew, and she likes to come here. She says it relaxes her." One relative was a "boor." "If she had not been a relative she would not have been a guest."

2. *Relatives regard each other as custodians of the family reputation.* Because the reputation of any family member is a part of the composite reputation of the whole family kinship group, relatives often take on voluntarily and sincerely a responsibility for each other in matters of social etiquette, general education, and occupational or professional guidance. Sometimes this partially self-protective obligation is assumed in such a way that it can be called only "interference." But often the gentle, well-meant suggestions and advice of intelligent and mature relatives, who want to see each generation a credit to the family, are of invaluable help especially to children, but also, sometimes, to adults.

The Howerths "ganged up" on Aunt Bettie in an attempt to cure, in the kindest possible way, an eccentricity which embarrassed them. At table, she never used the service silver, but always helped herself from the serving dishes with her own fork—an unpleasant and regrettable habit. Other aunts enlisted the aid of a nephew. In conspiracy, they decided upon this plan: At dinner time, he was to use his own fork to help himself from the serving platter; he would then be reprimanded for it and taught some Emily Postian principles, thus calling to Aunt Bettie's attention her own weakness in etiquette.

With like intentions, an uncle took in hand his eight-year-old niece who was developing into a rabid little card sharp. She bullied her elders into playing with her, concentrated profoundly, and beat them triumphantly. The uncle finally connived to get her into a game at which he himself was an expert. He won and insisted upon playing again and again, thus gentling her into a situation where she could learn to take defeat gracefully and without too much pain.

One girl mentions gratefully the aunt who, when the girl was going through the difficult and doubting period of first exposure to science, patiently helped her to reconcile science and religion. Many girls speak almost with adoration of the young aunts who taught them how to arrange their hair and to dress attractively when they were in the trying stage of gawky early adolescence. And a number of others, mostly boys, spoke of occupational or professional guidance, from relatives, that shaped their whole future. Often one notices in a youngster a much more striking identity, biologically speaking, to an aunt or uncle than to a parent. This may mean that in terms of like predispositions, that aunt or uncle can be a better counselor to the child than the parent, however well meaning. In very close-knit families, children profited greatly from this feeling of custodianship of the entire older generation for the entire younger generation. Greta's story speaks for itself as to her relatives' influence in her life and in her cousins'.

With so large a family there was a variety of talents, professions and interests. From these I reaped many benefits, both large and small.

As I learned how to draw from my uncle, I acquired other things from other people. My aunt provided me with embroidery to work on her visits. As I grew older the family became more than a mere source of entertainment. Since my parents were the younger members of their respective families, my cousins would often come over with their friends or their problems. My father often acted as liaison between parents and their offspring. No one ever seemed to avoid any subjects because I was present. On one occasion I would hear an aunt or uncle asking that my father persuade one of my cousins to act in a certain way. At another time I would receive the other side of the story. I liked having people come to my parents for advice. After these sessions of settling problems, I saw them in a newer light, although I had taken for granted that most of their ideas were right.

Children in families with relatives like these find their social resources multiplied manifold.

3. *The degree of cohesion of the kinship group varied considerably, and on the basis often of clearly indicated conditions.* At one extreme was the clannishness of Sylvia's family, of whom she writes:

Every one of my father's six brothers and sisters visited us periodically with their own families. My grandmother's eleven brothers and sisters also visited, but less frequently because they had to come from greater distances. One of my grandfather's cousins was a frequent visitor with her three grown-up offspring. The house was open to any of them at all times. I never knew what it was like to have dissension or family feuds, and such family disagreements still seem impossible to me whose relatives were such pleasant company.

At the opposite pole was the exclusiveness of the Brown household. The Browns entertained only two relatives, and at the end of a visit remarked, "Thank goodness we have no more relatives within three hundred miles."

Seven conditions are mentioned in the documents as

affecting this degree of cohesion. First are the families where some bar to general acceptance—minority or specific culture groups—tended to hold the members closely together. Represented there were Negro, Jewish, and recent immigrant families. They clung to an older pattern of kinship relationships, and perhaps depended upon it because of their special barriers to the free choice of friends as substitutes.

Second are immigrant families of relatively recent entry where the children, although surrounded by kinfolk, could not speak or understand the language of their relatives, or elected not to do so as a phase of their "emancipation" from the Old World culture. Certain immediate families cut themselves off completely from all relatives. In these cases the different units of the kinship group had assimilated with varying degrees, with a resulting disparity in points of view which tended to separate them. Also, there were foreign-born parents who had left most of their relatives in Europe, and thus were barred from kinship membership.

Third was the family turned transient by the father's occupation, and correspondingly strongly kinship conscious. With little opportunity to make lasting friends, relatives were clung to and visited, often over long distances. On the other hand, a number of kinship groups, widely separated from each other in distance, were not very clan-minded. They made their own friends in their respective areas, and felt no special urge to take on kinship contacts or responsibilities.

Families in which the members of separate immediate family units had achieved widely different social, economic, or educational levels, were also not closely knit together.

Large families, large in the sense that the present-day parent generation has many siblings, seemed to have a tendency to remain living fairly close together and to keep a close feeling of kinship. One document reads:

Ours is a large family, my mother coming from a family of nine children, my father from a family of eight. The aunts and uncles, all married, have provided my brother and me with forty-nine cousins. The result, ours being a close family, is that rarely a day has passed without some relative stopping in to visit.

Country families seemed to have a great many visits from their kinfolk. Several of the children in these families, though, sensed that this was a physical unity only: that the kinfolk regarded their homes as resorts and escapes from the city's dirt and noise.

4. *Friction and incompatibility between the immediate family units and kinfolk are referred to with marked frequency.* Considered as a whole, the sixty-eight documents bring to light a confusion for the families between the patterns of action and thought toward kinship members established in an era when blood ties were close, and the families' desires, because of certain factors in current American life, to free themselves from the behavior demanded by this pattern. Their conflict may be expressed this way. We *think* that the privacy of our homes and the sanctity of our personalities should be respected. We *want* nothing to hamper our individuality of thought and expression. It is our duty to prevent ourselves from being imposed upon and interfered with. But we *feel* that deep sensitivity to blood relationships. Our identification with, and responsibility toward, kinfolk have not been bred out of us. These people do belong to the family in spite of any desires for independence and anonymity, and even when we are tired, rushed, harassed, and preoccupied by a thousand interesting activities of our own. From this friction develop many of the irritations appearing in the family situations involving relatives.

How general this irritation is can best be indicated by a summary of the overtones of the relationships between immediate families and kinfolk. This is, by necessity, a quite superficial tabulation, although simplified in one respect by the frequency with which a family's relationship with all of its relatives conforms to the same pattern. That is to say, our material serves to show that most families like, tolerate, or hate their relatives as such, with somewhat less differentiation than one would suppose. Taking the documents, then, one by one, the relationships between family and kinfolk could on the whole be called companionable in eighteen cases; generally pleasant in seventeen; and tolerant in four. In ten cases, relationships were mostly constrained; in twelve, frankly hostile. Seven cases showed such variability in relationship from relative to relative as to constitute a separate group.

It would seem, then, that out of sixty-eight families, thirty-nine enjoyed agreeable relations with their kinfolk, and twenty-nine, wholly or partly disagreeable ones. But this is too optimistic a conclusion. Writers of case histories are hampered in truthful revelation by the same feelings of identification with blood-kin that influence their behavior toward them. An expression of frank hostility may be taken pretty nearly at face value, as may "I never knew dissension in my family." But, in the case records placing between these two extremes, one must suspect a cover-up, both in absence of expression and in circumspection of behavior described, of a great many cases of unpleasantness and hostility. Taking this into consideration, one could modestly estimate that relatives were sources of irritation in at least half of the families represented in this study.

Two further conclusions which emerge from our material bear upon this problem of friction within the kinship circle. They constitute the next two sections of this chapter.

5. *Viewed through the children's eyes, their families derive from two sources, which tend to be different, and often antagonistic.* Despite the present emphasis upon marriage as a relationship between the contracting partners, operat-

ing on their own initiative, the children see their parents as representatives of two kinship groups, between which tensions are frequent in number and often pervasive in significance. Recognition of this is constant in the material analyzed.

Mother's relatives and father's relatives usually have little in common. Often they are very different kinds of people. And always they are "in-laws" to one of the parents in the family. Children see signs of strained relations between their parents because of this situation. The youngsters themselves form their own individual preferences and think them over.

Mother distinctly disapproves of father's brother and does not like to have him in the house. She acts coldly when he does come. Her dislike is based upon his being a divorcé, she says. However, the child notices, mother's own brother, who is cordially welcomed by her, is "separated" from his wife. A strange young man appears at the door and claims cousinship. Father looks him over, estimates disparagingly, and concludes, "He must be one of your relatives, dear." He is; and he proves to be a family nuisance. Mother's parents and her sisters and brothers come to the house with a warm and eager rush. They enliven the household and delight the children. Father's relatives never cause any friction, but the children do not know quite how to treat them because they seem always to be "trying to control their blood pressure." Dad's crude and uneducated European relatives make his son want to better himself educationally. However, they are sincere and kindly people, whereas Mother's university-trained brother "had to marry" a very objectionable girl and led a slovenly life thereafter. A girl philosophizes upon what she believes to be a universality: that though a wife's relatives are welcomed at all times, her husband has to ask permission to have his kinfolk visit.

These small dramas, which may be acted out in any

family with visiting relatives, can become more tense when the two sides of the family are of different nationalities or of different religious faiths. Mary, whose father was Italian and whose mother was French, writes:

> My mother's two brothers were quite different from my father's brothers, but quite interesting because they traveled so much. They were musicians, worked irregularly, and had no ties. They always brought their music and their instruments; one played the guitar, the other played the clarinet. It seemed to me that they relaxed better and made more music when my father was not around. We children tried to teach them American songs, and they tried to teach us French songs—and even enjoyed the failure. They always made my mother ignore our bed hour—that is, if my father was not there.

The cases in the present study did not happen to reveal differences in religious faiths, but they did show that even differences of degree in religious fervor within the same faith, and between relatives, create special tensions. One can usually choose friends with beliefs and behavior similar to one's own. But relatives will not change theirs for peace's sake, and too often are imbued with an extraordinary missionary zeal in dealing with kinfolk, perhaps because, in a spirit of old-fashioned kinship, they wish some day to find the whole family group intact in a better world, and to be spared the shame of owning relatives domiciled in a less favorable climate.

The significance of this material for the study of the behavior of children resulting from intercultural marriages is obvious.

6. *Relatives live at different economic and social levels.* Money seems to have been a cause of unhappy relations with kinfolk in many of the families represented in this study. Bitterness sprang from three different sources.

First, siblings who grew up in one home, under like economic conditions, married and prospered unequally. In their visits to each other's homes these differences caused self-consciousness. Children were well aware of mother's effort to show off her home to its best advantage to a well-groomed auntie, and of auntie's habit of looking down her nose at the servantless and untidy house. Said one auntie, "You have a charming home here, dear, but you should really have someone in to help you." Relatives, with their special prerogatives, can make suggestions like this.

Second, brothers and sisters who had separated to maintain their individual homes became rivals, each with an eye on the holder of the family fortune. A college boy writes vividly, and with scorn, of the scene surrounding the reading of his uncle's will.

Frank's uncle, his father's brother, had lived in his home during the last twelve years of his life. During his lifetime he had built up a sizable fortune. When he died, all the relatives, down to several-times-removed cousins, appeared at Frank's home for the funeral and the reading of the will. There were the distant relatives who had not even known the deceased personally; the cousin named after his uncle "for very obvious financial reasons"; the aunt who assumed that she was now head of the family; the "painted doll," the divorced wife of the deceased who had been supported "on a lavish scale since their divorce"; and the unpretentious uncle who had evoked the wrath of his rich and departed brother by refusing to accept money from him while he was living. Frank watched their transparent attempts to be funereally somber and kindly disposed to each other as bereaved persons, all in a setting of "mingled anticipation and rivalry," until the will was read, revealing that the family fortune had been left to a home for stray dogs.

A third source of difficulties among relatives, because of money, comes from the fact that parents do not always come from families of like financial status. Mother's relatives always bring lavish gifts to the children. Father's family is nice, but they come empty-handed, and somehow they do not look the same either. You are not so proud to show them off to your friends. When they visit at the same time, neither mother nor father nor anyone else seems quite comfortable. Jean Trent speaks of difficulties in her family. Her father's parents looked down on her mother, because she was an orphan when she married. The other daughters-in-law and their families could do things for the parents. But mother was antagonistic toward them too, because they depended upon her husband for financial support and lowered her own little family's income level.

One of the most significant results to children of these deficiencies in financial status evolves from the fact that relatives with some means assume that this gives them a kind of control over their relatives, and particularly over the children. When these people have no children of their own to spend for, they are more than ever dangerous to family relations. In this study there was introduced the wealthy childless aunt who wished to adopt her widowed relative's children because she could offer them a better life. Such a situation stirs the imagination of children and palpitates in their dream-life, no matter how much they may not want to leave home. This particular aunt, when denied her desire, made an all-out effort to spoil the children. This put the school-teaching mother at a disadvantage and resulted in stormy scenes between the two. There appeared, also, an aunt and uncle who visited periodically and gave money generously to their niece, whose parents, less financially graced, did not believe in allowances. The girl always had either too much money for her own good, or no money at all. To this day she holds a strong resentment against the parents for permitting such a situation. To complete the picture, there were children roused to loyal defense of a home when a relative noted its inadequacy; and of a parent whose motherly softness was always resilient against the hard sophistication of a well-off "career Auntie."

The social status of relatives is noted as a fact in itself, apart from income differences. Ordinarily, children were quite proud of the kinfolk who lent distinction to the family. Artists, professional people, and the frequently mentioned "beautifully groomed" business woman were sources of satisfaction to children living in average servantless homes. They thought a bit better of their family after such a visit. At the other extreme, they fairly writhed with self-consciousness at the relatives who did not do the family justice. The father of one of the writers bought a relative a decent dress because he was ashamed of her looks. The relative was so insulted that she left the house. Commented the child, "This was exactly what father hoped would happen."

7. *Relatives are not acceptable equally to all members of a family.* This fact is significant both for marital relations and for child behavior. It is most significant when relatives come to live with the family. Out of the sixty-eight cases, twenty-four had one or more relatives regularly living in the house permanently, or for long periods, so that they were considered as members of the immediate family.

The material at hand shows that in some cases the attitude of family members toward relatives is entirely individual, as in one home already overcrowded, where the rest of the family extended the invitation to relatives cordially and willingly, but the high-school son, inconvenienced by the noise and confusion, was sullen in his attitude toward the whole situation. In other instances, the presence of relatives precipitated a horizontal cleavage, as in families of more recent American vintage. Here one finds foreign-born parents welcoming Old World relatives, but the children indicating somewhat less enthusiasm. Such cleavages, which caused children to be sulky and snobbish toward the welcomed guests of their parents, do not improve parent-child relationships.

Sometimes the whole family was irritated by the arrival

of a relative fondly accepted by a hospitable mother, who actually had herself to bear the brunt of most of the inconvenience caused by the visit. Aunt Annie was very acceptable to mother. In fact, mother turned the house upside down for her.

This shifting about irritated father, for I overheard him say, "To hell with . . ." but mother shut him up. Mother suggested that I start calling Aunt Annie "Precious." Father said, when he heard about it, "For Christ's sake, why don't you let the boy alone?"

Aunt Annie's winter visits were, generally, in January but never before Christmas. Mother saved presents for her until she came. Each year, auntie would say, "Oh, how lovely everything is. I feel so ashamed that I haven't something for all of you, but I have been so sick all winter that I couldn't get out to do my shopping." Then mother would say, "Hush, hush, Aunt Annie, as if anyone would expect you to buy for all of us here. Don't be silly." Aunt Annie would wipe her eyes and say to my mother, "I don't know what I would do without you, Adelle." One night when we were going to bed, I overheard father talking to grandpa. "It's a hell of a wonder," he said, "that she can't remember the kid." Grandpa replied, "With all her money, she could remember us all."

SUMMARY

1. Four changes have occurred in American family structure in modern times: (1) The decline of the extended or kinship group family; (2) the rising predominance of the immediate family; (3) the decline in the size of the immediate family; and (4) the changing forms of family dissolution.

2. These changes constitute a major revolution in the size of the group which socializes the child.

3. A study of sixty-eight young people reveals the following: (1) Modern youth still feels a marked degree of identification with kinfolk as such; (2) kinfolk regard each other as custodians of the family reputation; (3) the degree of cohesion of the kinship group varies considerably; (4)

friction and incompatibility between the immediate family and kinfolk are referred to with marked frequency; (5) viewed through the children's eyes, their families derive from two sources, which tend to be different, and often antagonistic; (6) relatives often live at different economic and social levels; (7) relatives are not acceptable equally to all members of a family.

CHAPTER V

The Small Family System

It is a bad plan that admits of no modification.—SYRUS

THE importance of the size of an interacting group has long been recognized in a general sort of way. A large industrial plant, one is told, presents problems of labor relations different from a small one. Small classes, as every pedagogue knows, permit teaching methods that are not feasible with larger ones. There is an optimum size for discussion groups. Small memberships in college fraternities result in fraternal relationships not customarily found in larger chapters. The size of the group *is* important. The present, and the succeeding chapter, are concerned with the size of the family group and its significance. Two contrasting sizes are analyzed, with particular reference to their significance for child development.

The present chapter deals with the small family, which has come to be the representative type of family, by size, in American life. It is the type known from experience by most readers of this volume, and studied most extensively by contemporary students. In this chapter, three main topics will be dealt with: first, the prevalence of small families in the United States; second, their distinguishing characteristics; and third, their importance for child development.

THE NUMBER AND PROPORTION OF SMALL FAMILIES

For purposes of this study, the term "small family" means any family with three or less children. Most of the data on family size are to be found in the statistics on size of households. The term "household," as used by the United States Census Bureau, means that "entire group of persons who occupy a house or apartment or room that constitutes a dwelling unit. It includes the related family members and also the unrelated persons, if any, such as lodgers, servants, or hired hands, who share the living quarters. A person living alone, or with unrelated persons, is a household. Institutions, transient hotels, large rooming houses, etc., are not counted as households."[1]

Utilizing Census data for the year 1940, one finds that 48.9 per cent of all households had no related children under eighteen years of age, that 21.3 per cent had one related child under eighteen years, 14.5 per cent had two such related children, and 7.3 per cent had three. This means that 43.1 per cent of all households had three or less children under eighteen. Combining the facts another way, one finds that of 17,922,760 households with related children under eighteen, a total of 15,108,500 had three or less children. Summarizing the data in terms of children under eighteen years, 19 per cent were the only child in the household under that age, 25.8 per cent were one of two, and 19.5 per cent, one of three children under eighteen in the same household. Estimates for 1947 change these percentages only slightly.[2]

Information bearing upon the prevailing size of families can also be obtained from the Census Bureau's data on fertility. This shows that, of all women who, in 1940, were between forty-five and forty-nine years of age, and who reported the total number of children ever borne, one out of six (16.7 per cent) had borne but one child; one out of five (20.0 per cent) had borne two children; and one

1 Bureau of the Census, *General Characteristics of the Population of the United States*, April 1, 1950, Series PC-7, No. 1, p. 3.

2 Bureau of the Census, *Types of Families*, Table 5, Special Report of the 1940 Census, and *Current Population Reports*, Series P-20, No. 11.

out of six (15.3 per cent) had borne three. More than half (52 per cent) of all women reporting had borne three or less children.[3]

The prevalence of small families established by college graduates is shown in a study of 1,327 married graduates of Cornell University in the classes of 1919, 1920, and 1921. Of this number, 19 per cent had no children at all, 22 per cent had only one child, and 31 per cent had only two.[4]

THE SMALL FAMILY SYSTEM

The phrase "small family system" was made a part of the sociological literature with the appearance in 1913 of a small book by that title, written by C. V. Drysdale.[5] It was used originally to identify families with some degree of contraceptive sophistication who were utilizing their knowledge to limit the number of offspring, and students of population still emphasize mainly the characteristic of size, and its relation to problems of the birth rate and population change. Subsequent studies of family life, however, have shown that size is correlated with various other phases of family behavior, until now the term has come to mean a way of family living with definite characteristics, practices, and values.

Selected Features of the Small Family System

Most of the characteristics of the small family system are matters of general agreement. First is its overall theme. The term "theme" is used here in the sense of a dominant affirmation (or attitude value) which tends to control be-

[3] Bureau of the Census, *Differential Fertility, 1940 and 1910,* Special Report of the 1940 Census, Tables 1-4 and 15-18.

[4] W. A. Anderson, *Marriages and Families of University Graduates.* Ithaca: Cornell University Press, 1950, p. 28.

[5] C. V. Drysdale, *The Small Family System.* New York: B. W. Huebsch, 1913.

havior or stimulate activity in a society.[6] In the small family system, the overall theme is planning. Planning is the substance of its procedure and its thinking—planning of size; of the spacing and timing of the birth of the children; of the emphases and programs to be followed in child rearing; of the main objectives in education, with careful attention to its status-achieving and promoting possibilities; and of preparation for subsequent careers. From this point of view, the family is a consciously controlled and directed experiment in living, performed by man, rather than an experiment performed by nature on man, as is the case in more passive and fatalistic cultures.

Second is the fact that parenthood in the small family is intensive rather than extensive. This emphasis begins at the onset of pregnancy, as the mother receives continuing prenatal care. After the child is born, the pediatrician is consulted on matters of diet, immunization, as well as the slightest sickness. Later on, the "child psychologist" may be consulted on the "everyday problems of the everyday child." Should Junior show symptoms of deviant behavior, the psychiatrist is called in. All this marshaling of scientific aids is utilized so that each pregnancy may eventuate in a normal child, that every possible child shall survive and develop to the utmost of his capacities. Such a history of intensive care is today the common lot of the child in the small family, in marked contrast to another and an older system of extensive parenthood in which many children were sired in the hope that some would survive.

Coupled with the program of intensive planned parenthood often are careers for mothers, before or after, or both, marriage and childbearing. It is pertinent to recall here that married women now exceed single ones in the labor force of the United States, and that one out of every four

[6] Morris E. Opler, "Themes as Dynamic Forces in Culture," *American Journal of Sociology*, November 1945, p. 198.

married women is employed gainfully outside of the home. Such employment usually is for the purpose of earning a supplemental income, to be utilized in the realization of family plans. At the upper economic levels, careers of mothers may take the form of club, communal, or various social welfare activities.

Another characteristic has to do with the type of interaction that prevails within the small family. Recent studies have shown that size determinant is an integral part in group interaction.[7] In a small group, according to Bales and others, for example, if the participants "are ranked by the total number of acts they initiate, they will also tend to be ranked by the number of acts they receive."[8] These and other more abstract and generalized studies give full warrant to the idea that the small family tends to make for a coöperative and democratic type of relationship. Each member, and especially the child, can receive a good deal of attention and consideration. Each is given a voice in group discussions, or at least has the opportunity to be heard. It may be more than a coincidence that the democratic and the small family have appeared together in point of time. Furthermore, family planning, motivated so largely by hopes for the future of its child members, naturally emphasizes the importance of coöperative relationships between parent and child. The child is the hope of the

[7] Robert F. Bales, *Interaction Process Analysis: A Method for the Study of Small Groups.* Cambridge, Mass.: Addison-Wesley Press, 1950; also, "A Set of Categories for the Analysis of Small Group Interaction," *American Sociological Review,* April 1950, pp. 257-63; Robert F. Bales, *et al.*, "Channels of Communication in Small Groups," *ibid.*, August 1951, pp. 461-68; Bossard, *The Sociology of Child Development*, pp. 145-49; John James, "A Preliminary Study of the Size Determinant in Small Group Interaction," *American Sociological Review,* August 1951, pp. 474-77; Alexander Paul Hare, *A Study of Interaction and Consensus in Different Sized Discussion Groups.* University of Chicago dissertation, 1951; William M. Kephart, "A Quantitative Analysis of Intragroup Relationships," *American Journal of Sociology*, May 1950, pp. 544-49.

[8] Bales, *et al.*, "Channels of Communication in Small Groups," *American Sociological Review,* August 1951, p. 468.

family plan. The essence of good parent-child relationships is to have the child coöperate voluntarily rather than be high-pressured into the family program. Here is another reason for small family parents to take recourse to books and courses on child psychology, the better to understand children and to promote such coöperation.

Coupled with this greater freedom and democracy of expression in the small family is the individualizing of the activities and roles of its members. Small family living makes for individual emphasis, in development and in thinking. The family members are noncompeting: father, mother, and child each goes his own respective way.

This lack of competition within the family turns its "green" eyes outward, accounting for what Margaret Mead[9] has called the sidewise look by the parents, meaning that they compare and measure their children primarily with children in other families in the same residential area, the same social class or clique, or the same school. This reinforces the pressure by the parents on the child, already inherent in the planning procedure which underlies small family living.

This sidewise look applies characteristically to kinfolk and certain other close associates. Relatively little attention is given to kinfolk unless they fit into, and can contribute to, the planned goals of the small family. A study made of the attitudes toward kinfolk of sixty-eight university students revealed that much importance was attached by them to the fact that relatives live at different economic and social levels.[10] This attitude on the part of the students obviously is a reflection of that of the parents.

The planning emphasis in the small family; the sidewise view which characterizes its thinking, particularly in re-

[9] Margaret Mead, *And Keep Your Powder Dry*. New York: William Morrow and Co., 1943, p. 109.

[10] James H. S. Bossard and Eleanor S. Boll, "The Immediate Family and the Kinship Group," *Social Forces*, May 1946, p. 383.

gard to its child members; the relative lack of contacts with kinfolk: all combine to lead the small family to make an appraising selection of home sites and residential areas, on the basis of their contribution to family plans. School facilities, recreational opportunities, social contacts, are three of the important considerations which underlie these selections. To a very large extent the contemporary suburb, with its standardization of some specialized pattern of living, is the product of these selections. Small families tend to group themselves on the basis of their family plans and ambitions.

As an illustration of what has just been said, a study of a Philadelphia suburb, made under the general direction of the author, may be cited. Cheltenham Township is a residential suburb, adjacent to Philadelphia, ten miles north of the center of the city. A careful analysis of the area shows the following:

1. People move into the area as families, not as individuals.

2. Families moving there are small. One out of five (21 per cent) had one child; a third (34.5 per cent) had two children; and three out of four (77.5 per cent) had three or less children.

3. Eighty-four per cent moved into the area after the first child was born; 71 per cent, after the oldest child was two years of age.

4. Seven out of ten families (71 per cent) owned their homes in the area.[11]

The small family system is a quality system. It prevails primarily at the middle- and upper-class levels. Its driving force is one of ambition, in an open-class system, in which a large proportion of the population aims at raising the status or pretends to have a status higher than is actually

[11] Arthur H. Jones, *Cheltenham Township*. Philadelphia: University of Pennsylvania Press, 1940, chaps. V and VI.

attained. Small families invariably are under stress, stress to achieve and to get ahead. This stress or pressure falls with particular heaviness upon the children, who are the potentials of the family's status-raising program. Most children in small families grow up under the shadow, so to speak, of the family level of expectation. Because the parents do so much for the children, they expect a great deal from them in turn. Children are pushed to the utmost, often without regard for their capacities, limitations, interests or needs. Because of the small number of children, the parents allow no margin of error or failure, as tends to be the case in the larger family.

An added factor here is that the parents tend to impose not only their own ambitions, but also their unfulfilled desires, upon their children. The man with a lifelong but unfulfilled wish to be a doctor drives his son toward the medical profession, willy nilly; the mother who never rated socially when a girl now grooms her daughter for a social career, regardless of the latter's abilities or interests. The drive of these unfulfilled desires of the parents, and how they may complicate the lives of their children, are particularly obvious to educators at the college and university level.

Significance for Child Development

The literature on child development in the small family tends to fall into two main parts. The first part deals specifically with the problems of the only child; the other, with the more general results of the small family system.

Almost one-fifth of all completed families (wife forty-five years of age and over) today have only one child. This represents a tenfold increase during the past two centuries. Both popular comment and scientific studies agree that he differs in certain respects from other children. There is an extensive literature on the only child, and this is summarized in one of the author's earlier publications.[12] Suffice it to say here that there is a continuing recognition of him as a problem. The two types most often recognized are: (a) the "spoiled," egocentric, difficult, and unsocial child; and (b) the sensitive, shy, hesitant, and often unduly dependent kind. The two groups of causal factors usually emphasized are his lack of necessary association with other children, and the complementary condition of receiving too much attention from adults, chiefly the parents. As a result, the only child does not receive adequate training in competing with other children in the family, and the parents are apt to be oversolicitous as well as spending too much time with the child. Operating to the only child's advantage is the fact that the parents are able often, because there is just one child, to make possible superior advantages of various kinds.

1. Turning now to aspects of growing up in a small family that are not necessarily restricted to the one-child family, certain facts and problems seem obvious. First, there is no doubt that children in small families enjoy advantages beyond those available to children in large families at corresponding economic and social levels. Furthermore, they receive more individual attention from their parents. With fewer to consider, their value seems greater; their health and safety and security seem more important. These general considerations, when translated into specific opportunities and services, comprise many of the factors that are important in child development, and, to the contemporary parent, they outweigh other considerations, as the birth statistics of Western culture clearly show. Mature reflection and long-continued study of the small family system suggest, however, additional problems which must be considered.

2. The small family child's earliest social experiences

[12] Bossard, *The Sociology of Child Development*, pp. 101-4.

(that is, with other persons) is in a small group. This is an obvious fact, but its implications would seem to be of very great importance. These implications grow out of the size and composition of the small family group as compared with the characteristics of most other groups in which one lives and works. A small family consists ordinarily of two or more adults, and from one to three children. Life within this group tends to be organized so that the child or children occupy the center of the stage. Their efforts tend to be eased and encouraged by adults. They enjoy "protected" competition. Much is done for them by their parents. Parents often have to double as parents, as playmates, and as friends. On the basis of these early experiences, the child forms his conception of himself, his role, and his importance in the group. He grows up in a world that largely revolves around him, and he thinks of himself accordingly.

A somewhat exaggerated illustration of the point in mind is found in the following excerpt from a life-history document in the files of the William T. Carter Foundation:

> I grew up as an only child. In our house lived my father, my mother, two uncles, and two servants. Until I was twelve years old, this was our household. A great many other adults came and went, as visitors or in some other capacity. Always, I was the center of attraction, and the main recipient of attention. This was the situation in which my habit patterns developed, habits which created so many problems for me as I grew older, for, unless I could always be the center of attention in a group, I would either sulk, behave conspicuously, or withdraw from the group.

Compare situations of this kind with those which obtain today in group life outside of the family. Let us begin with his school groups. Whereas most children in earlier years in the history of this country grew up in a large family and then entered a small school, today an increasing number of children leave a small family to enter a large and complex school situation; where once he went to school through quiet lanes and streets in company with other siblings in his family, today he may go alone through a maze of heartless and hectic traffic. Warren S., for example, is twelve years old. He has a sister aged six. To reach his school, he walks a mile and a half, crossing three heavily traveled lanes of traffic, only one of which has police supervision. When he arrives at school, he is one of 918 in his class. He is in Section 37 in English. His mother cannot understand why he cries and asks not to go to school.

Or, consider the industrial situation which the small family child enters today. The chances mathematically are that he goes to work in a large plant or office building, along with thousands, or even hundreds of thousands, of other persons. He is a single cog in a huge machine, a role diametrically the opposite of that he enjoyed in the small family.

Another type of situation which a large proportion of young men, and an increasing proportion of young women, are compelled to enter, is service in the armed forces. Stouffer and others have called attention to the problems of adjustment of American youth during World War II. In five years, from 1940 to 1945, the American army grew from 16,624 officers and 249,411 enlisted men to 772,863 officers and 7,305,854 enlisted men. Army life involved a totally new way of life for most of these people, with its authoritarian organization, its demand upon rigid obedience, its highly stratified social system, and its emphasis upon traditional ways of doing.[13] Small wonder that one out of five came to be rejected for psychiatric reasons.[14]

It is not meant to imply that the small family child always finds himself a problem at school, in indsutry, or in military service. What is being emphasized here is the dis-

[13] Samuel A. Stouffer, *et al.*, *The American Soldier*. Princeton: Princeton University Press, 1949, Vol. I, p. 54.

[14] Edward A. Strecker, *Their Mothers' Sons*. Philadelphia: J. B. Lippincott Co., 1946.

parity between the small family life situation and those which most young people enter today as they leave home; as well as between the individualized dominating role they enjoy in a small family setting, and that which most of them are destined to play at school, at work, and in the armed forces. There seems to be, then, this curious paradox about the small family system, that, while it represents an adjustment to the high expectancies and ambitions of modern living, it is a correspondingly inadequate training ground for performance in the realities of its everyday work. In short, people have small families in answer to the demands of modern life, but small families provide a poor kind of training to meet its requirements. To the extent that this is so, one finds here an illustration of how some civilizations tend to be self-destructive.

3. One of the most important features of child development in the small family is the undue pressure upon the child or children. Everything that has been said about the small family characteristics underscores the high level of expectation of the parents. Most every parent is ambitious for his children: the small family parent is so to an exaggerated degree, both because there are so few children on which he can focus his ambitions, and also because the whole family life is organized around the children's future development. Because these expectations and pressures often disregard the actual capacities, interests, and limitations of the children, they are the source of many serious strains and corresponding problems. Ambitious parents may complicate the lives of their children, too, and it is no secret that they often do.

There are many concrete aspects around which these family pressures cluster. Some of them center around the interest in family continuity, with undue solicitousness over the health or marriage of a child. Perhaps the mother has refused to bear more than one child, she may have aborted one, she may have tried to avoid having the child but failed; all these and other circumstances may create feelings of guilt, of undue anxiety, of abnormal apprehensions. The result invariably is an unhealthy and unnatural concern with and for the child. Not all interest in family continuity is conditioned by circumstances of this kind; obviously, much of it is a wholly normal concern, focusing heavily upon children in small families only because there are so few of them.

Or consider families in which there is an established business, or where the family history shows a succession of generations represented in the same profession or social position. Here is a family which has held an honored position for several generations in the law, or medicine, or the armed forces, or social circles. Naturally parents and grandparents who achieved such positions want their decendants at least to maintain such status, if not to raise it. Pressures of this kind often come, not only from members of the immediate family, but also from the larger kinship circle. When the child's capacities and interests coincide with those of his family, there is only the tension of intense pressure; it is when they do not, when the child either cannot or is not interested in functioning at the level of family expectancy, that more serious problems are created. The late William A. Percy wrote with great poignancy of such a situation in his own case, pointing out his father's (one time United States Senator from Mississippi) disappointment in a son whose interests ran in a different direction.[15]

4. The size of the small family creates, or intensifies, a number of emotional problems, four of which will be summarized briefly. There is, to begin with, a high degree of emotional concentration in the contemporary small family, due not only to the limited number of members, but also

[15] William A. Percy, *Lanterns on the Levee*. New York: Alfred A. Knopf, Inc., 1939.

because the immediate family has become so largely the sole important kinship unit. So far as the children are concerned, this means that the love and solicitude of the parents are centered on very few persons: in the case of the only child, on but one person. In any particular family, the intensity of such concentration depends upon the emotional output of the parents and the number of the children.

This accentuation of the problem of relations of members to each other in small family groups is particularly apt to lead to difficulties if the size of the group is three (the one-child family), for it raises inevitably a two-against-one issue. Most often this means that one parent and the child combine against the other parent. Especially do such situations obtain when one parent is antagonistic to another.

The Vernons have been married for nineteen years. Mrs. V. frankly states that she never has loved her husband. They have one child, a son of eleven, whose birth was the result of an unwanted pregnancy by the mother. During the son's entire life, the mother has clung closely to him, and has cultivated, subtly to be sure, a latent antagonism in the boy toward his father.

In other instances, a husband shows signs of jealousy of a child, and visits his displeasure upon both mother and child, with a resultant common resentment against him. In still other cases, the husband and child may compete with each other for the attentions of the mother. Such was the case in the Laird family.

Mr. Laird married a woman three years older than himself, after having been much "spoiled" by his mother. When their one child was born, and the mother gave normal attention to the child, the husband became petulant and resentful. Soon he began to increase his demands upon the mother, as though vying with the baby for attention. As the child grew older, and began to sense the pattern of behavior of the demanding father, she, too, became more and more demanding. As a result, by the time the child was thirteen, the mother's health was impaired by the increasing demands of the father and daughter competitors. Mrs. Laird was a highly conscientious and motherly person, who sought to be both a good mother and a dutiful wife.

Again, there is the frequency with which competition develops for the affection of the children in small families. This competition ordinarily is of two kinds: one where the parents compete with each other; second, where other kinfolk are involved. Both kinds of such rivalries may grow out of personality clashes in the child's family background, but they are most apt to be pronounced and serious when cultural differences obtain, such as religious, class, economic, or national group differences. In cases of this kind, the child becomes a pawn in a game between conflicting cultural groups, with his affection, loyalty, or possession the symbol of victory or defeat.

The emotional problem in the small family probably most emphasized in the literature is that of the child's social weaning. By "social weaning" we mean here the readjustment of parent-child relationships in keeping with the child's growing maturity.[16] This is a part of the normal process of growing up, and occurs usually between the twelfth and the twentieth year. While it presents some difficulties for both child and parent, in the large family any reluctance that parents may have to seeing their child grow up and away from them is limited because of the ease with which parents can transfer their possessive feelings to the younger children. In the small family, such transfer is more difficult or impossible, so that the process of weaning often is delayed, if not prevented entirely.

Finally, there is the relation of the small family system to the discipline of the children. The emotional implications here are of very great importance. In small families, the overwhelming proportion of the disciplining must be done by the parents. If the child needs a lot of disciplining, or the parents are unusually dominating, or both, an undue

[16] Bossard, *The Sociology of Child Development*, p. 422.

amount of disciplining of one child is done by one or both parents. The result is a concentration of deeply conflicting emotions: of deep devotion and love by parents who do so much for their children, and of marked resentment by children against extensive disciplining. This antithesis in the child's intimate background may well be the source of many of the deep-seated conflicts that characterize the current generation. It is in these respects in particular that the small family stands in such striking contrast to the large family system where the children largely discipline each other.

5. People are prone to identify themselves with the groups to which they belong. Size of group is an obvious group characteristic, and it means a great deal to its individual members. Students in a large university, members of a large fraternity, soldiers in a large army, and citizens of a large country, tend to consider themselves important because they are a part of a large organization. Conversely, members of a small group, particularly of so meaningful a group as the family, may feel, even if not wholly at the level of consciousness, a certain insignificance. This is perhaps the larger background of those feelings of loneliness and insecurity which are generally attributed to the small family child. He is a chronic victim of loneliness, of intimate contact with peers at odd moments when one can "take down one's hair." This lack of intimate contacts with peers is, in turn, a part of a larger isolation. Gruenberg has written of this:

> In the small city family, the child grows up in relative isolation. He may perhaps see many people of all sizes and ages. And under present crowded conditions, the household may include various relatives or a grandparent. But the child has direct and vital dealings with very few persons.[17]

[17] Sidonie Matsner Gruenberg, "Changing Conceptions of the Family," *The Annals of the American Academy of Political and Social Science,* May 1947, p. 130.

Perhaps the basic fact here is that the child in the small family views the world from a very narrow ledge. His insecurity grows out of the smallness of his group, the limited group of dependable peer supporters, the lack of feelings of nearness to kinfolk, and the uncertain durability of his immediate family. There is nothing perplexing about the widespread prevalence of people with feelings of inferiority and insecurity. Many of them are small family people, reared in relative isolation: lonely folk, almost faceless and nameless, in the lonely crowd.[18]

The complement to this relative isolation from peers is the fact that small family children spend so much of their earlier years in the company of adults. Adults play with them, walk with them, study with them, educate them, and discipline them. They see much of life through adult eyes; they sense the nature of adult pressures and tensions; they adjust to adult demands. And the adjustments made by children to adults differ from those made to other children. The literature on the oldest child has revealed this: how the child assumes the tolerance of elders yet thinks of them as aliens; how the element of power comes to be emphasized unduly; how it means association with persons who are preoccupied with other problems, and who will agree to patterns of behavior which relieve them of attention and responsibility.

6. A final point, often overlooked, is that the impact of crises often varies in seriousness with the number of persons who can share them. "Misery loves company" is not only a trite old saying but also points toward a valid sociological principle. The shadow which divorce casts over the lives of children in our contemporary culture has received considerable emphasis: rather less emphasis has been given to the impact of other family crises, particularly if there are

[18] David Riesman, *The Lonely Crowd*. New Haven: Yale University Press, 1950.

but one or two children. Nine-year-old Beatrice summarized the situation rather aptly in the following conversation with her mother:

Beatrice: "Mother, can we adopt another little girl?"
Mother: "I don't know, but I doubt it."
Beatrice: "I wish we had another girl living with us."
Mother: "Why?"
Beatrice: "Well, if there was another little girl, it wouldn't be so bad when father and you go yackety-yack all the time. If there was another little girl, we could comfort each other when daddy and you do that."

In the small family system, experiences tend to be shared with so few people. The child in the small family has so few people, particularly peers, to talk over his problems and to help him over a psychological hurdle. The important fact about so many life experiences is that they need to be shared, if their true meaning is to be assessed. This is as true of joys as of sorrows; of achievements as well as of failures; of triumphs as well as of disappointments. It is at this point that one wonders to what extent the size of the group helps to determine whether one becomes an extrovert or an introvert, whether one finds life's truest meanings in contacts with other people, or whether one is driven within one's self for these satisfactions. Obviously, other factors are important in the development of these contrasting types: our question here is one of the identification of a contributing cause.

SUMMARY

The small family system constitutes, then, a distinct type of family situation for the rearing of children. Such children are likely to enjoy certain superior advantages and opportunities, particularly in so far as individual care and relative economic resources are involved. On the other hand, they have to pay a price for all this, chiefly in the form of problem-creating circumstances. There is the danger, purely on the basis of the arithmetic of the situation, of acquiring an exaggerated opinion of their importance in group life. There is the continuing factor often of an undue pressure to achieve, and to excel. There is the atmosphere of concentrated emotions, as well as the necessity of dealing unduly with adults, preoccupied with the weight of their pressures in their own lives. Finally, there is the comfort or the inadequacy of sharing life and its experiences.

The small family system is a quality system. It is based on the idea of achievement. It is an upward, climbing system, adapted to the requirements and opportunities of an open-class system. It is a rationalized system, giving sway to long-range planning rather than a passive hopefulness or a careless disregard. It is a system of prudence, based on the insecurities of a rapidly changing culture.

CHAPTER VI

The Large Family System*

The murmuring of many voices, the upturning of many faces.
—CHARLES DICKENS

CURRENT thinking concerning child and personality development has become so family-minded that it even counts its tasks in terms of families rather than of children; this in spite of the obvious fact that a family with twelve children is twelve times as important statistically as a family with one child. Examination of Census data on types of families by size will reveal the contrast that has just been made. Of all households (35,087,440) enumerated in 1940, only 2.2 per cent (765,560) had six or more related children under eighteen years of age. Reckoning in terms of household units, families of such size seem relatively unimportant. Counting in terms of children, however, a total of 5,134,159, or 13 per cent of all children under 18, were found in these families. To put it another way, one out of every 46 families had six or more children under 18 years of age, but almost one out of every seven children was reared in families of such size. If the same comparison is made for households with five or more related children under 18, the percentage of all households is 4.2 but the percentage of children found in these households is 22.1. This might be compared with the fact that 19 per cent of all children under 18 were enumerated in households with but one related child, and with 25.8 per cent of all children in households with two related children under

* Author's Note—In the research paper reported in this chapter, I have had the assistance of Winogene Pratt Sanger, sometime Research Associate of the Carter Foundation. She should be noted as co-author of this chapter.

18 years of age.[1] Comparable data for 1950 are not available at the present writing. It is anticipated that they may change, but not materially alter, the relative proportions prevailing in 1940. Obviously, then, the large family is more important, as a family situation in the development of American children, than has been generally appreciated. It was this conclusion which led to the formulation, in 1948, of a pilot study of the large family, with particular reference to its role in the field of child development, as one of the research projects of the William T. Carter Foundation at the University of Pennsylvania. This chapter is a first report on selected aspects of this study. The completed study will be presented in book form at a later date. This chapter will explain briefly the case material upon which this study is based, the methodology utilized in the gathering of the material, and certain tentative conclusions formulated at this stage of the study.

THE FAMILIES IN BRIEF SUMMARY

Twenty-five families are included in this study. Eighteen of them are Protestants, six are Roman Catholic, and one is Jewish. Fifteen are native-born white of native-born parentage, six are native-born white of foreign-born or mixed parentage, and four are foreign born. Residentially, they range from New England to North Carolina: all east of the Mississippi. Seventeen are small-town families, six are city products, and two are farm families. By father's occupation, they represent considerable diversity, with the majority in the lower rather than the upper half of the occupational hierarchy. By size, all but one of the families had six or more children; eight have ten or more children. The twenty-five families had a total of 222 children, of

[1] Bureau of the Census, Department of Commerce, Special Report of 1940 Census. *Types of Families*, Table 5.

whom 121 were boys and 101 were girls. The children range in age from two years to fifty-three.

SOME METHODOLOGICAL NOTES

Two persons have collaborated in the study to date. One, of male sex, is the older of two children; the other, a woman, is the product of a family of twelve, and is the oldest of ten children. The methods utilized have consisted of the following: (a) the formal recording of basic data concerning the families; (b) written analyses of the families, centering around twelve suggested topics, furnished by a sibling member or members of the families; (c) non-directed interviews with the informants. These interviews have been highly informal, and were repeated as need for information and willingness to contribute it have warranted. In the case of twenty-one families, there has been one informant; in four cases, more than one.

Three conclusions concerning methodology have emerged thus far. One is the concept of *the interacting size of the family,* meaning the numbers of persons living together within the household at a given time. This concept is important because the interacting size varies often from the number of siblings ever born, and/or of other persons who have ever lived in the household. One reason for this is the distribution in point of time of the birth of the siblings. In one of our families, for example, with fourteen siblings, four older children had left home and married before the last two were born; whereas in another family, seven siblings were born within nine years, so that all lived together for a number of years. For many purposes of sociological analysis, size of immediate family does not consist of the total number of parents and siblings ever born, but the number of persons living together at any given time. A large family partakes in this respect of the nature of an audience at the reading of a scientific paper: the number is fluid and changes at irregular rates and times. Or, it resembles the traveling personnel of a transcontinental Pullman car, with passengers boarding and alighting at various points en route.

A second conclusion is that a family situation does not consist primarily of a number of concrete facts, but rather of a series of viewpoints which change from one person to another, and from time to time. Many concrete facts about a family remain the same, but the shadow which they cast varies with time and the place of the observer. In studying the internal life of a family the order of birth of the informant is highly important. Concretely and tangibly, a family is made up of people and things; psychologically and socially, it consists of attitudes and relationships, which are subtle often and change with varying degrees of rapidity.

Third, in our methodological evaluations, the chief reliance is upon relatively free associational writing for those persons who write readily, and the nondirective interview in all other cases. Persons differ markedly in their ability to verbalize, particularly about intimate aspects of their lives. Some can do so best on paper, others via the conversational route. For some items of information, the formal questionnaire method is permissible, and we have used it to some extent; but for an understanding of complex human situations, other methods are preferred. We have indicated elsewhere the main reliances in our study of family life.[2]

SELECTIVE TENTATIVE CONCLUSIONS

Twenty-five cases is too small a number to have any statistical significance. What is presented is rather a series of highly tentative conclusions, which can be formulated

[2] James H. S. Bossard and Eleanor S. Boll, *Ritual in Family Living*. Philadelphia: University of Pennsylvania Press, 1950, chap. X.

into a series of hypotheses, to be tested in more pretentious and specialized studies.

1. Our first and overall conclusion is that the large family is not like any other family, differing only in size, but that there is a large family system, that it involves a distinct way of life, in clear distinction to the small family system, and that virtually every aspect of family life is different in the large family system.

The far-reaching implications of this statement are apparent. If the family is as important in conditioning the life of the individual as has been generally assumed, and if the large family system constitutes a distinctly different way of life, then it produces an entirely different personality type. And if this is true, then the shift from the large to the small family system in past decades involves no less than a fundamental change in the type of personality produced. Specifically, this means a distinctively different kind of child, with different behavior patterns and problems.

2. The large family may be planned, too. A surprising proportion of our families seem to be, not as to specific number but for general size. This is not the place to enter into a discussion of the motives and factors that affect family size. However, since so many of the past studies in this field have taken the form of a statistical exercise in the identification of some one or other factor, mention might be made of our own hypotheses. First, the motivation involved in bringing human beings into the world is more a projection of a person's philosophy of life into the future, than of a specific statistical circumstance. Such a philosophy, whether worthy, rational, or the reverse of these, is the product of past experience, plus the hope of the future. Life unfolds in terms of the whole rather than as particles making up an aggregate. All life is dominated by a dynamic cohesiveness, in which the past, present, and future are

indivisibly related.[3] It is quite true, of course, that the working out of this philosophy depends upon the technical aids known to a person. In this case, this means his degree of contraceptive sophistication.

Second, our study suggests that there is an individual rather than a husband-wife attitude toward family size. The past literature seems to assume that it is the attitude of the married pair which constitutes the unit for study, due perhaps to the fact that past investigations have dealt largely with small families in which some degree of family planning is accepted by both parents. In the case of the large families in this study, one is impressed with differences, and often decided ones, in the attitudes of the two parents toward family size. In one of our families, for example, the mother is proud of her progeny scattered about, but the father will not take his children to town because he is ashamed that there are so many. In another case, the father sees his eleven children as living proofs of his prowess, while the mother slyly hopes that our study will reveal other ways of satisfying men like him.

3. When, as, and if the large family is not planned, it tends to develop certain patterns of an active acceptance of fate. In fact, one of the things which early strikes one about large families is the tendency to take many crises, especially minor ones, in stride. This is true much more than in small families, perhaps for two main reasons: one, the fact that crises occur so much more frequently, and, second, that they are shared in by so many more persons. For example, the spilling of ink on a tablecloth becomes in the small family, a major crisis, with father, mother, and child involved. All three work on the mess, with the parents doing the major part. The same incident, in a large family, leaves father undisturbed with the evening paper

[3] Marshall C. Greco, *Group Life*. New York: Philosophical Library, 1950, chap. II.

and mother intent on her sewing. The child who spilled the ink wipes it up, aided perhaps by another child. So many minor anxieties and crises occur that children, and parents, in large families develop immunity against all but the major casualties.

Large family living, then, makes for adjustment to the changing vicissitudes of a realistic world. Things are always happening in a large family, its members live in an ever-changing milieu, so that they are under the necessity of adjusting repeatedly to changes in role, in status, in responsibilities, in group and individual circumstances, and in possibilities of individual development. Since there is less change within the small family our comparison suggests that while the small family system represents a group adjustment to social change, the large family system is the best training ground for it.

4. The large family seems to be peculiarly vulnerable to major crises, chiefly because of its size, especially when the children are young. Such vulnerability grows not out of the prevalence of divorce or separation, as is the case in the small family system, but out of the death or disabling sickness of one or both of the parents. While there was not one case of divorce or separation in our twenty-five families, there were eleven cases of this other kind of crisis. In one case, both parents died; in five cases, the mother died; in five cases, the father died—all during the dependency of the majority of the children. Furthermore, in five of the ten cases where one of the parents died, the remaining parent remarried, with the resulting complications of step-parents, stepbrothers and/or stepsisters. In all but one of the ten cases, relatively serious problems of readjustment were created by the death of a parent; in all eleven cases, the economic results were of major importance.

5. One of our main conclusions is that the large family emphasizes the group rather than the individual. What one

can do, as a large family member, depends upon what others do, and plan to do. Most large families operate on a close economic margin, if margin at all, which means that economic necessity makes coöperation a virtue. At every turn, it is not only one's own efforts, but the modifying forces of the behavior of other family members that determines what one can do or cannot do. The condition of the hand-me-down that must be worn, the acquiring of a new dress, the use of the living room for your date, of being able to go to town alone, of getting to sleep early, of taking a night school course—all these are grist of the group mill.

Once the central importance of the group concept is recognized, many implied emphases in large family living become apparent. Two of these will be touched upon here. First, the larger the family group becomes, the more internal organization and dominance of some one or two persons appear. A large group of persons, of differing ages and sexes, living within a limited space, on a limited income, and with limited living facilities of various kinds, requires some degree of organization, administration, authoritarian control, and executive direction. This may mean a dominant role for the father, the mother, or occasionally for an older sibling. The degree of dominance developed and accepted may vary considerably, but some degree seems inevitable. Our present hypothesis is that the extent to which such executive dominance appears is a correlate of size, other things being equal. This would tend to suggest that the earlier authoritarian type of family was the product, at least in part, of the large family system, creating an authoritarianism that was then transferred to the larger society, just as the small family system emphasizes individual development and a democratically minded society. Along with this authoritarian type of family go certain complementary virtues of behavior. Conformity is valued above self-expression. Coöperation is needed more than individualism. Listening is the rule rather than talking, which suggests that the current cocktail party pattern of everyone talking and no one listening may be a by-product of the small family system.

A second implication of the group concept, as applied to the large family system, is the specialization of role and function which occurs among its members. Apparently the degree of such specialization correlates with increase in the size of the group. Durkheim developed the underlying principle of this in his analysis of the division of labor, pointing out that the larger the number of people living together, the greater the division of labor and specialization of function there are apt to be.[4]

Specialization, within the large family, takes many forms. Earlier, it was quite customary in many large families to direct members, especially male members, into differing occupations. Thus, one son might be given to the church, another to the army, another to the law. Considering, however, only the more prosaic forms of specialization, we find it universal in our families. One aspect is to be found in the tasks assigned customarily to different members. Such assignments are based partly on specialized aptitudes or skills, partly on differences of interest, and partly on age and sex differentials.

From these assignments to specialized tasks within the family, and the siblings' adjustment to them, emerges the unity of larger patterns of behavior. Thus, in one of our families, one girl was the household drudge; another, a son, the father substitute; another, the "gadder-about"; another, the silent, stubborn one, with reputed deep emotions, whom it was best to leave alone; a fifth, the whiner, who tried always to shirk his duties; the next, the informer, who carried tales to parents and kinfolk.

[4] George Simpson, *Emile Durkheim on the Division of Labor in Society.* New York: The Macmillan Co., 1933, Book II.

This specialization of role among the siblings is particularly important in a large family, not only because the degree of specialization increases as a correlate of size, but also because the number of siblings limits the range of choice of those lower in the order of birth. Only the oldest child has a relatively unlimited choice. Since no one wants to duplicate the role of another sibling, each succeeding child's choice is limited by the choices of his predecessors in the order of birth. Specialized roles are pre-empted by the older siblings: they come to be firmly held with the progress of time. Thus the younger children in a large family may have greater difficulty in finding satisfactory roles within the family group. Also, they may be under greater temptation to develop patterns of rebellion. At any rate, our hypothesis is that such specialization of role, and the individual response to it, come early in life for members of large families; that such experience is of importance in shaping the patterned form of adjustment to life; and that both the early acceptance of assigned role in the group, or rebellion to it, are important determinants in shaping the personality. Often, the subsequent effort to escape an early assigned role and transfer to another becomes one of life's basic drives.

6. Durkheim points out still another principle of value in the study of the large family system. The greater the degree of specialization, he says, the greater the degree of interdependence that comes about. This in turn demands *consensus*, a term and idea which Durkheim has contributed to sociology. It is this *consensus* which gives unity to the group, binds the members together, and "the greater the diversity of relations..., the more it creates links which attach the individual to the group."[5] It is our hypothesis that the larger the family group, that is, the more persons are living together in a family, the more family consensus tends to develop, the stronger its hold upon individual mem-

[5] *Ibid.*, p. 109.

bers becomes, and the stronger the position of the father as its directive symbol becomes.

7. Discipline in the large family may be exercised in the name of the constitutional monarch, but much of it is executed by the siblings. Children in a large family discipline each other, adjustments must be made to peers, not primarily to adults. Competitions between siblings are lifelike, not "protected." The disciplinary pressures are often more subtle than overt. The group is impatient with nonconforming members; there is ridicule for the odd one; there is disdain for the vexing transgressor.

The complement to this sibling-rearing-by-siblings is a pattern of parental behavior quite different from that which obtains in the contemporary small family. The oversolicitous mother is strangely out of place in a family of twelve. The nagging parent, the type who says, "Mary, go out and see what Johnny is doing and tell him to stop," is too much occupied in a large family to "ride" any one child. Both parent and child in a large family are apt to be less demanding and less possessive in their attitudes toward each other. The stark realities of large family living laugh to scorn the neurotic sins of the small family. In short, our hypothesis here tends to agree with George Bernard Shaw's comments years ago: "The old observation," he writes, "that members of large families get on in the world holds good because in large families it is impossible for each child to receive what schoolmasters call 'individual attention.' The children may receive a good deal of individual attention from one another in the shape of outspoken reproach, ruthless ridicule, and violent resistance to their attempts at aggression; but the parental despots are compelled by the multitude of their subjects to resort to political rather than to personal rule, and to spread their attempts at moral monster-making over so many children, that each child has enough freedom, and enough sport in the prophylactic process of laughing at its elders behind their backs, to escape with much less damage than the single child."[6]

8. *Are the older children in large families penalized by the parents' inability to launch them properly on their adult careers?* Contemporary students of the family appreciate the importance of distinct stages in the family history, each with its own crises, preoccupations, and problems. Parenthood is one such major stage, with three rather distinct substages comprehending its span. These are the childbearing, the child-rearing, and the child-launching substages.

In the case of the small family, these three are distinct and well defined, both in point of interest and of time, particularly so when the small number of children are born close together. The case material suggests that the fundamental problem of the older children in large families lies in the fact that by the time they reach the need-to-be-launched stage, their parents are still occupied with the tasks of the child-rearing and childbearing stages. There are, to be sure, those few remarkable parents, so energized or financed, that they can bear, rear, and launch a dozen children with noticeable effectiveness, but they are nonexistent thus far in our study. Mostly, the older children in large families launch themselves, if indeed they are launched at all, or, in recent years, they are launched in and by the armed forces of their country.

9. Reference to the family cycle and a consequent long-time consideration of family life suggests another question. *Does the large family facilitate a more balanced conception of child-rearing problems, particularly in the case of the younger children?* Our material tends to show that many children make for extended accumulation of parental experience, and such accumulated experience tends to teach

[6] George Bernard Shaw, *Misalliance.* New York: Brentano's, 1914, pp. xix, xx.

that various problems represent a temporary phase of the growing-up process, often best cured by liberal doses of judicious neglect. Parents of small families often act neurotically about these phases and tend to communicate their neurotic concern to the child; parents of large families learn to take many family and child development problems in stride.

10. Much of what has been said in this chapter might be interpreted to suggest that all is sweetness and light within the large family. This certainly is not the case, and our observations reveal various other aspects. Life in the large family tends to be decidedly complex. The laws of family interaction presented in the succeeding chapter will show with mathematical precision that the number of personal interrelationships in a group grows more rapidly than does the number of persons. These numbers in turn have to be considered against the background of available space of living quarters. We are proposing in the next chapter a spatial index for family interaction, which expresses quantitatively the spatial setting for family and other intragroup relations.

Thinking prosaically, in terms of numbers of persons, sets of personal interrelationships, square feet of living quarters, number of bedrooms and bathrooms, it must be evident that the large family, especially when living at moderate and lower income levels, faces many problems of internal stress and strain. Our studies of rituals in large families at lower income levels reveal that many of them are routinized adjustments to living under cramped quarters.

The limitations of this chapter permit presentation of but a few of more than thirty hypotheses which have been formulated on the basis of the pilot study. All of them center around the main contentions of this chapter: (1) That the large, like the small, family involves a system of living, with distinguishing characteristics, problems, and patterns of adjustment; (2) that these are correlates, tending to vary with changes in the size of the group; (3) that these systems of family living are of particular importance in the study of personality types.

SUMMARY

1. Counting in terms of children rather than families, the large family is far more important as a family situation in child development than is commonly realized. Almost one-fourth of the children in this country are reared in families with five or more children.

2. A pilot study of twenty-five large families suggests that the large family involves a distinctive type of family system, differing in most respects from the small family system.

3. Many large families are planned, for general size. Parents expect and want a large family. Religion, national tradition, general philosophy, and specific ideas influence family attitudes toward family size.

4. Large families tend to take crises in stride, largely because crises are more commonplace than in the small family.

5. Large families tend to be more vulnerable to major crises, especially when the children are small.

6. Large family living emphasizes the importance of the group rather than of the individual.

7. The large family makes for greater specialization among its members, which calls for greater consensus among them.

8. Children in the large family tend to discipline each other.

9. Parents in large families are not able often to launch adequately the older children on their adult careers.

10. The large family makes for historical perspective in child rearing.

11. Life in the large family often becomes complex, particularly if the family lives in cramped quarters.

12. Systems of family living, and changes from one system to another, are of great significance in the study of personality types and behavior patterns.

CHAPTER VII

A Spatial Index for Family Interaction*

When you get on too much pressure,
All is lost by a collapse.—EUGENE FITCH WARE

"This is an awfully small space to house so much incompatibility," writes an unhappy wife to her marriage counselor. She lives with her husband and seven-year-old son in a two-room apartment.

"To insure a happy marriage," comments the seventy-eight-year-old father of twelve children, "a family needs to live on a place large enough so that its members can get out of earshot of each other."

These two comments will serve to pose the problem of the spatial setting for family living, and the relationship between this spatial setting and the number of persons in the group. To facilitate research in this direction, this chapter presents the concept of a spatial index for family interaction.

BASES OF THE CONCEPT

This index is based upon, and is an extension of, two sociological laws which have been published within recent years. One of these is identified here as the Law of Personal Interrelationships. This has been stated as follows: "With the addition of each person to a family or primary group, the number of persons increases in the simplest arithmeti-

* For suggestions incorporated into this chapter, acknowledgment is made to Winogene Pratt Sanger, sometime Research Associate of the William T. Carter Foundation, and to Robert O. Blood, Jr.

cal progression in whole numbers, while the number of personal interrelationships within the group increases in the order of triangular numbers."[1] The mathematical formula involved was set forth as follows:

x = the number of personal interrelationships
y = the number of persons

$$x = \frac{y^2 - y}{2}$$

This law considers only the interpersonal relationships that exist in a group.

The other law is identified here as the Law of Potential Intragroup Relationships. This recognizes the fact that there are relationships within a group other than those between two persons. There may be a relationship between one and all the other group members, singly or in all possible combinations; or between any combination of members with any other combination of members. My colleague, Dr. William M. Kephart, has presented recently this second law. "Although the number of potential relationships increases disproportionately as the size of the group increases, such relationships are never infinite in number, the quantity always being mathematically determinable."[2] The total number of potential relationships that can exist in a given group is represented by the following formula:[3]

$$\text{P.R.} = \frac{3^n - 2^{n+1} + 1}{2}$$

Sociologically, both of these laws would seem to be of considerable significance. The fundamental implication of each is that an arithmetic increase in the number of per-

[1] James H. S. Bossard, "The Law of Family Interaction," *American Journal of Sociology*, January 1945, p. 293. *See also* the author's *The Sociology of Child Development*, p. 146.

[2] William M. Kephart, "A Quantitative Analysis of Intragroup Relationships," *American Journal of Sociology*, May 1950, p. 546.

[3] *Ibid.*, p. 548.

sons in the group is accompanied by a markedly increasing acceleration in the number of relationships within the group. The following series will illustrate this point.

For the Law of Personal Interrelationships, the series follows:

Number of Persons	= 2	3	4	5	6	7
Number of Personal Relationships	= 1	3	6	10	15	21

For the Law of Potential Relationships, the series follows:

Number of Persons	= 2	3	4	5	6	7
Number of Potential Relationships	= 1	6	25	90	301	966

The foregoing laws have been presented in terms of group relationships. It is obvious that the family is a group within the meaning of these laws, and their application in the rest of this chapter will be to the family.

THE CONCEPT OF THE INTERACTIVE SPACE INDEX

The concept of the interactive space index adds to these laws the data on the physical area of the home (i.e., floor space) within which the family functions, expressed in terms of square feet. For the determination of the index, three groups of facts are necessary: (1) the number of persons within the household or family group, (2) the resultant number of interrelationships, and (3) the number of square feet of floor space in the living quarters. The index is obtained by dividing the second number into the third of these variables.

For example, the Brown family consists of six members. Applying the formula of the Law of Family Interaction, it is found that there are $\frac{36-6}{2}$ or 15 sets of personal interrelationships. Measurement of the living quarters of the Brown family reveals a total of 1,380 square feet. With 15 sets of personal interrelationships, our interaction space index then is 92, or an average of 92 square feet for each personal interrelationship within the family group. The Black family, on the other hand, with four members and six sets of personal interrelationships, living in an apartment of the same size, has an interaction space index of 230. The Jones family, with three members and three sets of personal interrelationships, shows an index of 460 in a domicile of equal space.

This index is a quantitative expression of the spatial setting of intragroup relations. It is, in other words, an index of the pressure of the physical nearness of persons who are interacting, or, better still, a quantitative indication of the degree to which the home space may be presumed to place pressure upon the family members in their relations with each other. It is presented as an advance over the commonly used ratio of the number of persons per room in a household. The sociologist's primary concern, and especially that of the student of family living, is not so much with the number of persons per room as with the number and complexity of interrelationships within a given space. The two differ, and increasingly so, with the addition of each person to the group.

ASSUMPTIONS AND IMPLICATIONS

The fundamental implication of this index is forecast in Emile Durkheim's *De la division du travail social* (1893), where he points out that increase in the number of contacts multiplies the occasions when people find themselves interrelated, when problems arise necessitating adjustment, and when life has to be lived in conformity with rules and regulations.[4] This implies rather clearly the basic importance of the spatial setting of social interaction.

More specifically, the thesis advanced here is that the spatial dimensions of living quarters are related to the

[4] *Cf.* George Simpson, *Emile Durkheim on the Division of Labor in Society.* New York: The Macmillan Co., 1933, Book II.

stresses, strains, and frustrations of family living. This does not imply that family members are necessarily aware of this factor, although material on family quarreling, gathered under the auspices of the William T. Carter Foundation, reveals a considerable number of references to "nothing but four walls to look at," and other expressions implying the cramped quarters in which the family lives. It is as a background factor that the spatial index, with its quantitative expression, becomes a measurable tool for research in the problems of family living. It is particularly germane in a situational approach to the study of family behavior.[5]

ALLOWANCE FOR VARIABLES

Any use of the family interaction space index as a research tool must recognize at least five variables in regard to the families studied. These are the sex, age, marital status, and occupation of the family members, and the stage of development of the family cycle.

The role of the sex composition of the family is obvious, and grows out of the cultural differences in the behavior and status of the sexes, even within the intimate area of family life. There are aspects of daily living which for many people call for privacy, complete or partial, from the opposite sex. Being cultural, these vary from one cultural and subcultural area to another. All kinds of specific combinations of family personnel arise to present problems. A family with two children of opposite sex has a sleeping space problem different from what exists if they are of the same sex. The presence of two in-laws of the same sex creates space demands somewhat less than if they are of opposite sex. The space that must be reserved for sleeping purposes encroaches upon the space available for other purposes. Perhaps, as a beginning, the spatial index might

[5] *Cf. The Sociology of Child Development,* chap. II.

be divided by two, especially when two sexes, unmarried to each other, live in the same household.

The age factor is more difficult to compute, and is connected specifically to the family cycle, as well as to the sex differential. Differences in age coincide with different stages of life development, which means differences in needs, interests, and activities. A father may insist that the television dominate the room, with appropriate light shadings, so that he may witness "the fights" at the same time that Junior has to prepare for an algebra quiz. Grandfather is ill, sleeps fitfully, and insists upon a quiet house. The baby, aged eight months, is tucked away for the night soon after six in the evening. Mary Ellen is expecting her beau some time after eight. These, and many others, are the realities of the variables which must be considered in a spatial index for family interaction.

The significance of marital status, too, is obvious. The married pair have spatial needs that differ from those of unmarried adults living in the same households, and the spatial interests of newly married couples change with the coming of children. Occupation is important chiefly because of its bearing upon the time spent within or away from the home, as well as the times of leaving, returning, and sleeping. Perhaps most important of all the variables is the stage of the family cycle. This not only is interwoven with the other variables, but is significant because it determines the composite personnel, activities, and time schedules of the members of the family group.

Ultimately it may be possible to determine the role of these variables with some degree of precision. In the meantime, as a first step in research, their importance can be minimized by utilizing the index with families similar in respect to these variables, but differng in their spatial setting. Such families could then be studied with a view of determining the role of differences in the spatial index.

SUGGESTIONS FOR RESEARCH

The concept of the spatial index for family interaction suggests various lines of specific research. One of these would be an inquiry into the forms of adjustment which families make who live successfully in cramped quarters. This would be particularly significant in the further study of the large family. Most large families are found in the lower income groups, which means that the spatial index will be relatively low. Particularly is it true that today the great majority of large families in urban centers live at the lower economic levels.

The study of family rituals, and the differences in these rituals which obtain on a class basis, are particularly revealing. One such study of class differentials in family rituals of 156 Philadelphia families has been made and published.[6] The homes represented in the lower class range from two-room apartments to a six-room house, and the families vary in size from four to thirteen members. The ritualistic adjustments are found to include methods of arising, bathroom procedures, the eating of meals, work, and recreation. "The rituals arising from these situations are, for the most part, rituals of expediency, to keep the home going, and to facilitate escape from home into a more exciting or promising outside world."[7]

The study of rituals, just referred to, suggests that other class differentials in family living are the outgrowth in some measure at least of variations in the family interaction spatial index.

Complementary to such studies would be those which explored the relationship of the index to the conflicts, complaints, irritations, and recriminations that occur within

[6] James H. S. Bossard and Eleanor S. Boll, *Ritual in Family Living*. Philadelphia: University of Pennsylvania Press, 1950, chap. 6.
[7] *Ibid.*, p. 133.

families. To what extent are these related to frustrations in family interaction, as affected by the multiplication of physical contacts and of failure to work out living habits expedient to them? It would seem that an index based on the ratio of personal relationships to spatial dimensions is far more significant than the number of persons per room.

Again, it is pertinent to inquire not merely if the number and intensity of family tensions vary with changes in the interactive spatial index, but also if, and what kind of, changes in the nature and kinds of tensions occur with changes in the index. Are there characteristic problems at varying levels of the index? All of this suggests that the spatial index may have considerable significance in the field of marriage counseling.

The reference to levels of the spatial index suggests that ultimately spatial norms might be established for the interactive needs of the family. This has been done on a health basis, in terms of the number of persons per room, so that a similar quest for scientific standards in the field of family interaction would seem to be equally feasible, and significant.

Many other questions suggest themselves. What is the relationship between the proposed index and the courtship patterns of younger members of the family? What forms of adjustment are necessitated here, and how do they vary with spatial considerations? To what extent are class differentials in courtship patterns and in premarital sex experience related to differences in the interactive index? How is the index related to the increase of leisure time of members of working-class families? To the increasing demand in many families for special purpose rooms? To the reputed transference of family functions from the home to the community? To the use of passive commercialized entertainment? To the homework and school progress of adolescents in the home?

The suggestions for research just made might be thought of as so many hypotheses to be tested through inductive processes. The spatial index for family interaction is offered as an objective and quantitative device to facilitate such research.

SUMMARY

1. This chapter presents the concept of a spatial index for family interaction. It is based on two recently published laws of group interaction. To them it relates the idea of the space in square feet of the home in which the family lives.

2. Its basic assumption is that the spatial dimensions of living quarters are referred to the stresses, strains, frustrations, and adjustments of family life.

3. In utilizing this concept, allowance must be made for the sex, age, marital, occupational, cyclical, and other facts about the family.

4. The concept suggests various lines of specific research for students of family problems, personality development, behavior problems, marriage counseling, and housing experts.

CHAPTER VIII

The Child with a Sequence of Parents

Say not you know another entirely, till you have divided an inheritance with him.—JOHANN LAVATER

THERE is an area of child development, and of family life study too, largely undeveloped, both in the literature and in programs for adjustment and guidance. It consists of the field of remarriage, and of the problems of the development of children who are involved in the sequence of marriages of their parents. The present chapter is devoted to this subject. The first part of the chapter will summarize briefly the salient facts about remarriage: its extent, its increase in recent years, the age of those remarrying, who remarries whom, conjugal combinations in remarriage, and the social atmosphere around remarriage. The remainder of the chapter is devoted to the problems of the children in remarriages. Included will be some of the facts about children in remarriage, the factors affecting their relations and adjustment in the new home, some comments on the significance of the problem, and a possibly constructive comment.

I. The Salient Facts About Remarriage

THE EXTENT OF REMARRIAGE[1]

One out of every five marriages in the United States in

[1] For a more complete statement of the supporting data on this and other aspects of remarriage, see the author's chapter on "Remarriage: Changing Nature and Problems," in Forrest L. Weller's book, *Courtship and Marriage.*

recent years has been a remarriage for one or both of the spouses; in approximately one out of every fourteen, both have been married before. Considering married pairs of all ages, in one out of every eight cases (13 per cent), one or both of the spouses have been married previously.

These statements are based upon a tabulation of 820,012 marriages, made by the author, of all marriages reported in New York State, exclusive of New York City, over a period of years (1916-24, 1929, 1936, 1945-48), and in Nebraska during the years 1949-50. Table I presents the

TABLE I. REMARRIAGES: NEW YORK STATE, 1945-48, AND NEBRASKA, 1949-50[2]

			Percentage of Remarriages			
State	*Year*	*Total marriages*	*One or both previously married*	*Groom previously married*	*Bride previously married*	*Both previously married*
New York	1945	47,725	21.6	6.4	6.8	8.3
New York	1946	78,433	19.4	5.9	7.3	6.2
New York	1947	69,534	20.7	6.7	7.2	6.8
New York	1948	63,751	20.7	6.2	7.3	7.1
Nebraska	1949	12,743	28.9	6.8	8.5	13.6
Nebraska	1950	13,828	28.1	6.3	8.4	13.4

data for a four-year period in New York and a two-year period in Nebraska.

Supporting these conclusions is a report of the Federal Census Bureau, based on a sample study in April 1948, of 25,000 households in forty-two states and the District of Columbia. "Twenty-one per cent of the married persons in April, 1948, who had been living with their present spouses less than five years, had been married more than once," states the report. The percentage for those who had been

[2] Annual Reports, State Department of Health of New York, 1945-48 (Albany, N.Y.); and Annual Reports, Bureau of Vital Statistics, State Department of Health (Lincoln, Nebraska).

living with their spouses more than five years was eleven, and for all married pairs was thirteen.[3]

Most remarriages are second marriages, but a certain proportion are third, fourth, fifth, etc., marriages. Of persons marrying more than once, approximately one out of sixteen is marrying a third or additional time.[4] Of these, the most frequently found combination is that of widows marrying widowers, each for the third time. Next in order are third marriages where the bride has been both widowed and divorced. The terms "consecutive monogamy" or "sequential marriage"[5] have been suggested to designate these cases. One might also use the term "chronological Mormon," suggested by a waggish friend.

THE INCREASING EXTENT OF REMARRIAGE

Remarriage has been increasing in extent in recent years. The proportion of remarried women among those previously widowed or divorced was one-sixth greater in 1940 than in 1910, and in New York State, outside of New York City, the percentage of all marriages that were remarriages increased from 14 in 1940 to 20.7 in 1948. The chances of remarriage have risen in all age groups, and particularly in the ages from twenty-five to thirty-four, inclusive. The chances of marriage are greater for those previously married than for those single; age for age, they are greater for the divorced than for the widowed; in each age group, they are greater for men than for women.[6]

[3] U.S. Bureau of the Census, *Marital Status, Number of Times Married, and Duration of Present Marital Status,* Series P-20, No. 23, March 4, 1949, p. 1.

[4] Based on an original study, by the author, of 39,963 men and 42,610 women who remarried in New York State, 1945-48, and Nebraska, 1949-50.

[5] A. H. Hobbs, *The Claims of Sociology,* Harrisburg: The Stackpole Co., 1951, p. 102; Paul H. Landis, "Sequential Marriage," *Journal of Home Economics,* October 1950, pp. 625-28.

[6] "The Frequency of Remarriage," *Statistical Bulletin,* Metropolitan Life Insurance Co., Vol. 30, January 1949, pp. 8-10; "The Chances of Remarriage for the Widowed and Divorced," *ibid.,* Vol. 26, May 1945, pp. 1-3; "The

These facts seem surprising at first glance because, in times past, most persons remarrying were those who had been widowed, and, as is well known, the death rate has been falling during the years under consideration. Marital dissolutions because of the death of the husband or wife have dropped from 30 per 1,000 married couples during the early 1890's to about 19 in 1948.[7] It would seem logical, therefore, to expect a decline in the rate of remarriage.

Certain factors, however, have been operating contrariwise. To begin with, there is the increasing prevalence of marriage in general. Census data on the marital status of the population reveal the extent of this trend. In 1890, when official data on this matter were first recorded, 53 per cent of the population fifteen years of age and over was married; in 1948, that percentage was sixty-six. Second, there is every reason to believe that there has occurred in recent years some change of attitude toward remarriage, as well as divorce, which is an important "feeder" to those remarrying. Both changes have been in the direction of greater tolerance. Finally, there is a change in the previous conjugal condition of those remarrying. A generation ago, most persons remarrying were those who had been widowed; today, first place goes to those who have been divorced. And, as already pointed out, the divorced are more apt to remarry, and do so sooner, than the widowed. Table II shows the extent of this change in previous conjugal condition of those remarrying in one state.

AGE OF THOSE REMARRYING

Remarriage is occurring at earlier ages than formerly.

Chances of Marriage and of Remarriage," *ibid.*, Vol. 25, January 1944, pp. 7-9; State of New York, *Sixty-ninth Annual Report of the Department of Health*, Albany, N. Y., Vol. 2, p. civ.

[7] "Have Broken Families Increased?" *Statistical Bulletin*, Metropolitan Life Insurance Co., Vol. 30, November 1949, pp. 1-3.

This is due to the increase of divorced persons among those remarrying. Since divorce occurs at earlier ages than widowhood, and because the divorced remarry sooner than do the widowed, the effects upon the age of remarriage are inevitable. In New York State, for example, by comparing

TABLE II. PREVIOUS CONJUGAL CONDITION OF PERSONS REMARRYING, NEW YORK STATE, 1916-24 AND 1945-48[8]

		Previous Conjugal Condition by Percentage		
Year	*Total*	*Widowed*	*Divorced*	*Widowed and Divorced*
		Grooms		
1916-24	49,195	81.4	17.6	.9
1945-48	34,460	43.2	54.9	1.9
		Brides		
1916-24	47,267	75.8	23.3	.8
1945-48	36,774	41.5	56.4	2.0

the ages of those remarrying in 1938 with those in the postwar years 1945-48, it will be found that the percentage of men remarrying under thirty years of age almost doubled, rising from 10.8 to 19 per cent. Among women, the same comparison shows an increase from 25.1 to 32.3 per cent. Considering the 71,234 men and women who remarried in New York State, exclusive of New York City, during the years 1945-48, a third of the men (33.5 per cent) and one-half of the women (48.3 per cent) remarried before their thirty-fifth year.[9]

WHO REMARRIES WHOM

Persons previously married show some preference for persons of the same previous conjugal condition as their

[8] Annual Reports, State Department of Health of New York, 1945-48.

[9] Annual Reports, State Department of Health of New York, for years ending 1938 and 1945-48.

own, when they remarry. Widowed persons mate more often with the widowed than with any other previously married group. They seem to avoid divorced persons, choosing single mates next in the order of preference. Divorced persons mate more often with divorced persons than other previously married groups do, but mate most frequently with single persons. About one out of three persons who have been both widowed and divorced marry single mates: the preference here is heavily in favor of persons who have been married before. Table III shows the selections, by previous conjugal condition, of 196,658 persons who also had been previously married.

The age combinations in remarriage offer an intriguing field for study. Ordinarily four out of five husbands are older than their wives, but when single men marry widows, an unusually large proportion of the wives are older than their husbands. To a lesser but still noticeable extent, this is true when single men marry divorced women, and when divorced men marry widows. When divorced men marry single girls, they select mostly girls younger, and often considerably younger, than themselves. The same thing is true of widowers. When persons previously married mate with each other, they tend more often to marry in the same general age group. One seems to sense, in both the men and the women who had been married previously and chose single mates, an effort to turn back the hand of time, and to start again, with a young mate.

CONJUGAL COMBINATIONS IN REMARRIAGE

The term "remarriage" is a kind of catch-all, used to include all persons who marry more than once. For certain statistical purposes, such a general classification is permissible, but socially it is rather misleading. For there are many varieties of remarriage. First, one must distinguish between the single, the widowed, the divorced, and the

TABLE III. MATE SELECTION, BY PREVIOUS CONJUGAL CONDITION, BY PERSONS REMARRYING, NEW YORK STATE, 1916-24, 1929, 1936, 1945-48

Years	*Previous Conjugal Condition*	*Number*	*Total Per Cent*	*Previous Conjugal Condition*			
				Single	*Widowed*	*Divorced*	*Widowed and Divorced*
1916-24, 1929, 1936	Widowers	49,231	100	47.8	43.9	7.6	0.5
1945-48	Widowers	14,887	100	33.3	46.0	18.8	1.8
1916-24, 1929, 1936	Widows	43,608	100	44.2	49.6	5.6	0.6
1945-48	Widows	15,277	100	40.2	44.9	13.4	1.5
1916-24, 1929, 1936	Divorced men	13,955	100	61.2	17.5	20.7	0.6
1945-48	Divorced men	18,929	100	59.2	10.8	29.2	0.9
1916-24, 1929, 1936	Divorced women	17,279	100	60.7	21.7	16.7	0.8
1945-48	Divorced women	20,763	100	59.0	13.5	26.5	1.0
1916-24, 1929, 1936	Divorced and widowed men	695	100	37.7	39.3	19.3	3.6
1945-48	Divorced and widowed men	644	100	26.8	34.8	32.1	6.2
1916-24, 1929, 1936	Divorced and widowed women	656	100	39.3	43.1	13.7	3.8
1945-48	Divorced and widowed women	734	100	33.2	38.1	23.1	5.5

widowed and divorced, each of which categories may combine with any other one in remarriage. This means that there are fifteen different possible combinations on the basis of these four previous conjugal conditions in both sexes. But each of the previously married persons may or may not have children. Adding this differential increases the total of possible combinations to forty-eight. Furthermore, it has been pointed out that unusual age combinations are relatively prevalent in remarriage. If each of the preceding categories is further divided into three age groups—young, middle-aged, and old—the resultant number of possible combinations is 432. It would be entirely proper to go on and distinguish each of the previously married groups on the basis of the number of times that widowhood and divorce have occurred, singly or in combination. These are important distinctions, and they would increase the number of possible combinations in remarriage to an almost fantastic number. Enough has been said, however, to make it clear that many different kinds of family situations are included under the term of remarriage, each differing from the other in important aspects.

THE SOCIAL ATMOSPHERE SURROUNDING REMARRIAGE

A remarriage is never just a marriage; it is always a *re*marriage. It differs from a first marriage, not in its legal aspects or in the customary domestic sequelae, but in the way it is regarded by all who note its occurrence. It is invariably the occasion of comment. "She got married *again.*" "He married a widow." "She was a divorcée." "She married a widower with two children." Newspaper write-ups of remarriages always mention the fact, with perhaps an additional paragraph about the former mate, together with names, dates, and circumstances. Personal comments at times are critical. The community may not wholly accept the idea of remarriage, especially at the unconscious level. Friends may have taken sides in the divorce of a participant of the remarriage. Kinfolk may be concerned, perhaps disturbed, for various reasons. Business and professional associates seize the opportunity to belittle a competitor. Unhappily married persons may envy secretly one who has the opportunity to embark on a new matrimonial venture. All round, there is a sense of awareness, often subtle to be sure, as if there were something not quite proper about the new marriage. Remarriages tend always to be on the defensive, as it were.

Most important of all, it is a remarriage in the minds of the spouses. They too have a sense of awareness, of themselves and of each other. There is apt to be a whole complex of attitudes, conceptions, and perhaps uncertainties, much of which remains in a twilight of self-consciousness, and never fully aired in open discussion. Moreover, for those previously married, there is the memory of a màrital past. We live with our past, always. One never wholly forgets, and it is through our memories that we look, as through a colored glass, at the present and the future. Experience is not only the arch we build upon, but it is also the measure by which we assimilate new experience. Thus the past may hang heavily over a new union, as did that of the first wife in Du Maurier's *Rebecca;* or it may predispose to a happiness which earlier realities completely denied. A divorced person may be embittered, disillusionized, or disappointed; the separation from the first mate may not be complete; or its frustrations may give way to a strained eagerness to make a success out of another venture. Whatever the outcome, remarriages involve problems of adjustment, both of the self and in relation to the mate, which are added to those which may appear in first marriages. The social atmosphere surrounding remarriage tends not to be wholly helpful.

II. Remarriage and the Child

The principal concern of this chapter, and the principal problem in many remarriages, is that of the child. This is true, whether one is concerned with the happiness of the marriage or with the development of the child or children. Four groups of facts about children of parents who remarry will be pointed out by way of beginning.

1. The presence of children often encourages remarriage. Widowed fathers, and divorced ones too, left with children, need a housekeeper and caretaker for their children. Widows and divorcées, with children, may need economic maintenance. The younger and more numerous the children, the greater the need to remarry, as well as the greater the urgency for haste. But these are the very conditions which limit the range of choice of mates. Eligible men and women, who are desirable as marriage partners, hesitate to assume the responsibility for a "ready-made" family. This seems to be more true of women than of men, since they must bear so much of the brunt of rearing another's children. This results at times in the selection of women of lower status and qualifications than that of the father and his children.

2. The presence of children increases the difficulties of a satisfactory adjustment in remarriage. This is axiomatic, since the number of problems of adjustment increases automatically with the increase in the number of persons living together. More will be said of this presently: suffice it here to point out that the two facts just mentioned, considered in combination, create the heart of the problem of many remarriages. The presence of children increases the necessity for remarriage and, at the same time, increases the risk of failure.

3. There is considerable evidence to show that the extent

and urgency of the economic need for the widowed, particularly mothers, to remarry is declining. It has already been pointed out that, due to the decline of the death rate, the proportion of marriages broken by death has been falling steadily. Coupled with this is the increasing prevalence of the small-family system, which means that on the average there are fewer children per widowed parent. Also, there is the increasing extent of industrial pensions, workmen's compensation, and federal social security payments to cushion the economic impact of the death of the father.

4. A final group of facts results from the increase in the percentage of persons remarrying who have been divorced. Divorce tends to occur in younger age brackets than does widowhood, after fewer years of married life with the former mate, and probably with fewer children involved. These factors would make for a smaller total of children found in remarriages, but this tendency is offset, at least in part, by the marked increase in the rate of divorce. Moreover, children of divorce differ from children of widowed parents in one important circumstance when the parents remarry. They must adjust to new parents, i.e., stepparents, while their real parents are still alive. Children of widowed parents are not confronted with that problem.

NUMBER OF CHILDREN INVOLVED IN REMARRIAGE

The number of children involved in remarriages in the United States cannot be stated with any degree of accuracy. Various estimates have been made which are suggestive. Cohen concluded two decades ago that about one-third of the divorced have children, and that these average about one child.[10] Marshall and May, who included desertion and nonsupport cases in their study of divorce in Maryland,

[10] Alfred Cohen, *Statistical Analysis of American Divorce.* New York: Columbia University Press, 1932.

found that only 15.4 per cent of the couples involved were childless.[11] Davis estimates the number of children of divorced couples in the United States in 1946 at 306,000, and a total of 1,533,000 from 1940 to 1946, inclusive.[12] He further estimates that about 34 per cent of these are under ten years of age, and about 70 per cent are under fifteen.

Examination of certain scattered sources bearing on this point suggests that these estimates may be too low. Reports from a state like Nebraska, for example, which publishes data on the number of children in families where divorces are granted, show that the total number of children almost equals the total number of divorces. For the two-year period 1949-50, the total number of divorces granted was 5,011; the total number of children involved was 4,778. While it is true that the birth rate in a state like Nebraska is higher than in large urban centers where divorce is relatively more prevalent, the ratio between divorces granted and total number of children involved is so high as to suggest that past estimates of the number of children involved in divorce may need to be revised.

It is possible that our judgment has been influenced by the large proportion of childless couples among those divorced. In the Nebraska data just cited, almost half of the cases (48.8 per cent) were childless; another quarter (25.9 per cent) had but one child each. Only one-tenth (10.6 per cent) of the couples divorced had three or more children each, yet these accounted for more than two-fifths (42.3 per cent) of all the children involved, averaging almost four children per divorce.[13]

[11] Leon C. Marshall and Geoffrey May, *The Divorce Court.* Baltimore: Johns Hopkins University Press, 1932, Vol. I, p. 31.

[12] Kingsley Davis, "Children of Divorced Parents," in *Law and Contemporary Problems,* Duke University School of Law, Vol. X, No. 5, 1944, p. 713.

[13] Annual Reports, *op. cit.,* 1949, p. 75, and 1950, p. 75.

These percentages are in striking similarity to those reported in a study of marriage and divorce in Wisconsin for the years 1915, 1920, 1935, 1940, and 1945, which shows that 45.8 per cent of the divorced couples were childless, 24.2 per cent had one child, 13.9 per cent had two children, and 16.1 per cent had three or more children.[14]

The foregoing discussion has centered upon the number of children in divorces granted, and not the number of those involved in the remarriages of their parents. We know here only that the divorced are younger than the widowed, have fewer children on the whole, and remarry more quickly. Considering the entire range of remarriage, a recent special report of the Census Bureau is of value. As of 1948, the study shows that "only about 25 per cent of the women who married for the first time during the two years preceding the survey had children under 18 years of age in the home, as compared with about 56 per cent of those remarried. A likely reason for the difference is the fact that a large proportion of the children of remarried women were children of a previous marriage."[15]

Accepting the most modest of the estimates, and keeping in mind the fact that the totals are but as of a given year and need to be considered in their cumulative totals, it must be evident that children in remarriages constitute a sizable part of the field of child problems and child development. Obviously, the stepchild is not a sentimental figure from the pages of fairy tales and medieval history, but as current as the morning newspaper; instead of declining, it is, like a great many other problems, changing in nature and in our appreciation of its import.

[14] George W. Hill and James D. Tarver, "Marriage and Divorce Trends in Wisconsin, 1914-1945," *Milbank Memorial Fund Quarterly*, January 1952, pp. 13-16.

[15] Paul C. Glick, "First Marriages and Remarriages," *American Sociological Review*, December 1949, p. 732.

FACTORS AFFECTING STEPPARENT-STEPCHILD RELATIONS

The stepchild has always been recognized as a special problem in family relations and child development. Not that the circumstances have always been unfortunate or unhappy, for one can find almost every conceivable kind or degree of situation. There is, on the one hand, the case of Lincoln and his stepmother. A year after the death of Abraham's mother, his father married a widow with three children. When she came to her new husband's home, she found "two unkempt children," of whom Abraham, aged ten, was one. "The children were scrubbed and better clad. The home took on new character at once," writes one of his biographers. "She transformed the home of the cheerless widower and his two motherless children into a spot of pleasant associations and happy memories. Her own three children . . . lived in perfect accord with the children already there. It was a good day for Abraham Lincoln and the world that brought Sarah Bush Johnston to the rude cabin of Thomas Lincoln."[16]

In striking contrast is the following case, taken from a collection of case histories of juvenile delinquents:

> As far back as I can remember, my life was filled with sorrow and misery. The cause was my stepmother, who nagged me, beat me, insulted me, and drove me out of my own home. My mother died when I was four years old, so I never knew a real mother's affection. My father remarried when I was five years of age. The stepmother who was to take the place of my real mother was a raw-boned woman, devoid of features as well as emotions. She was of Polish stock, and had the habits and customs of the people of the Old World. She came to America when about thirty years old; was married at the time, and had seven children. Her husband was in ill health, and he died soon after arriving in Chicago. After burying her husband, she found herself without financial resources for herself and children. Realizing her predicament and the neces-

[16] William E. Barton, *The Life of Abraham Lincoln.* Indianapolis: Bobbs-Merrill Co., 1925, Vol. I, p. 118.

sity of immediate action, she ventured out to find a husband, a man to support herself and her seven children; literally to slave and labor and bring home the bacon. Her venture was not so successful at first. Men were not wont to fall for her precious few charms. And, besides, did she not have seven children as an added burden?

My father was in a similar predicament, my mother having died and left three children. His thoughts went in quest of a woman to be his wife and a mother to his children. So it happened that Fate brought about a meeting of the two. A hasty courtship ensued, and in a short time they were married. My father worked for the Gas Company, and my stepmother proceeded to establish a home.

To this day I wonder how my father could have picked out such a woman for a wife. My conclusion is that she, in her desperation, used all her charm and coercion to get a man—any man who was able and inclined to work. My father, being fond of his whiskey and beer, and being in need of a mistress, became intoxicated and thus blinded to her nature and circumstances, and yielded to her coercion.

She brought her seven children to our home. With us three children, my brother, my sister, and myself, there were twelve to feed and clothe. We all lived in four rooms in a basement. My father did not whimper. All he asked for was his regular meals, a bed to sleep in, and his daily can of beer and whiskey. His mind was like a motor, always on one course. He didn't think of his children as boys and girls to be loved. He thought of us as just "kids," who had to be provided for, and he was the good provider. There his parental duties ended. Never did he show any love or kindness. We "kids" were worth boarding and tolerating because sometime we would be financial assets.

For six months things went rather smoothly. Then my troubles began. My father and stepmother began to argue and quarrel about us children. I didn't know much about it at first, for I was more interested in playing with the cat behind the stove, but I soon felt the change. From a quiet woman, the stepmother changed to a hellcat full of venom and spite. The first time she struck me was when I was in my favorite nook behind the stove, playing with the cat. She pulled me out and beat me, striking me in the face and on the back with her hard and bony hand. That was the first time that I ever knew fear. After many beatings I became more and more afraid, and I crouched behind the stove in fear. Well do I remember my first fears and horrors of her. I became unhappy and did not caper and play with my brother and sister as I had been wont to do. My father gave me no comfort. He spent his time at work, at the saloon, and in bed. Never did he pet me or cheer me.

The stepmother favored her own children in every way. They received what luxuries were to be had, while my brother and sister and I had the crumbs to pick off the table. She let her children eat at the table, and made us wait. Whenever one of her children would do a wrong they would tell her that I did it, and then I, instead of the culprit, would get the beating. My father couldn't interfere, because if he did the stepmother would threaten to leave. That would have been the best thing for his children, but of course he didn't want her to go.

Things went on this way. We fought with her because she favored her children at meals and beat us for their misdemeanors. Hard indeed it was for me to get enough to eat. Often when I would go to the store to buy food for the family I would take a little biscuit or anything I could without my stepmother knowing it. So that much was I ahead when I got my portion at mealtime. My father worked steady and received good wages, so there was no good reason why we could not have enough to eat. But the stepmother was saving and fed her own children and let us go starving and half naked on the street.

The stepmother also made us (brother, sister and myself) do all the hard work in the house. And then she would beat us if we complained. That is what embittered me against her and her children. I developed a hatred against her that still lasts; a hatred that was so burning that when she would look into my eyes she would read it there, and in that way she knew my feeling. The Lord knows I tried to love her, but my nature could not stand her caresses in one of those sympathetic moods which she seldom had. Occasionally she would seem to feel sorry for her abuses and cruelty, and would ask me to kiss her; but my feelings protested. My fear and hatred made me avoid her and resent her caresses. Then she would get angry and beat me.[17]

Between these two extremes, there are endless varieties of family situations involving stepchildren. What are the factors which, acting singly or in combination, produce these situations?

[17] Reproduced from Clifford R. Shaw, *et al.*, *Delinquency Areas.* Chicago: University of Chicago Press, 1929, pp. 55-57.

Perhaps the foremost question which presents itself is this: Are conflict and tension between stepchild and stepparent inevitable? Is it true, as Wulffen suggests, that hatred of the stepmother for her stepchild is rooted in sex, that the stepchild reminds the stepmother of the husband's love relations with his first wife, and that her animosity toward the child is an expression of her sexual jealousy of the first wife?[18] Or, there is Wittels' contention that the stepmother cannot "do right" by her stepchildren because of her own maternal drives. "The fact is," he writes,

> that the structure of the human family is of a very peculiar kind, with the inevitable result that a second wife cannot do right by the children of her predecessor, even when animated by the most earnest desire to be a true mother to her stepchildren. If she has herself been married before and has had children by her first husband, she will, by force of nature, give them the preference. . . . If she has not been married before, or has had no children by her first husband, she will want to bear children of her own. Should she remain childless, she will have a sense of inferiority to her predecessor, and this will react on her relation toward her stepchildren. If, as usually happens, the second wife brings children into the world, she would have to be an angel from heaven not to feel more loving toward the fruit of her own womb than toward stepchildren who are, in any case, prone to regard her as an interloper.[19]

Contemporary scholars in the social sciences would reject this viewpoint in large measure, contending that, since there is considerable variation in the nature and seriousness of the problem from one culture to another, there is nothing necessarily inevitable about it, but that it is rather the product, at least to a large extent, of cultural factors.

1. The cultural factors include: first, those institutional forms and practices affecting the stepparent-stepchild re-

[18] Erich Wulffen, *Woman as a Sexual Criminal.* New York: Ethnological Press, 1934, p. 281.

[19] Fritz Wittels, *Set the Children Free.* London: George Allen Unwin, 1932, pp. 202-3.

lationship; and second, the content and weight of popular thought and tradition regarding it. Concerning the first of these, the following points have been emphasized. In many societies, there is a sharp distinction between the reproductive unit of parents and children and the authentic institutional family, with the former playing a minor role, and the latter carrying on the functions which in this country are associated with the family. In some of these cultures, children belong to the group and are not the private property of their biological parents; in others, the father and mother, while accorded some importance, are but one of several persons of each sex who are responsible for the child, so that the loss of a biological parent has less meaning for all concerned, and substitute parents are readily available. Similarly, where the family consists of several successive generations, the loss of one individual member, even if a biological parent, is not particularly disturbing. Again, in those areas where polygyny is practiced, where it is the custom of all the children to call all of the wives "mother" so long as they live with a common husband, the addition or loss of an additional mother has relatively little significance. "Where it is the accepted behavior for a child to run up to any one of several nursing women and suckle at her breast, or seek comfort and help from her, then to all intents and purposes she is his 'mother'—he does not stop to ask her if she is his flesh-and-blood mother. This system tends to widen the family circle and draw into it many who in our society are on the periphery."[20] Finally, there is the

[20] William C. Smith, "The Stepmother," *Sociology and Social Research*, May-June 1949, p. 345. *See also* "The Stepchild," by the same author, in the *American Sociological Review*, April 1945, pp. 237-42; as well as his chapter on "Remarriage and the Stepchild," in Morris Fishbein and Ernest W. Burgess, *Successful Marriage*. Garden City: Doubleday and Co., 1947, pp. 339-55. Of importance in this connection is Davis' chapter in "Children of Divorced Parents," published by the Duke University School of Law, *op. cit.*, pp. 700-21. *See also* James H. S. Bossard, *The Sociology of Child Development*, pp. 51-73, for distinction in structural forms of the family.

practice of the *sororate* in certain cultures, whereby the dead wife's younger sister steps into the breach, becomes the father's second wife, and, by established custom, becomes the mother of her dead sister's children.

Considered in this comparative light, a good deal of the problem of the stepparent in our culture results from the prevalence of the small procreative family unit in which we have given to the biological parents the entire responsibility for the child, and into which we have concentrated all the emotions peculiar to blood relationship. While this makes for a deepened parent-child relationship, it also makes for great disturbance when the family unit is broken, and increased difficulties for those who, in substitute roles, seek its restoration.

Reinforcing the role of the institutional forms and practices are the chilling hand of folklore and the heavy weight of the popular stereotype. By this is meant the complex of attitudes and conceptions concerning stepparents built up in the popular mind through the years. To begin with, the very word *stepchild* has an ominous sound, singling out the relationship as a singularly unnatural one. Next, virtually the entire range of reference in the literature, from fairy tales to this morning's newspaper, have built up a concept, particularly of the stepmother, as a characteristically callous, cruel, inconsiderate, and unfair kind of person. To such an extent has this been done that when a telling reference is to be made of discrimination or neglect of anything, it is spoken of as a stepchild. Thus a governmental department is spoken of as the stepchild of the New Deal, arthritis is designated as medicine's stepchild, and music is called the stepchild of education.[21] "The stereotype of the stepmother," says Smith, "presents her as being inconsiderate and lacking in motherliness. Then, when a woman goes through a marriage ceremony and becomes a step-

[21] Smith, *American Sociological Review, op. cit.,* p. 237.

mother, she is automatically placed in a definite category which defines and characterizes her. We define her first and then make her fit the definition. We forget all that the psychologists and educators have taught us about individual differences; we make no realistic examination of the total personality concerned but react to the generalized category, even though it does not accord with actuality. This hangs a millstone about the neck of the stepmother and makes her role an exceedingly difficult one."[22] Curiously enough, this stereotype is completely at variance with that of the foster mother. It is usually assumed that adoptive parents will be good, just as it is assumed that stepparents will be bad, parents.

2. Just as there is a generalized social attitude toward the stepparent, so there are the individual attitudes of those involved. These constitute a second group of factors, and they are seldom as simple as statistical reporters would have one believe. Growing as they do out of the individual's experience, combined with his definition of the present situation and anticipation of future ones, they tend to be uniquely individual and variable. In a brief analysis, one can at best but designate polar points in their development. First among these would be the child's attachment to the former parent. This may range from a continuing idealization of the past parent to a tragic sense of relief that what has been will be no more. There is the dull, aching acceptance of the inevitable toll of death, or the not necessarily final arrangement of the divorce court. The former home may have been a well-integrated one, with the past parent a wise counselor or a sympathetic friend; it may have been a place of bitter quarreling, an intermittent drunken brawl, or the foreboding quietness of inexpressible hate. The child may have had complete emotional security, or been buffeted between quarreling parents and shifted about

[22] Smith, *Sociology and Social Research*, *op. cit.*, p. 346.

under pressure of economic uncertainty. It is on the basis of his particular combination of experiences with past parents and home situations that the stepchild develops the attitudes which he brings to the new relationship.

The new parent has had his or her experience, with resultant attitudes, too. He may have been a solitary, unattached figure, like George Washington,[23] who revels in the companionship of a ready-made family; or a distressed widower who wants mostly a caretaker for his children and sex for himself. She may be an unmarried teacher, skilled in dealing with children, and of an age when motherhood is improbable; or a grasping widow, with three children of her own, whose economic support has to be underwritten; or a sensitive, shy divorcée, pathetically eager to please and make a "go" out of a second try; or a selfish prowler, on the financial make, with an older man as her prey, and his children as the enemy to be outsmarted. Men and women marry and remarry, for many reasons. Moreover, there is involved also a conception of children per se, their nature, their importance in family life, their rights as children, and their obligations to adults and parents. These loom particularly large in remarriage, where children are involved in so many ways in the establishment of new family situations.[24]

The attitude of the natural parent who remarries is apt to be overlooked. If widowed, there may have been the background of a tragic accident or a lengthy sickness. Bills may have mounted, with some of them still unpaid. The psychic shock of bereavement may have been combined with the nightmare of economic uncertainty and the distracting needs of young children. Remarriage may have occurred too soon, giving rise to feelings of guilt and in-

[23] Douglas S. Freeman, *George Washington.* New York: Charles Scribner's Sons, 1951, Vol. III, particularly chaps. I and II.

[24] For a more complete analysis of attitudes toward children, see the author's *The Sociology of Child Development*, pp. 91-93.

ternal tensions. If divorced, long months of conflict and bitterness may have gone before, perhaps there was embarrassing publicity, there may be the guilt of a divorce engineered for the purpose of a specific remarriage, or the acceptance of a new husband while on the rebound from the first. All this suggests that the parent who remarries may be worn, worried, or distraught. Then, too, the parental attitude may have changed. The mother who dotes on her son suddenly finds him a nuisance when a new suitor appears: she fears the child will lessen her chances. The father who was a "real daddy" to his little girl now terms her unreasonable, since the blonde he is courting is critical of the child's manners. Thus the child, upset by having lost one parent, now finds the other one irritable from tensions or distraught with fears, or changed under the competing spell of romance.

3. A third set of factors are the *operational* ones. This term is applied to the circumstances involved in the establishment of the new relationship. These, too, cover a wide range. One set has to do with how and when the child was introduced to the new situation. The parent may have arranged for early and repeated meetings between child and prospective stepparent, with efforts to ease the adjustment between the two. The parent may discuss pending prospects or plans, and explain the reasons for the remarriage. Or the new parent may come without preparation or warning. Neither child nor new parent may have seen each other before they begin life together in the same household. Adults realize that their reaction to many things turns more on how they are done than on what is done: they tend to ignore similar reactions in their children.

A second set of operational factors has to do with the role of outsiders, both during the interval between the parents' marriages, and afterward. Many children are obliged to make one or more adjustments between the break-up of the first home and the establishment of the second one. Sometimes they are shifted from pillar to post, so that any kind of stability may come to be welcomed. There may have been a housekeeper, with ambitions of her own, whose thwarted feelings may cause her to stir up the child or children. The other divorced parent may interfere in the home life of his former mate, particularly through their child or children. There may have been relatives, with whom a temporary sojourn was so happy that they are unwilling to terminate it. There may have been a grandmother who pampered, so that a sterner regime will be resented. Or there may have been the chaos of neglect and irresponsible caretakers, so that the new parent's effort to restore a semblance of order and discipline will be strenuously opposed. The accumulated effect of successive shocks, disturbances, and by-play of antithetical forces in the background may have made the child difficult to manage, at least for a time.

Another operational factor concerns the number and sets of children involved. One child may be amenable to the new parent, three may "gang up" on the newcomer. If both parties to the remarriage have children from a previous marriage, the difficulties increase manifold. Not only do the two sets of children have to adjust to each other, but the possibility of favoritism to "my" children against "your" children is very apt to arise. Much depends in such cases on the ages and sexes of the two groups of children, considered in relation to each other. Finally, there are those cases where ultimately there are "your children" and "our children," or "your children, my children, and our children."

Thus far, no mention has been made of the role of economic pressure, but it must be evident that factors of this kind are operating constantly. When and where economic resources are adequate, parent-child relationships tend to be less strained than when they are not. Research in the large-family system, reported elsewhere in this volume, reveals this in the natural family: its importance in remarriage families is still more obvious. In families of moderate and lower incomes, each child becomes a serious addition to the family budget. In the vast majority of families, parents make sacrifices for their children. Such sacrifices are made more readily for one's own children. The man who marries a widow with two children may love the widow and like her children, but resent the financial drain of the latter. A stepmother may complain about the behavior of her husband's children: what really annoys her is their competition with her own love for clothes. Economic pressure is often rationalized so as to appear in other guise.

4. Finally, there are the personal traits of the persons involved. Age and sex, of children and of parents, have already been referred to, and they are highly important. It seems obvious that when both parents and children are young, adjustments can be made more readily all around. Adolescence appears to be a particularly trying period. Daughters in this stage seem often to resent it when their fathers form new attachments; sons feel similarly about their mothers. Modern psychoanalysts have a term for this, but its nature and prevalence have been obvious through the centuries.

The sex of the participants is an important factor in a number of ways. There is general agreement that the position of the stepmother is the most significant, both in determining the outcome of the remarriage and the adjustment of the children. Stepmothers probably fare better when they marry a man with sons; men who marry widows with daughters seem to have fewer difficulties than if there are sons. When two groups of children, hitherto strangers to each other, are brought together to live in the same household, their ages and sexes become highly important. Living quarters are more likely than not to be cramped, which means living at close quarters, and on doubling-up bases. Here again, the resultant problems are much simpler if the children are young, and of the same sex.

Possibly most important of the personal traits in this connection is the capacity to get along with people at close range. Whatever terms the experts in human behavior use to classify individuals and their traits, there is a fundamental difference between people in this respect. There are persons who can adjust quickly to new situations and get along readily with other people. When such persons come together in family life, they tend to make a go of it, regardless of past experiences and present circumstances. But many people have this faculty in lesser degrees, and they, too, find themselves cast in the role of stepparent and stepchild. It is the combination of people with differing degrees of this faculty that constitutes the grist of the family mill, in cases of remarriage as in cases of first marriage.

SOME SUGGESTIVE DATA

There is nothing about remarriage and the stepchild relationship that is outside of the pale of possible adjustment. Many of the problems are similar to those of marriage per se; all are the product of factors that can be understood and dealt with constructively. Admittedly, both remarriage and the stepchild present added problems, and it is of no avail to minimize their unique difficulties, but this means only that greater efforts must be made by all persons concerned.

The evidence on how remarriages turn out, while not conclusive, is distinctly encouraging. Selected studies which reveal a lower rate of success than for first marriages show a difference that is not marked, and confine their conclusions to cases where the persons remarrying were divorced rather than widowed.[25] Other studies, principally those by Locke, conclude that bereaved persons make as good an adjustment in subsequent marriages as the adjustment of persons who have been married but once; that divorced women who remarry make as good an adjustment as women married the first time; and that divorced men, while presenting a record of lesser success, do not differ greatly from the record of once-married men.[26]

All of this information bears on husband-wife relationships in remarriage, and tells us nothing of the rate of success or failure of adjustment of stepchildren in these situations. It is possible to find illustrative cases showing every conceivable kind of stepchild treatment, but these only reveal the variety of life situations, and no preponderance of result in any given direction.

Various studies have emphasized that the presence of a stepparent in the home is a factor in the causation of juvenile delinquency,[27] but most of these studies have been general in scope and statistically unrefined, so that they do not throw much light on the role of this specific factor apart from the general family configuration. Healy and

[25] Paul Popenoe, "Divorce and Remarriage from a Eugenic Point of View," *Social Forces,* October 1933, pp. 48-51; Hornell Hart and E. B. Hart, *Personality and the Family.* Boston: D. C. Heath and Co., 1935, p. 109.

[26] Harvey J. Locke, *Predicting Adjustment in Marriage.* New York: Henry Holt and Co., 1951, p. 309. *See also* Harvey J. Locke and William J. Klausner, "Marital Adjustment of Divorced Persons in Subsequent Marriages," *Sociology and Social Research,* November-December 1948, p. 101; and U.S. Bureau of the Census, *Marital Status, Number of Times Married, and Duration of Present Marital Status,* Series P-20, No. 23, March 4, 1949.

[27] Clairette Armstrong, *Six Hundred and Sixty Runaway Boys.* Boston: R. G. Badger, 1932; John E. Slawson, *The Delinquent Boy.* Boston: R. G. Badger, 1926; Earl T. Sullenger, *Social Determinants of Juvenile Delinquency.* New York: John Wiley and Sons, 1936; White House Conference Report, *The Adolescent in the Family.* New York: D. Appleton-Century Co., 1934; S. P. Breckinridge and Edith Abbott, *The Delinquent Child and the Home.* New York: Russell Sage Foundation, 1912.

Bronner, in their careful analysis made a generation ago,[28] and Smith in his more recent summary and evaluation, both agree that it is the character of the parent or stepparent that is of greater importance than the fact of their presence in or absence from the home.[29] The fact of the matter is that no satisfactory study of the problems of the stepchild, and the significance of family situations in such cases, has been made. Such a study would need to distinguish between cases where the children's parents have been divorced, and where death has terminated the procreative family; as well as between the various sex and age combinations that prevail. What, for example, is the relative significance of the stepfather and the stepmother; with male as compared with female stepchildren; with pre-adolescent, adolescent, and post-adolescent children? What is the significance of class differentials? And, finally, what is the significance of all of these situations, not only in regard to specific problems, such as delinquency, but with reference to general behavior patterns? As this is being written, two cases of stepchildren come to notice which are suggestive of some of these broader behavior implications.

Mary is eighteen years old. Her mother died three years ago. A little more than a year later, her father remarried. The new wife is young, attractive, and friendly to Mary. Relations within the new family are pleasant, but Mary's behavior has changed completely since her father's remarriage. She has become quiet and reserved, spends a good deal of her time in her room reading, and now applies herself with greatly increased seriousness to her studies. She has withdrawn from a number of her social contacts, despite increased gaiety in the home. Mary inherited a substantial income from her mother, so that no problem of finances is involved.

[28] William Healy and Augusta F. Bronner, *Delinquents and Criminals: Their Making and Unmaking.* New York: The Macmillan Co., 1926, pp. 124 ff.

[29] Smith, *American Sociological Review, op. cit.,* p. 238.

William's father and mother were divorced, after a legal battle of considerable bitterness. In-laws on both sides were actively involved. Sometime later, William's mother married again, and William lives with his mother and stepfather. William is eleven years old. Recently, he had the following conversation with a classmate:

William: "Have you found the material for our theme?"
Companion: "Yes, I asked my father."
William: "I'd ask my father, but my grandmother won't let me talk to him. He would be able to help me if I could talk to him. I have another father that I live with, but I don't talk to him, not much. It gets me."

Neither of these cases would be labeled a problem by most persons, in the sense of presenting a crisis situation, yet obviously both young people's behavior is being affected. Mary is withdrawing from normal contacts; William is in a state of puzzled confusion, meeting his situation, too, with partial silence.

CONCLUDING COMMENTS AND A SUGGESTION

For a number of years the author has been observing, asking questions, and recording data, on children of remarriage. From this material, two conclusions and a suggestion are selected for presentation at this point.

1. At upper-class levels, it is frequently supposed that adequate financial provision for the child is all or most of what is needed. Thus one finds these children sent away to expensive boarding schools, packed off to Europe or swank summer camps during the vacation period, supplied with an automobile and a generous bank account, all with the seeming conviction that these constitute the full parental duty. Obviously, all this fails the child in the things that matter most—love, understanding, sympathy, companionship, and a sense of awareness of his importance in the parents' range of attention.

2. At all social levels, but most frequently at the lower

levels, there is a policy of silence, or an inadequate "talking out" of the matter. The parent marries, the new parent arrives, with little explanation—only a fait accompli. This is not only an instance of poor "public relations," but it overlooks an important fact about children. Ordinarily children pay little attention to their parents: they think of parents only as they have need for them. They seldom, if ever, think of their parents as having problems and needs of their own; yet they have the capacity to understand them, if they are explained to them. It is the failure to do these things, to take the child into one's confidence, to explain what is happening in terms that the child can understand, that accounts for a poor start in many stepchild situations.

3. The suggestion to be presented grows out of what has just been said. It involves a policy of child preparation for the remarriage of parents. The failure to do so is in strange contrast to our practice in other situations resembling it. For many years, the policy of careful case work in the placement of a child in a foster home has been fully accepted. No children's agency of any repute would "dump" a child in a foster home without preparation of child and parents. Even societies for the prevention of cruelty to animals now will not place dogs at their disposal for placement without some preliminary preparatory contacts with the new family. Despite the welter of social agencies for every conceivable kind of specialized service, there is an almost complete dearth of facilities or interest in the child of remarriage. This is a curious and serious lack.

SUMMARY

1. One out of every five marriages in the United States in recent years has been a remarriage for one or both of the spouses.

2. Remarriage has been increasing in recent decades. While the decline of the death rate has resulted in a lower

rate of widowed, this has been more than counterbalanced by the higher rate of divorce and remarriage of divorced persons. Also, remarriage is occurring at earlier ages than formerly.

3. The social atmosphere surrounding remarriage is not always helpful in the promotion of a successful adjustment. Remarriages succeed in spite of, rather than because of, friendly attitudes toward them.

4. The child is the central problem in many remarriages. The presence of children often encourages remarriage, and at the same time increases the difficulties of a satisfactory adjustment. An increased proportion of parents with children by a previous marriage who have been divorced and then remarry is changing the overall nature of the problem of the stepchild.

5. Reckoning number of children involved rather than number of marriages with children, the total number of children of divorced parents may equal the total number of divorces.

6. The problem of the stepchild seems to vary a great deal from one culture to another, suggesting the role of cultural factors in their determination. Other factors are the attitudes of the persons involved, the circumstances attending the remarriage and the child's life in the new family, and the personal traits of the family members.

7. There is little scientific evidence on the significance of remarriage for child development. Similarly, very little attention has been given to constructive efforts in dealing with the stepchild, particularly by way of preparation for the new experience.

CHAPTER IX

Interclass Marriages and Child Development

For a man by nothing is so well betrayed
As by his manners.—EDMUND SPENSER

TWO recent developments in sociology may revolutionize social studies in the field of the family and of child development. One of these is a realization of the reality and importance of social classes; the other, the cultural approach to the study of the family and its problems. Each of these will be described briefly, after which the remainder of the chapter will be devoted to their meaning for family relations and child development, with particular reference to marriages between persons of differing social class backgrounds.

SOCIAL CLASSES: THEIR MEANING AND PERVASIVENESS

For many years social science studies of life problems were developed on the assumption that most people lived at about the same level and had the same general interests and problems. Such exceptions as were made recognized chiefly a submerged and a criminal element. In recent years there has come a realization that living patterns in our society are far more numerous, and that the so-called normal and self-maintaining population lives and thinks at a number of different levels. Gradually the term "social class" has come to be applied to these levels, and as a descriptive rather than a snobbish term. This newer usage has not been easy, because of its past connotations, so that even now its employment in a scientific sense is apt to call forth symptoms of emotional resistance.

As currently used by sociologists, two basic ideas or sets of criteria are used in the definition and determination of social class. One is that of evaluated participation, which means the relative place of persons on the basis of their participation in the social system of the community; the other is that of certain status characteristics, such as occupation, source of income, type of home, and residential area.[1] Behind both of these is the essential fact of differences in ways of living and thinking, i.e., cultural differences. It is in this sense, then, that the term "social class" is used in this chapter: to mean differences that encompass the entire range of social behavior. Thus conceived, social classes are freed from emotional connotations, and become objective realities, expressing themselves in relatively fixed patterns of behavior.[2]

Utilizing their techniques in both of these approaches, modern students have identified six social classes. This classification utilizes the old tripartite system of upper, middle, and lower classes, and subdivides each into an upper and a lower group. The result is six social classes, known as the upper upper, lower upper, upper middle, lower middle, upper lower, and lower lower. Whatever future scholarship may reveal about the number and variety of social classes, and whatever terms may come to be applied to them, this classification allows a sufficient number of social levels for generalized studies, and will be utilized in this chapter.[3]

A good deal of the study of class differences at these

[1] W. Lloyd Warner, Marchia Meeker, and Kenneth Eells, *Social Class in America.* Chicago: Science Research Associates, 1949, chaps. 1 and 2.

[2] Bossard, *The Sociology of Child Development*, chap. XIII.

[3] For a more complete description of these classes and the criteria used in their identification, see W. Lloyd Warner and Paul S. Lunt, *The Social Life of a Modern Community*. New Haven: Yale University Press, 1941.

levels that has been done thus far emphasizes their role in family life, and particularly in child rearing. What this means is that these differences are ingrained in people from early childhood, so that class ways of living and of thinking come to be thought of as "second nature." Class differences, in other words, are not superficial: they are both deeply rooted and pervasive. The cultural determination of personality operates on a class rather than on a generalized basis. Behavior patterns are class patterns: individual patterns are variations of the class mode.

THE CULTURAL APPROACH TO THE FAMILY

There are three distinct ways in which the family may be studied. One approach is concerned with its overall organization—its size, structural forms, and systems of continuing relationships. Second is the conception of the family as a unit of interacting personalities, with the emphasis primarily upon the processes of interaction between its members, the role of these processes, and the nature of their operation. The third approach deals with the content of family life. This is spoken of as the cultural study of the family, and it is concerned with how the family lives, what it thinks and believes, and what it aims to do. These three approaches have developed historically in the order in which they have been named: the cultural approach is only now in process of taking form.[4]

The cultural approach to the family is proving an extremely valuable one, because it is constantly emphasizing that a family is not merely a biological experiment, as some people seem to think, or a sociopsychological relationship, as is often implied, but a group of related people in process of developing attitudes, values, and modes of conduct, as all members of families learn by experience.

[4] For a more complete discussion, see *The Sociology of Child Development*, chaps. II to VI.

These patterns involve to some degree almost every aspect of human living together, but they center chiefly about family matters, such as courtship and marriage procedures, sex attitudes, husband-wife relationships, status of men and women, parent-child relationships, family solidarity, attitudes toward aged parents and other kinfolk, entertaining, drinking, worshiping, recreational interests, methods of child rearing, and goals of child development. It is the last two named in particular that become focal points, because they involve the crystallization and conscious projection of these patterns upon the next generation. It is this complex of ways of family living and thinking that comprises the family culture. In popular parlance, it may be spoken of as the internal life of the family.

This inner life of the family differs in certain respects from that of other major social institutions in our society. Their inner life is more formal, more prescribed and organized. Within the church, for example, there are precise forms and orders of service, formally established articles of faith, definitely stated commandments, duties, and taboos, and behind all is an omniscience that can never be deceived. The state has its laws, police courts, and entire regulatory system; and the school has its schedules, curricula, books, and course outlines. The family, on the other hand, operates largely on the basis of tradition, ritual, mores, intuition, history, folkways, and consensus. The stability of the family depends upon the extent to which its members accept these less formal and more intangible pressures; the higher the status of the family, the greater is the expectation of their acceptance; the more rapidly changing the society, the more consensus has to reinforce the waning force of the other factors. In other words, in this wide range of intimate matters which comprise family life, so vital to the individual and his relations to others, there is the least reliance upon formal requirements, and the greatest reliance upon consensus among its constituent members.

INTERCLASS MARRIAGE: MEANING AND EXTENT

Stated in simple terms, an interclass marriage is one between two persons who have been reared at different social class levels. Thus, were a society debutante, whose parents are listed in the social register, to marry her father's chauffeur, who is the son of the village garbage man, everyone would recognize it as an unusual combination because the persons marrying come from such differing backgrounds. Cases of this kind are obvious because of the marked disparity in backgrounds; they are spectacular because of the prominence of some of those concerned; but less conspicuous and striking interclass unions are occurring all the time, attracting the attention chiefly of those who know the persons and their past. The essential fact about such marriages, whatever the classes combined and the degree of their disparity, is that two persons, reared in different backgrounds, accustomed to diverse ways of life, accepting different sets of life's choices and values, come together: first, to share life in its most intimate areas, presumably until death do them part; and, second, in the event of parenthood, to coöperate in life's major responsibility—the rearing of children. This is the real meaning of an interclass marriage.

The extent of interclass marriages in not known because class status of those marrying is nowhere recorded. All that one can say is that, reading between the lines of the various studies of factors in the selection of marital mates, the operation of class status is apparent, as are also the numerous exceptions to it. It seems reasonable to assume that the number of interclass marriages in a country like the United States is large, and may have been increasing in recent years. It is relatively large because ours is an open-class system, in which social "terraces" have been less sharply defined and maintained than in other and older cultures; because of our democratic traditions; and because of the individualistic emphasis in American marriage, whereby the choice of mates is much more a personal than a family one. The number of such marriages may be increasing for many of the same reasons that mixed marriages are, reasons inherent in the increasing freedom and range of social contacts between young people in school, college, and the armed forces.

In this connection, it is particularly important to bear in mind the importance of marriage as a status-achieving device. In a mobile and open-class society, the achieved statuses, and the devices by which they are obtained, receive much attention. Among these status-achieving devices marriage has high rank, especially for women. The peasant girl who marries the prince in the ancient story books has given way to the show girl who marries the banana king's heir and the screen star who invades the Four Hundred. In fact, success in the artist world is one of the most promising short-cuts open, especially to women who wish to consummate status-raising marriages.[5] Café society has been defined as a mixture of producing artists, easy money, and old names, with publicity as its foundation.[6] Instances of this kind are glaring, but status-achieving marriages are made by both sexes and between all levels in our society. In fact, the irritations of many lower-class families with the marriages of their children is that they have not married out of their own class.[7]

[5] James H. S. Bossard, "Marriage as a Status-Achieving Device," *Sociology and Social Research*, September-October 1944, pp. 3-10.

[6] "Café Society," *Fortune Magazine*, December 1937, pp. 127 ff.

[7] Betty Smith, *Tomorrow Will Be Better*. New York: Harper and Brothers, 1948.

ASPECTS OF INTERCLASS MARRIAGES

Many facts seem wholly obvious when stated in general terms: their reality does not appear until they are translated into concrete circumstances and cases. Two aspects of married life in which marked differences in class behavior have been studied will be presented to illustrate some concrete facets of interclass marriage. Two of these are sex and the social use of alcohol.

One of the significant conclusions of the Kinsey report on the sexual behavior of the human male was that there is not one pattern of sexual behavior in the United States, but scores of patterns, each of which is confined to a particular segment of our society. Stratifying the population on the bases of education, occupational class of person, and occupational class of his family when he lived there, Kinsey and his associates report marked variations between these social classes in frequency of sexual outlet, masturbation, heterosexual petting, premarital intercourse, intercourse with prostitutes, frequency of marital intercourse, sources of erotic arousal, nudity, manual manipulation, oral eroticism, positions in intercourse, and conceptions of the significance of the sexual relationship.[8] Many of these might be combined under the felicitous term of a friend, who speaks often of "bedroom manners," and their basic importance in married life.

Perhaps most significant of all are the conclusions of Kinsey, *et al.*, that the majority of persons follow the pattern of their particular class or segment, conceive of it as the normal and right one, and consider other patterns as wrong, unnatural, and immoral. What this means is that when persons of different class backgrounds are joined in

[8] Alfred C. Kinsey, Wardell B. Pomeroy, and Clyde E. Martin, *Sexual Behavior in the Human Male*. Philadelphia: W. B. Saunders Co., 1948, chap. 10. The reader is also referred to Clellan S. Ford and Frank A. Beach, *Patterns of Sexual Behavior*. New York: Harper and Brothers, 1951.

marriage, neither mate is likely to have philosophic insight into the differences in patterns of sexual behavior, and the reasons for them. Each thinks of the other as an abnormal individual rather than as a class type. Persons with experience in marriage counseling or familiar with divorce court testimony know how often differences of this kind are at the root of domestic conflicts and tragedies. In fact, the Kinsey report is emphatic in its contention that these class differences in attitudes toward sex behavior complicate the entire range of the treatment of sex problems and sex offenders in our society.

The social use of alcohol in its various forms is a problem in a great many American homes. This is the second aspect of class differentials in marriage selected for consideration. Dr. John Dollard, of Yale University, has analyzed the drinking mores of social classes. "What is most evident about drinking behavior in these various class groups," he writes, "is that it differs a good bit."[9] Drinking in the upper classes, he continues, is not usually a moral issue, but the attendant behavior is important. Aggressive or antisocial conduct is frowned upon. Lower-upper class persons, being in a more insecure or frustrating position, drink more recklessly than established, older families. In the upper-middle class, moral restraint and occupational (chiefly professional) requirements tend to operate, but social nearness to the upper classes and partial identification with them lead to some compromise, with the result that men indulge to an extent on social occasions, but the women do so somewhat less. As for the lower-middle class, the shadow of its nearness to the lower classes emphasizes the customs and virtues which separate it from them. Both sexes in the lower-middle class show a strong taboo against drinking,

[9] John Dollard, "Drinking Mores of Social Classes," in "Alcohol, Science and Society," *Quarterly Journal of Studies on Alcohol*, New Haven, Conn., 1945, p. 99.

and are the most stringent in exercising social control over it.

"A workingman has the right to have his beer," loudly wails a lower-class laborer in his cups, and his insistence is characteristic of the two lower classes. Here there are fewer taboos, except the occupational restraints in certain occupational groups, like railroad workers. Drinking at home and in taprooms is a social privilege and a compensation for the rigor of manual labor. It is not required to "drink like a gentleman." Fights resulting from too much drinking are frequent, as is violent treatment of wives and children. Week-end binges are not unusual, and at times they lead to acts of criminal behavior or to arrests for disturbing the peace.[10]

There are, of course, many individual exceptions to the foregoing summary statements. Similarly, differences in ethnic backgrounds affect the drinking customs. Such groups as the Germans, Irish, Jews, and Italians tend to have distinctive attitudes which now reinforce and now run counter to the characterization of class mores that has been presented. The point to be emphasized here is that, regardless of individual preferences, a person is prone to judge drinking behavior on the basis of a class measure. When, then, persons from distinctly different class backgrounds marry, the differences in these measures come to express themselves as judgments of the individual mate rather than as symptoms of class rearing.

ILLUSTRATIVE CASE STUDIES

It will help to underscore the nature and reality of interclass differences in family life to summarize briefly two case studies. Both are taken from the files of the William T. Carter Foundation.

[10] *Ibid.*, pp. 95-104.

1. *The Darnell-Linden Family.* This is a family resulting from the marriage of two persons of quite dissimilar backgrounds. The part of the case record presented here is that which sets forth the family backgrounds of the wife and husband respectively.

Jean Darnell came of a middle-class family consisting of father, mother, two daughters, and one son. The family lived in a middle-class suburb of a large city, and moved but once in thirty-five years. Both her father and mother had professional education and experience, although Mrs. Darnell gave up her employment when she was married. Higher education was considered an individual asset and the basis of community prestige. All the Darnell children were encouraged to apply themselves to their studies, cultivate steady work habits, and earn good grades. Rivalry for school success was keen among the three children. The family attended the Episcopal church, and faithfulness in attendance was emphasized. Good grammar, avoidance of "cuss" words, proper observance of the Sabbath, moral behavior, good sportsmanship, and the selection of "proper" companions were virtues constantly emphasized by the parents and grandparents. Proper etiquette at the table, due respect for elders, and regular living and sleeping habits were also insisted upon, without deviation. Jean was graduated from high school and from college with a good record, then entered a profession, in which she served until she was twenty-six years old, when she married Harry Linden.

Harry was born and reared, figuratively and literally, on the other side of the railroad tracks. His family consisted of father, mother, and six children, of whom Harry was the oldest. Harry's mother's mother had kept a rooming house, and Harry's father had been a roomer there. He was twenty-five, and Harry's mother was fifteen, when they were married, and had their six children in rapid succession. Harry's father was one-quarter Indian, and his mother was born to a Protestant-Catholic marriage. Both parents had been keenly aware of the problems of mixed marriages, and the father in particular had to submit to various jibes because of his Indian ancestry. Occupationally, the father insisted on finding outdoor jobs, so that the family were always moving, shifting from city to small town to open country and back to each in turn. As time went on, and particularly during the depression, he was employed irregularly. Relief grants and odd jobs by the children helped to tide the family over the worst spots. Gradually he began to drink heavily, and when he was under the influence of liquor he became quite abusive of his wife and children. Meanwhile, Mrs. Linden was very proud of the fact that she was still youthful looking. She insisted on handling the family finances, but was not a good manager and made various unwise expenditures, for which she was unable to pay. The bill collector at the door was a familiar sight for the Linden children. The children were early encouraged to work, the boys doing odd jobs and the girls finding employment as waitresses at resort towns. School was not emphasized and there were no plans for the education of any of the children beyond the legal requirements. None of the children did any reading outside of school, and the use of good English was sneered at as "putting on airs." The girls were encouraged to marry as early as possible, and all of them did so before they were eighteen. When the boys reached puberty, they were given money for liquor and dating by the paternal grandmother. Each of the three boys had sex experiences at an early age, and frequently, as time went on. Two of the boys left school at the end of the second year in high school, only Harry finished his high school course, after which he entered the armed forces. When he was twenty-three years old, he met Jean under romantic circumstances. They were married soon afterwards, and had three children in four years.

2. *The Willis-Torr Family.* This family differs from the preceding one in that the husband has the higher social status. Ralph Willis is an attorney. He was graduated from a well-known university and took his law degree at another university law school. His family, while of moderate circumstances, have held an honored place in their community, functioning successfully at the professional level for three generations. During his second year at law school, Ralph became engaged to a girl of excellent family and a social status equal or superior to his own. Subsequently, his fiancee tired of waiting for a young attorney to establish himself, and eloped with an older man who was succeeding in business. Ralph was crushed for a time, but pulled himself together and went on with his legal practice. He lived at home, conforming to his family and class patterns. This meant associating with the right people, attending the Presbyterian church regularly, observing the community's moral code, and living comfortably but unostentatiously, and always within one's means. During the next several years, most of his friends who were still single now married and estab-

lished families. In the course of his law practice, he came to meet Jane Torr through her father and married her after a brief courtship. A child was born about six months after their marriage.

Jane was the daughter of a genial saloon keeper. She lived in a section of the city whose name quickly identified its residents as lower class. She had taken a commercial course in the local high school, but her father had frowned upon her employment after graduation. Jane was a Roman Catholic, but not unduly devout. She was pleasing to the eye, but her dress somewhat departed from the limits of good taste. The life she had known comprised that of a working-class area, partly upper lower, but more largely lower lower, class; and that which she knew most intimately was that which centered in the friendly camaraderie of her father's saloon. Her idea of being well dressed was to "knock someone's eye out"; her speech was sprightly, inclined to bluntness, and a bit salty at times. Her idea of success in life was for her husband to obtain large fees, to live so to advertise one's prosperity, and to have a good time. Specifically, the latter meant a lot of guests, good eating, and drinking.

After their marriage, Ralph purchased a home located in a somewhat isolated spot, about three miles out of town. Jane's successive pregnancies, with four children in less than seven years, prevented serious marital difficulties during these years.

CHILD DEVELOPMENT AND INTERCLASS MARRIAGES

The meaning of interclass marriages for child development is an unexplored field. Obviously, the problems presented are similar in nature to those found in religious mixed marriages, but greater in degree and range because the differences between the mates are more extensive and pervasive. Religion is but one phase of the life of an individual, whereas class is as broad as life itself. Often, too, differences in religion are a part of the class differentials united in marriage, that is, interclass marriages are often interreligious ones.

As an initial step in the study of child development in interclass family situations, this chapter summarizes a study based on twenty-five case records. Fifteen of these are families where the parents obviously are of different class backgrounds, and ten are constrasting cases in which both parents are the products of similar class conditioning. In nine of the first group of fifteen cases and in six of the control group, the case records extend over more than a five-year period. In eight of the fifteen cases, the husband is of higher class status; in seven, the wife. All but two of the fifteen families are separated by two or three classes in the sixfold classification utilized in this chapter. The customary class combination in our cases is upper middle class with upper or lower class. The limited number of cases precludes any statistical summary, and this study is of possible empiric interest only for the hypotheses which it suggests. No summary is made here of the ten cases where both parents had the same social-class rearing. These were utilized solely for purposes of contrast and to facilitate insight into the cases of interclass marriages.

1. Our cases suggest that interclass marriages affect child development primarily in two ways. One is through the nature of husband-wife relationships, and the adjustment that each makes to these relationships. These constitute what might be called the interactive background for child development. The other way is through the effect of such unions upon the processes of child rearing. Child rearing is a phase of family operation, a cultural as well as a personal partnership, quite apart for the romantic relationships between the parents. One finds families, for example, where the husband-wife relations are far from the best, yet both parents do make a conscious effort to coöperate for the "sake of the children." Most often, however, husband-wife relations and child rearing are but two parts of the same family story.

2. Perhaps the basic fact about family life resulting from interclass marriages is a fundamental lack of inner harmony. Such lack appears in all of our fifteen cases, and in clear contrast to our ten control families. There is no

harmony because there is no basis for harmony, and where no basis for it exists no amount of effort or of pretending can create it. Harmonious family life involves the complete acceptance by both mates of each other: when significant cultural differences exist between them, the marriage in a certain sense is not complete. If there is one thing which psychoanalytic insights have given to us it is that the psychic atmosphere of the home (another name for family harmony or its lack) is a pervasive reality. So subtle are its operations often that the child's behavior reflects it, through an identification of the unconscious of the child with the uneasy unconscious of the parent. Often, too, children sense this atmosphere without understanding it, and they may do so at a remarkably early age. Adults deceive their children far less often than they suppose. A part of the case record of the Tindale family illustrates this.

> Mrs. Tindale was the daughter of an upper middle class family, who had married a man of lower class status. Many things about her husband's behavior annoyed her, and the mannerisms of one of his best male friends was particularly trying to her. She sought, however, to control her feelings, and to show no signs of her disapproval. One night, after the friend's visit, she was unusually well satisfied with her apparent self-control. As she was putting her five-year-old daughter to bed, she was very much surprised to hear her say: "Mother, why don't you like Mr. Blank?"

This lack of harmony, let it be emphasized, is cultural, not necessarily personal. Interclass marriages may bring together personalities which complement, rather than conflict with, each other. There are these two aspects of every marriage: first, two individual personalities, each with its own traits, temperament, and disposition, are brought together; and, second, two cultural backgrounds, each with its own ways of doing and of thinking, are united in a new cultural synthesis. It is the cultural combination in marriage, and the conflict between the two cultures of the mates in the interclass marriages, with which we are concerned in this chapter.

3. An interclass marriage may be maintained because the marital partners work out an adjustment whereby each goes his or her way, within socially acceptable limitations. This is referred to in erudite circles as solution by personal schematization. While such adjustments maintain outward appearances and the semblance of peace, the real relationship is not lost upon the children, at least not indefinitely. A further adjustment is that the rearing of the children is turned over to one of the parents, usually the mother. This is the case in the Winters family.

Beth and George Winters were an oddly mated pair. Beth was a university graduate, a sorority member, campus figure, and member of Phi Beta Kappa. George had contrived to finish the second year of high school, drank to excess at times, and found his highest inspiration in the daily sports page. They were married after a secret courtship, during which he had been to Beth's house but once. After their marriage, George stopped drinking and went to work in a business which calls for salty language with tough-mannered customers. He prospered, set up a business of his own, and has made a good deal of money. He is proud of his capable wife, and she knows how to utilize the income he derives from his business. Having very little in common except a satisfactory physical relationship, they go their separate ways. The rearing of their two children has been monopolized by the mother; George's only participation is to say to the children: "You do what your mother wants." Both of the children understand the situation, and lately have shown signs of patronizing the father. Thus far, the children have not had biparental rearing, which historically has been emphasized as one of the major values of the monogamous family.

One result of adjustments of this kind is that it narrows the range of social contacts for the family. Where each parent tends to live his or her own life, common friends are few; where the parents come from different backgrounds, the friends of both may tend to avoid them. Such is the case with the Post family.

Henry and Mabel Post have been married eleven years. Henry's background was upper middle class, shading into upper class; Mabel came from a working-class family that might be labeled as upper lower. Henry's friends find Mabel "common" and "boring": they just "don't get to see Henry any more." Mabel says that Henry's friends patronize her, and she is glad to see little of them. Her own friends have gradually ceased to come to visit the Posts because they do not "feel welcome" when Henry is about. In recent years, the Posts have had few friends. Their ten-year-old daughter, and only child, tells her mother that she has no "family friends." She is at an age when she reaches out for *family* as a security need. She is aware that other children do things with their families and with other families, and it is true that there is much of this kind of socializing among the families of the children who go to her school. Within the past year, she has not wanted to go to school, and lately she has made friends with another girl whose father is dead and whose mother is working. These two girls have played truant several times.

Another form of adjustment to the personal schematization of the parents, suggested in the Winters case and three others in this study, is the marked concentration by the male parent upon his business or career. This results in turn in relative success for him, financial or otherwise, which may widen still further the breach within the family configuration.

4. In its milder forms, the lack of family harmony resulting from interclass differences manifests itself in a lack of definiteness in child rearing. True, one parent may have excellent ideas, but tends to be restrained or weakened or discouraged because of the opposition or lack of support of the other. One sees, for example, children who are serene and secure in their assurances because their parents, and visiting kinfolk, are in harmony on most ideas and values. A carefully selected private school may further

reinforce this. Several of our control families are of this kind. In contrast is the Whitten family.

The Whittens present the same situation in many ways as the Winters family just described. But Mr. Whitten is not the complacent husband that George Winters is. He is not as proud of his wife's academic and social achievements. With little formal education, and of lowly origin, he too has prospered, and he is pleased with himself. He sees no reason why his son and daughter should go to college, and he refers to his wife's social friends as "peewees." He does not approve of his wife's methods of child rearing or of her plans for the children. He permits her to have her way for the most part, but he snorts and displays in various ways his disagreement and disapproval. Often, when the mother asks the children to do something, or brings pressure to bear upon them, they look at their father and await his outburst. Even when he supports the mother, it is with a reluctant: "Your mother thinks this is important, so go ahead." Or there is a sarcastic "this is one of your mother's fancy notions" outbreak.

5. Relatively peaceful adjustments of the kind thus far referred to are in the minority among our fifteen cases. Most generally, these class differences lead to open disagreements, to quarreling, and various kinds of conflict. Controversy may flare up over anything: often the alleged cause is but symbolic of deeper issues and resentments. The mate of lower social status is apt to be sensitive and feel insecure; the one of higher status may be unable or unwilling to hide feelings of superiority. These attitudes are complicated often by economic considerations. A lower class husband may earn a good wage or conduct a profitable business and in time "have more" than his "high falutin' " wife; or an upper class wife may be employed and earn more than her lower status husband does, thus adding economic weight to social distinction. Again, the lower class wife may not know how to handle money wisely or to spend it in good taste. Or her bricklaying father earns more than her rising young physician husband or university instructor striving for his doctor's degree.

Helen and Jack Trenton have been married for seven years and have two children. Helen is upper middle class. John is upper lower at best. Their married life has been one long-continued battle, verbal for the most part but descending at times to physical expression. Periodically, Helen packs up the children and goes to the home of her parents, while Jack keeps the apartment and takes his meals with his mother. Each time thus far, Helen has returned to him. She intimates that Jack has a strong physical appeal, and it seems likely that the desire to resume sex relations is uppermost. To her parents and friends, she justifies her return as being for the sake of the children. As for them, they have been rather kicked from pillar to post in the course of these battles. When Helen is angry with Jack, she tells the children that their father is no good, lazy, shiftless, and doesn't want the nicer things in life. When they are with Helen's parents, they reinforce all this, and add adjectives of their own. To Helen and the children, Jack is always on trial as a person: they do not realize that it is his class pattern that they reject.

Methods and objectives in child rearing are among the most frequent bases of conflict between parents of different class backgrounds. Child rearing is class rearing, which means, first, that parents from different class levels have been reared in completely different ways; second, that they project their own experience to the rearing of their children in turn. These class differences in child rearing begin in infancy, and cover an extensive array of items. They include the frequency and duration of breast feeding, the time of weaning, the age and extent of bowel training, the age and extent of bladder training, the assumption of personal and household responsibilities, exploration of the body, sexual inhibitions, family attitudes toward the child, attitudes toward kinfolk, sense of family solidarity, the whole educational pattern, and social and recreational activities.[11]

[11] Allison Davis, *Social Class Influences upon Learning.* Cambridge: Harvard University Press, 1948; Allison Davis and Robert Havighurst, "Social Class and Color Differences in Child-Rearing," *American Sociological Review,* December 1946, pp. 698-710; Bossard, *The Sociology of Child Development,* chaps. XIII and XIV.

Conflicts in these matters are the essence of culture conflicts, and personal quarrels between the parents over them are largely conflicts between the cultural systems which they personify. These culture conflicts within the family project themselves upon the children, and express themselves in terms of internal, i.e., mental, conflicts in the children.

6. One of the common and more serious aspects of these situations is when the children, accepting the standards of the higher class parent, are ashamed of the other parent. The psychology and the sociology of shame are unexplored areas, and yet everyone knows from experience their obvious role in human behavior. Shame of parents is frequent among children, at times justifiably so. It may express itself in many ways—in disrespect to the parent, in ignoring of parental commands, but perhaps most often in the use of the avoidance technique. Avoidance is the child's best weapon when dealing with adults. It may take the form of avoiding the parent in the home, or not appearing with the parent outside of the home, or not bringing other children to the home lest they meet the particular parent. Shame of a lower class parent's occupation is quite common, as indicated elsewhere in this volume.

7. The mother is the crucial parent in mixed class, as she is in mixed religious, marriages. Our cases clearly show this. If the mother's class status is the higher one, things may be more difficult for her, but they tend to be easier for the children. The major responsibility for child rearing in our culture falls upon the mother; children are quite generally encouraged to look upward as they grow older; mother and children thus become partners in the family program for the future. Where the father's social status is the higher one, the difficulties presented are more serious. This is particularly the case with daughters. Fathers, especially upper class fathers, tend to be quite solicitous for

their daughters: in such cases a socially inadequate mother is likely to be a great trial for the father and an even more serious handicap for the daughters.

The Fisher family consists of an upper class father, a lower middle class mother, a son, and two daughters. The father is conscious and proud of his social position, and expects his children to "carry on." Mrs. Fisher has neither the ability nor the interest to function at this level, nor to aid her children. The son, the oldest of the children, has identified with the mother, and ignores all social obligations. This has been a sore disappointment to his father, and all his family hopes have come to be centered upon the two daughters. But entrance to upper class social life requires, among other things, a mother's skillful guidance, and this Mrs. Fisher cannot give to her daughters. Both daughters are aware of this, and have come gradually to ignore their mother. Their relation to the father is quite close, and in the last few years the mother has displayed unmistakable signs of jealousy toward her own daughters. The Fisher family seeks to maintain appearances, but it is not a happy one.

A not uncommon result in these interclass marriages is that, while the dominant parent takes the family "bit in the mouth" and rides intently ahead, the other parent develops an attitude of defeatism which is transmitted to the child, thus undoing much or all of what the dominant parent seeks to accomplish. There is good reason to conclude that this defeatist attitude is most often developed by the mother, since it is more in keeping with the wifely role in marriage.

8. The crucial time in the lives of the children in interclass marriages comes when the child grows up and gains insight into class differentials—and discriminations. Hollingshead has described this in general terms in his study of Elmtown's youth.[12] The behavior and ideas which the child learns at home, he brings to school, church, and other areas of youth activities. In these places, as Hollings-

[12] A. B. Hollingshead, *Elmtown's Youth.* New York: John Wiley and Sons, 1949. See particularly chap. 17.

head points out, other patterns are contacted, and comparisons are made. The child learns that some are more acceptable than others, work better than others, have higher social prestige. And some children learn the reverse, too: that their families do not rate, that their patterns are not socially acceptable. It is at this time, too, that children from interclass homes become aware of the differences between their parents: that one parent has the patterns that rate, while the other does not. This often is a cruel discovery, as several of our case records show. In fact, much of the research work which the author has done in recent years emphasizes the major importance of the child's experience when he comes to compare his parents with other adults. Our studies of the coming of guests to the home underscore the importance of such comparisons as a part of the growing-up process.[13]

The child may react in a number of ways to the discovery that one parent is of lower social status. It may be the parent he loves, and if the identification with the parent is strong enough, the child may accept the lower status too. In other cases he may become bitter, or more, may "lose face" in his own estimation, or may lose respect for the parent of lower status. One is reminded here of Samuel Johnson's statement that poor people's children never respect them. "I did not respect my own mother, though I loved her: and one day when in anger she called me a puppy, I asked her if she knew what they called a puppy's mother."[14]

9. None of the case histories drawn upon in the writing of this chapter has terminated in divorce, desertion, or separation. It must be obvious that these more serious forms of family disorganization frequently result from interclass

[13] Bossard, *The Sociology of Child Development*, chap. XI.

[14] Joseph Wood Krutch, *Samuel Johnson*. New York: Henry Holt and Co., 1944, p. 4.

marriages. Our cases represent instead forms of adjustment to class differentials in the family, with particular reference to the processes of child rearing. Such cases constitute a definite segment of the field of child development.

Taken as a whole, our interclass families are characterized by a good deal of intermittent quarreling and tension. This seems to grow out of a certain duality in the marital relations. In a number of the cases there appears to be a strong bond of physical attraction between the parents, and on this plane marital relations are satisfactory. It is in other respects that difficulties arise, such as in social life and child rearing. As a result, these marriages are not terminated: they fluctuate between spells of happiness induced by physical satisfaction, and periods of tension occasioned by cultural disagreements. These fluctuations are particularly trying to the children, the more so as they grow older.

10. One leaves the study of these families with a conviction of the very great difficulties that are involved. Pertinent data are far from easy to obtain, especially for a large enough number of cases, and of the kind that do not find their way to professional consultation rooms. Furthermore, studies of this kind constitute a form of *pure* social research which only the rare financial source will underwrite.

SUMMARY

1. The acceptance of the social class concept and the cultural approach are revolutionizing the study of the family.

2. A social class is a cultural level, a complex of ways of working, living, playing, and thinking, encompassing the entire range of social behavior.

3. Child rearing is class rearing, which means that class patterns are deeply rooted and firmly fixed.

4. The family, culturally considered, includes a great many aspects of life. There is a family culture pattern.

5. An interclass marriage is one between two persons who have been reared at different class levels. Its unique character lies in the fact that two persons reared in different ways of life come together, presumably permanently, in life's most intimate area.

6. Significant class differences, particularly important for family life, exist in sex behavior and in the social use of alcohol.

7. The meaning of interclass marriages for child development is largely an unexplored field. An original study of fifteen cases, with records of ten additional families where the parents are of the same social class, reveals significant findings. These emphasize the lack of family harmony, of definiteness and certainty in child rearing, a considerable amount of parental quarreling, and feelings of shame on the part of the children.

8. The mother appears to be the crucial parent in mixed class marriages, as she is in mixed religious ones.

9. The crucial period for the children is when they grow up to the point where they gain insight into the nature and importance of class distinctions.

CHAPTER X

Children of Overage Parents

A hearty unison can seldom be established except amongst comrades of the same age.—SANTAYANA

SOME years ago, a prominent anthropologist called attention to the relative neglect of the factor of age in the study of social organization.[1] In the years since, a number of sociologists have acted upon this suggestion and sought to analyze its role in various aspects of our social life. Wide gaps, however, still persist in the understanding of the significance of age and age differentials in human relations. One of these is the importance of the age of parents in family life and child development. This chapter presents the results of an initial study of one phase of this: viz., the relationship of overage parents to the problems and processes of child development. After defining the term "overage parent" and indicating the scope of the problem, the chapter explains briefly the types of overage parent situations, and then presents the suggestive findings of the study. These are grouped under three main headings: the physical, the psychosocial, and the cultural.

WHAT IS AN OVERAGE PARENT?

In a general manner of speaking, the term "overage parent" is self-explanatory. Obviously it is a relative concept, implying an unusually high age differential between parent and child. Its more specific definition calls for a more precise determination of what is an unusually high

[1] Ralph Linton, "A Neglected Aspect of Social Organization," *American Journal of Sociology*, May 1940, pp. 870-86.

age differential. Just what age differential makes a parent an overage parent?

We have utilized here the data from the National Office of Vital Statistics, which show that the statistically average mother in the United States bears her last child at age twenty-seven. For the purposes of this study, it is assumed that an overage parent is one who is more than twenty-seven years older than a particular child. This, of course, is an arbitrary figure, and the line might be drawn, with perhaps equal propriety, at any differential between twenty-five and thirty-five. Wherever the line is drawn, the age differential pertains to each particular child, so that, in the same family, one or both parents may be overage for some but not for all of the children born to them. In all the cases included in the study summarized in this chapter and labeled as overage, the age differential is in excess of thirty-five years.

SCOPE OF THE PROBLEM

How many young children with overage parents are there in the United States? What is their relative proportion to all young children? It seems pertinent to summarize, by way of background to the present study, some data to indicate the national scope of the problem. Such summary shows the following facts:

1. Of all husband-wife households in 1947, having one or more related children under eighteen years of age, 6.2 per cent had fathers fifty-five years of age and over.

2. A total of 3,494,000 children under eighteen years of age lived in these households. This was 9.1 per cent of all such children in the United States.[2]

3. There were almost two million (1,836,980) husband-wife households in 1940 where the mother was fifty years

[2] U.S. Bureau of the Census, *Households by Type, Composition, and Housing Characteristics in 1947*, Current Population Reports, Series P-20, No. 16.

of age and over, and where there were related children under eighteen years. This was 11.7 per cent of such households.

4. A total of 3,241,563 related children under eighteen years of age lived in these households. This was 9.2 per cent of all children in that age category.[3]

5. Among white women, births at ages thirty-five and over constituted 10.6 per cent of the total number of births in 1947.

6. Among white women thirty-five to thirty-nine years, 15.1 per cent of babies born in 1947 were first births, and 20.5 per cent were second births. These two birth orders accounted for more than one-third of the total number of children born to these women.

7. Among white women, forty to forty-four years, 21.7 per cent of all births were first or second births in 1947; among women forty-five to forty-nine, 11.5 per cent of the births fell into these two birth orders.[4]

Since some children with overage fathers do not have overage mothers, and some with overage mothers do not have overage fathers, it is not possible to tell from the foregoing data the total proportion of children with one or both parents who come within our definition of overage parents, but it is apparent that a very considerable percentage of children fall into this category.

THE PRESENT STUDY

The study presented in this chapter is a modest one, even though it has been in the making for a number of years. Its inception dates back to 1932. In the years since, material bearing upon this subject was gathered from many sources and was carefully recorded. Some of it is in the form of

[3] U.S. Bureau of the Census, *Types of Families*, Special Report of 1940 Census, Table 8.

[4] Metropolitan Life Insurance Company, *Statistical Bulletin*, November 1949, p. 10. Compiled from basic data obtained from the National Office of Vital Statistics.

personal observation, some consists of the comments of other observers. In addition, seventeen relatively complete case histories were gathered. Of the latter, six were obtained from overage parents; eleven were from persons with overage parents. The former ranged in age between forty-three and seventy-two years; the latter between nineteen and fifty-four. Altogether, information was obtained from forty-three different sources, and the study is based on this material. Observation of most of the cases, or contact with them, extends over more than ten years.

TYPES OF OVERAGE PARENT SITUATIONS

A wide variety of overage parent situations was encountered. They will be described briefly.

1. One form is where fathers are overage and the mothers are not. This type of situation is relatively common because of the tendency of men in all ages, and particularly in the older age brackets, to marry women younger than themselves. In some of these cases, the younger wife is a first marriage for her spouse, but more likely it is a remarriage for him, and he may have older children with a former wife or wives. Our material includes cases where the father was over sixty-five years of age when his young wife gave birth to a child.

Incidentally, a statistical study of 259,443 marriages recorded in New York State, outside of New York City, over a four-year period, 1945-48, revealed that 70,615 or 27.2 per cent of the men marrying were thirty years of age or over; that 27,472 or 10.6 per cent were forty or over; that about half of them married women rather considerably younger than they were; and that as men grow older, the age differential between them and the women they marry increases.[5]

2. A second type is where the mother is overage and the

[5] James H. S. Bossard, "Marrying Late in Life," *Social Forces*, May 1951, pp. 405-8.

father is not, or is at least less so than the mother. Older women, not yet past the age of child bearing, often marry younger men. In the New York study just cited, approximately one-fourth of the women in the age groups between thirty and forty-five married men younger than themselves.[6]

3. A third type is where both parents are older, and again it may be a first or a remarriage for either one or both. We recorded one case where a man of sixty-five was married, for the third time, to a divorcée of forty-three, who promptly presented him with a son. He has two grown children by his second wife; she had a ten-year-old daughter by her first husband.

4. Fourth are the cases found in large families. Here the younger children arrive after both parents are older. In 1947, for example, in the country at large, 24.7 per cent of all children born to women forty to forty-four, and 33.6 per cent of those born to women forty-five to forty-nine, were the tenth or later child.

5. A fifth type includes what are often called "little accidents." Here the parents have had their children when young, reared them to or near to maturity, and then, during the mother's climacteric, another pregnancy ensues.

6. Finally, we have recorded two cases where women past forty bore children out of wedlock, and proceeded to rear them.

It is apparent from the foregoing that overage in parents is associated with other factors. Among these are the extent of the age differential between the parents; their respective marital histories; the number, ages, and sexes of other children by the same parents; and the sex of the child in relation to the sex of the overage parents. In other words, overage in parents cannot be considered apart from these other circumstances in the family situation. This fact must be kept in mind in the succeeding pages of this chapter,

[6] *Ibid.*

although an effort has been made to isolate the operation and significance of the overage factor.

OVERAGE PARENTS AND CHILD DEVELOPMENT—SOME SUGGESTIVE FINDINGS

1. It is generally recognized that motherhood late in life may involve medical difficulties. Unfortunately our records include no medical histories of our cases, but they do contain a number of lay references to the difficulties that the mothers had in bearing children in the later reproductive ages. This was particularly true in the case of the first born. It would be a primary requisite of an adequately financed study of the development of children of overage parents to have obstetrical and pediatric histories of the cases included in the study. All that can be said here is that the family comments recorded in this study bear out the traditional medical point of view.

2. Overage parenthood is related to the problems of orphanhood and child dependency. This is obvious, since the more advanced the age of the parent or parents, the greater the likelihood of their death or incapacity before the child reaches maturity. Our data illustrate this clearly, although the number of cases is too small to be significant statistically. Lack of advantages and the necessity of assuming unusual responsibilities at an early age also result at times. In cases where one parent is considerably older than the other, there are the added possibilities of widowhood, remarriage, and the problems that are associated with them. The child of overage parents, it may be said by way of summary, faces certain insecurities beyond the range of those attending children of younger parents.

3. There is, of course, a reverse side to much of what has just been said. This appears in cases where the family is financially well situated. The overage parent may be a father who delayed marriage until he achieved an ad-

vanced position in the business or professional world, and parenthood comes to him in the flush of material success and/or personal prestige. Or he may be a well-established widower who marries a young wife who bears a second group of children to him. In cases like these, the children of overage parents may enjoy advantages that the same parent could not give at earlier stages of the life cycle. One of the cases included in this study is that of a man who rose in the ranks of a large corporation to be one of its responsible officers at the age of fifty-one years. He then married (his first marriage) a young woman of about twenty-five, with whom he had three children in the course of the next six years. During the entire period covered by our record of the case, his children were the "apples of his eye," for whom nothing was to be denied. Curiously enough, he has sought consistently to shield them from the kind of experiences he encountered, which he insists went into the making of his success, and upon which he rose to his present position.

4. Advanced age in parents is of primary significance in child development because of its meaning for parent-child relationships, and information bearing on this has been noted with particular care in our material. As a framework for the interpretation of this information, the time differential between parent and child is taken as the basic concept of measure. The idea involved has been well stated by Santayana: "Old and young, even of the same breed, find themselves at different phases in the vital cycle, and cannot agree in mood, opinion, impulse or affection. Contact means constraint on both sides, and a hearty unison can seldom be established except amongst comrades of the same age."[7]

Simply stated, two conclusions underlie the rest of this

[7] George Santayana, *Dominations and Powers.* New York: Charles Scribner's Sons, 1951, p. 69.

chapter. One of these is that the age or time differential between parent and child measures the difference in place between the two on the life cycle. This is indicative in turn of the nature and range of other differences between them. Many of these differences translate themselves into difficulties when they share the intimacies of family and parent-child relationships. The second conclusion is that, after a given point is reached, the greater this age or time differential, other things being equal, the greater the scope and degree of other differences and difficulties between them.

It must not be inferred from the foregoing that every added year of difference in age between generations increases of necessity the differences and problems between them, nor must this chapter be interpreted to mean that men and women should marry and have their children at the earliest biological-economic age possible. The thesis presented in this chapter is that, *after a given point is reached*, an increasing age differential between generations exaggerates the problems that arise between them. This given point need not necessarily be in the teens: it may be at or even past thirty. More of this will appear in the final chapter of this volume.

Some age differential between parents and children is inevitable, and so, as a consequence, are many of the conflicts between successive generations. Turgenev has given classic expression to these in his well-known *Fathers and Sons*. Various sociologists have conceived of the conflict between generations as an inevitable phase of the social process, resulting from the difference in their places in the life cycle.[8]

The differences and the problems raised in the relation-

[8] Edward A. Ross, *Principles of Sociology*. New York: The Century Co., rev. ed., 1930, chap. XVIII; Earl H. Bell, "Age Group Conflicts and Our Changing Culture," *Social Forces*, December 1933, pp. 237-43; Kingsley Davis, "The Sociology of Parent-Youth Conflict," *American Sociological Review*, August 1940, pp. 523-36.

ship between persons separated in the life cycle may be grouped under three heads: physical, psychosocial, and cultural. For most children, the difference in ages between them and their parents is from twenty to thirty years; in the cases included in this study, the differences range from thirty-five to seventy years. How does this greater time interval affect these physical, psychosocial, and cultural problems of adjustment?

5. Four problems of a physical nature in overage parent-child relationships appear in our material. The first involves the problem of nervous energy. Parenthood is a nervous-energy-consuming occupation. Children, like young puppies, seethe with energy. They make enormous demands upon those responsible for their care. These demands are of many kinds—verbal, physical, nervous. To meet these demands with reasonable adequacy is a drain upon one's energy, as every parent knows. And what every grandparent knows is that later in life the ability to meet these demands of young children is limited. This is one of the basic problems of the overage parent—the lack of energy to be an adequate parent. What forms of adjustment result? Our material reveals the following. Most of the care and rearing of the child is turned over to someone else. Or the overage parent makes a determined effort to measure up, and fails. In failing, the fact may be recognized, albeit rather wistfully; or irritability may appear; or the overage parent's inadequacies are rationalized into faults of the child.

A second series of observations revolves around the health problems of overage parents. These are significant here, not so much for their meaning to the parents as for their effect upon the children. It is necessary to recall here that children conceive of parents in terms of their need for them and tend to resent it if parents have problems of their own. The ailing, the infirm parent, then, is conceived of, not as someone who needs the child's help, but as a person who is ineffective in meeting the child's need for help.

Several of our cases emphasize how the health problems of the overage parent interfered with family routines. In one case in particular, the parent projects his physical discomforts upon the rest of the household, seeking in various ways to tyrannize them. The different members of the family adjust in different ways, with a resultant tension that grips the entire household, and that the young child member only vaguely understands. Our material does not contain a case where the overage parent suffers from a mental illness, but one can easily realize that in such cases the upset in the family would be even more pronounced.[9]

Akin to the problem of health is that of the living habits of the overage parents. Older people tend to develop set habits of living—time to get up, to go to bed, to eat, and the like. As time goes on, these become more and more rigid. The coming of a young child creates a great many problems in this respect. Once the child is at school, school activities and companionships make for irregularity in many aspects of the family regime. Moreover, children are noisy. Their companions are noisy. Or so they seem to elders. These are matters that interfere with the ordered life of older persons. The kind of situation that results is illustrated in one of our cases.

Thomas Orcott was 55 when his youngest child, a daughter, was born. Now she is 17 and her father is 72. She is pretty, vivacious, and popular. She has many friends among both sexes. Some of them gang up together in a particularly active round of social life. Her active life, and that of her friends, is a great trial to her father, with his rigid living habits. As a result, father and daughter have been in continual conflict in recent years, despite the restraining intervention of the mother. The 72-year-old father rails against her

[9] For an interesting account of how mental illness affects family life, the reader is referred to an article by Mary B. Treudley, "Mental Illness and Family Routines," *Mental Hygiene*, April 1946, pp. 235-49.

teen-age activities, calls them silly; flays her friends as uncouth barbarians; and issues one ultimatum after another to her. The 17-year-old daughter fights back, says he is unreasonable, an unnatural father, a selfish old man, out of joint with his times. In her softer moments, she is content to say that he is in his dotage. In the past year, he has embarrassed her greatly by being rude to her guests, ordering them out of the house on several occasions. One cannot contemplate this case record without a profound conviction that the real difficulty here is that the daughter is at a stage of the life cycle that calls for action and expression, and the father is at the stage that wants peace and quiet and orderliness.

Finally, there is the physical appearance of the overage parent. Two of our cases point up to this interesting fact, that the child, in comparing his parents with the parents of his child companions, sees that his overage parents differ in physical appearance. He discovers that his parents are old, that they do not look like other parents.

Virginia, an only child, is nine years old. Her mother was thirty-eight when she was born. Now, at forty-seven, she is highly attractive in an adult kind of way, but to her nine-year-old daughter the gray in her hair and some other signs of age are very conspicuous in comparison with the other third-grade mothers. Virginia is very proud and very family conscious. For several months now, she has spoken a number of times of her mother's difference in appearance. Apparently, she is having difficulty in assimilating the fact.

The case of Cordelia suggests that awareness of this kind may come early in life.

Cordelia is three and a half. One day, while sitting on the lap of her forty-nine-year-old father, she keeps looking at his bald head with its gray fringe. After several appraising surveys, she says to her father: "Daddy, you don't have hair like some men I might know."

Reinforcing these physical differences which the child sees is the fact that the overage parents tend to have different social contacts. In many neighborhoods and communities, parents of the same age socialize with each other. Their children go to the same school, play at the same playgrounds, and participate in the same activities. The social contacts of the parents coincide with those of the children. In many suburban communities, and with the small family system, all this becomes very important for the child's sense of security. But here again the overage parent may be a misfit, a fact which his child will quickly sense. His parents do not belong, they do not "go around" with the other parents. Such a situation may create problems for both the overage parent and the child.

Two of our cases are of this kind, but a third one shows a strikingly different outcome. In this case, the father, because of his age, maturity, and professional status, is an honored community figure, while the mother, older too than most mothers, is president of the Parent-Teachers Association. Here overage in the parents is associated with relatively high community status, a fact of which their two sons are well aware.

6. Various stages in the life cycle are characterized not only by differences in energy, health, living habits, and physical appearance, but also by differences of many other kinds. Of those which have been grouped as psychosocial, only a few can be touched upon here.

(a) One of these is what shall be called the attitude toward experience and the learning process. Youth is characteristically aggressive, experimental, hopeful, idealistic, progressive. Particularly important here is it to note that youth is experimental and idealistic, both of which are due to lack of experience. It was Galsworthy, I believe, who said that idealism depends on our distance from the problem. Youth, then, wants actual participation, and hope colors the expectation of such experience. This is youth's way of learning. Experience keeps a dear school, but youth is willing and eager to pay the price. Only modern youth, says Will Durant, knows better than the verdict of twenty centuries.

Part of this is of physical origin. Youth is full of energy, which craves expression. There are tensions seeking outlet, and it would be a mistake to assume that these are only sexual. The organism supplies the physical energy that is necessary for survival: another of the aspects of balance in the miracle of nature.

By contrast, age is conservative, realistic, skeptical, and sure. The old have had their contacts and experiences with life—enough to have many convictions, and perhaps some disillusionments. Now they see their young toying with the same problems, undergoing a similar experience. Because of their love for their own young, they seek to give them the benefit of their experience. Sometimes they do so in kindly vein, and only when asked; often they become dogmatic, or seem to be so.

Much of what the case material reveals can be reduced to a sense of irritated impatience on the part of overage parents with their children. Unlike younger middle-aged parents, who also may still be in experimental and idealistic stages, overage parents are relatively sure of many things: they cannot understand why their children cannot accept their judgment. Other things being equal, the older the parent, the more positive his opinions, and the greater his impatience with a child who insists on the folly of finding out for himself. The child, by way of contrast, thinks of the overage parent as dogmatic, opinionated, domineering, narrow-minded, unreasonable, and out of date.

(b) There is apt to be considerable difference in conceptions of the importance of specific aspects of experience. To the fourteen-year-old daughter in one of the case records, having a boy friend to carry her books home from school is one of the most important things in the world. Her sixty-five-year-old father, realizing that he cannot remember the name of the girl whose books he carried at that age, thinks her anguish is silly, and does not give her the sympathy she needs. Besides, he knows that many a street car named Desire passes by between fourteen and sixty-five. Our material is replete with differences of this kind, and they are as tragic to the child as they seem foolish to an aged parent.

(c) Similar to the differences in attitude toward experience are the anxieties of the two age groups under consideration. The history of the personality in terms of its successive anxieties has not yet been written, but one strongly suspects that each stage of the life cycle has its own characteristic ones. Certainly the anxieties of seventeen are different from those of seventy. Those of youth are concerned chiefly with possible lack of opportunities for cxperience: those of age are compounded out of trauma from past experiences and dread uncertainty of future ones. It is for this reason that overage parents tend to be oversolicitous, a fact which our case material amply illustrates. They are oversolicitous because they know the hurt of the world. They have been hurt themselves, and they want to keep their children from similar hurts. The older the parent, the greater the accumulation of hurt may be; the longer time there has been for hurts to fester, the more solicitous he may be for his child.

(d) Overage parents like these may have become cynical, or bitter, or else tend to withdraw from life and often encourage their children to do so. This is the viewpoint of one of the young people included in the study, who writes:

> My father is retired and spends much time at home. He is devoted to his family. He helps my mother with housework, so that they have a lot of time. As a result, they and their two children (I have a sister) have done a great many things together, and with other adults. As a result, I have grown up with adults instead of with other children of my own age.

I wanted to be accepted by other children, but I was never helped in this by my parents. As a result, I have become very independent, and have developed a "I'll take care of myself" attitude. My parents now seem two old people, whom I love, but who live in an isolated world of their own. I haven't been happy in this world, and I haven't been happy in the world to which I aspired. So I am fighting for a position in it.

As time has gone on, I have gone away to school and spend the summer traveling. I do not enjoy being at home. I feel as though I am in a vacuum. I escaped it once, but I always have a silly feeling that some day it will catch up with me again and I won't be able to escape.

This encouragement of the child to withdraw, relatively, from life by overage parents is common in our case records.

(e) If overage parents with such attitudes have ample economic means at their disposal, they may seek to insulate and/or isolate the child from contact with the realities of life. Several of our cases reveal such patterns. One overage father, recalling his experience in fighting his way to school when a boy, has his child chauffeured to and from school. Another, remembering his perennial shortage of funds, is overly liberal with his child. A third one, still smarting from the memory of a sadistic employer when he was sixteen, is unwilling that his child accept summer employment at age twenty.

(f) A common difference in anxieties between a young boy or girl and an overage parent centers around money. The latter, looking back on a lifetime of economic fluctuations and aware of the great importance of an economic reserve to cushion such fluctuations, and realizing too the baubles obtained for many expenditures, becomes overly concerned with money and its use. Youth, on the other hand, has not yet learned these things or, knowing them intellectually, rejects them emotionally. Moreover, there is perhaps never any time in the life of the individual when a few dollars may mean as much as in the teen years. Throughout the course of this inquiry, there has been much encounter with squabbles and tensions between overage parents, often moderately well off or better, and their teen-age children over matters involving small, often trifling, amounts of money.

(g) One encounters overage parents who tend to exploit their children by making relatively excessive and unusual demands upon them. Some of these demands may be economic, but probably more often they are of a psychosocial nature. A more pretentious study than this would be necessary to prove that the frequency of such exploitation increases with the age differential between parent and child. It seems reasonable to suppose that this is true, and several of our cases show its operation.

One case is that of Mrs. Lerner. Her eleventh and last child was born six years after the tenth child, and when she was forty-four years of age. From the very begining, Mrs. Lerner "took over" this eleventh child, who was her fifth daughter. Nora, the daughter, was to run all her mother's errands, wait on her, and devote all her time to her care. Mrs. Lerner was emphasizing constantly her own age, that she was not well, and that she couldn't get around without help. Nora is twenty-four now, exceedingly attractive, but has no social life, and devotes all of her time to the care of her mother. She has had less education than the other children. Her mother, a "healthy invalid" at sixty-eight, talks incessantly about the "ingratitude" of her other children, the devotion of Nora, and the indispensability of her devoted care. Friends and neighbors speak of Nora's devotion as "beautiful" or "pitiful," according to viewpoint.

(h) The tragedy of some children of overage parents is that they are not wanted. Such rejection may involve a variety of forms. The rejecting parent may be an old man, unwilling for any of a number of reasons to assume the duties of parenthood at his age; it may be an older woman who accidentally conceives, and her resentment against her husband finds expression in her treatment of the child; it may be a young wife of an older man, who hadn't planned such a development; or the rejection may come from the older children of the parents. Moreover, its existence may not always be evident; in fact, it may be accompanied by compensatory forms of behavior that seem to deny any possible interpretation of rejection.

In some of our cases, there can be no doubt. In one, the young mother voiced in no unmistakable terms her resentment against a fate which had her conceive with a seventy-two-year-old man. Another man of sixty-eight cursed his luck and threatened to kill himself when his young third wife became pregnant. Highly interesting is the case of a woman who became pregnant at fifty-two, and showed her resentment against her husband by not speaking to him during the rest of her life.

The most common form of rejection seems to be that of the other children, if there are any, of overage parents. This happens when a child is born late in the life of one or both parents, after the other children are fully grown or nearly so.

John Lott was born when his mother was forty-four years old. His parents had four other children, ranging from seventeen to twenty-four years. The Lotts live in a small town, and there has been a good deal of bantering comment about the late arrival. The other children have had to take a lot of teasing about the new brother. The attitude of the parents is tinged with feelings of shame, and three of the four siblings look upon the newcomer with mingled feelings in which there are ridicule and feelings of rejection. Only one of the siblings is receptive, markedly so, which appears in striking contrast to the attitudes of the others. John early displayed marked signs of aggressive behavior, as though he would compel you to notice him, whether you would or no.[10]

(i) A good deal seems to depend on the particular age

[10] Bossard, *The Sociology of Child Development*, p. 336.

when parenthood comes to the overage parent. If it comes during the late sixties and seventies, the young child will never have any conception of his parent except as an old person. Moreover, a father of that age may never take an active role in the child-rearing process. If, however, the child comes when the parent is in high middle age and at the height of development, the child is apt to witness and experience a process of aging and deterioration in the parent that may puzzle, irritate, confuse, or sadden him. The following is an excellent picture of an aging father through the eyes of his son.

Ralph Connor was born when his father was fifty-four years old. This means that when Ralph entered his teens, his father was past sixty-five. Concerning his father in these years, Ralph says: "As father aged, his self-discipline deteriorated. Manual labor makes exhausting demands as men grow older. His language relapsed in the direction of his antecedents and his habits became increasingly uncouth. His table manners were appalling and his attitudes were more hostile or irritable. He was over seventy when I was fifteen, and we did not anticipate the fact that a fairly definite senile trend had set in. It was not explicit until he was nearly seventy-eight, but may have been reflected in his somewhat pathetic rages, self-pity, demands, and inconsistencies for ten years previous. The family situation became increasingly tense, and as my older brothers and sisters left to marry or find congenial work, they broke rather definitely with father. My own break was less definite. I finished high school at an early age, and then, some time after that, left for college. It was a relief to get away, even though I was on a very heavy schedule of work supporting myself along with my studies. . . . As my father grew older, he also grew noticeably less hospitable to boys who came to call on my sisters, and perhaps somewhat suspicious of their designs. He complained that he did not know their parents, and he appeared to be interested primarily that they be out of the house by ten o'clock. This did not improve the situation between him and my sisters, who eventually met the situation by having their dates at the homes of girl friends."

(j) It is interesting to note how the past history of an overage parent may produce quite unexpected behavior as a parent. To William Grant was born at fifty-three his first child, to be followed a year later by a second one, both boys. Mr. Grant, a prominent professional man, was fifty-one when he was married. His background had been one of puritanic severity. Thanksgiving Day, for example, had never been observed in his family when he was a boy: it was too worldly a custom. Christmas Day was observed with solemnity, but no gifts. It is doubtful whether he ever had a toy as a child. His upward climb to a professional education and later professional eminence had been a long, arduous, and painful one. No reader would expect from this dour-looking man of eminence what our case record reveals! A father more delighted with his sons than many a father half his age, a man who entered with eagerness the games of his sons, who played with their trains at Christmas time more than did the children, who took them on fishing trips, who went camping with them, and who batted out many a home run in their ball games. Past sixty, William Grant discovered with his sons the joyous delight of children's play. For the first time in his life, he is being a child.

(k) Finally, there is the overage parent who finds it difficult, because of his occupational experience and what it has done to him, to be a parent. Reference has been made in another chapter to the fact that different occupations create different personality types, and that these types are not confined to the office and the shop but are carried over into the home as fathers and husbands. Says the captain of a ship, in speaking about his difficulties with his son: "When I give an order, I expect it to be obeyed."

The case material of this study is somewhat weighted in the direction of executive and professional men who are overage fathers, and it is replete with illustrations of these occupational types in the role of parents. The driving executive past middle age looks from the high rung of his ladder upon a mild and studious son; a successful money maker with a beautiful, svelte young wife cannot understand an introvert son who majors in English literature; the judge demands deference in his home; the teacher expects prompt obedience from his children; the vice-president, with three secretaries, and five buttons to press, wants his youngsters to come as promptly to his call as does his office help. Writes the general manager of a plant: "I want my son to be so well trained that, no matter how hard at play he may be, he will drop everything and come to me at once when he is called." Truly, it is difficult to be one kind of person eight hours a day at work, and another kind the next five hours at home—especially after the years have worn smooth the neural pathways.

7. The third main group of difficulties between overage parents and their children are cultural in character. By nature, these are similar to those which inevitably exist between successive generations—each having its own ways of doing and thinking; it is their degree and intensity which are noteworthy in many cases of present-day overage parents.

Two factors are significant in this connection. One is the time interval between the generations, the other is the rate of change in the culture. The time interval between generations determines, other things being equal, the difference in the cultural milieu in which successive stages in the life cycle take their cultural form. A parent who is twenty years older than his child grew up in a world twenty years earlier. Babyhood, childhood, adolescence, youth of parent and child all are separated by a twenty-year interval. Consider now by contrast two of our cases.

George Dern was born in 1891, which means that a late nineteenth- and early twentieth-century culture conditioned the formation of his behavior patterns. Moreover, the area in which he lived and the industry upon which his family depended for a livelihood passed through a lean stage during those years. In 1936, at the age of forty-five, he was married, for the first time, to a woman of twenty-two. In 1937, and again in 1939, she bore him sons. Today, 1952, these boys are twelve and thirteen, respectively. Their father, while happy in his marriage and parenthood, finds it hard to "understand" his sons. He grew up in the days before the first World War; his sons, in the years after World War II. True, it is borne in upon him in many ways that we are living in a different world, generally and intellectually. George Dern accepts this. His difficulty seems to be that of translating this acceptance into terms of the minutiae of everyday living.

All this is even more pronounced in the case of Walter Train, who married his nurse in 1924 when he was sixty-eight years of age. He had been born in 1856, married his first wife in 1879, and reared three children in the last quarter of the nineteenth century. His first wife died in 1901. A second marriage had ended in divorce. Now, at the age of sixty-nine, his third wife bore him a son. This son was four years old when the depression began in 1929, and eighteen when he joined the armed forces in 1943. The father died in 1941, at the age of eighty-five. His later years were full of disappointment about this last-born son. He was a rugged individualist who believed, on the basis of his nineteenth-century background, that success or failure turned wholly on the quality of the citizen character. The son, coming to maturity during the depression years and holding the views of many of the young people of that era, spoke a language that was both foreign and anathema to the old man. Time had forged an unbridgeable gulf between father and son.

The significance of the time interval in this connection depends in considerable measure upon the rate at which the culture changes. A forty-year difference in a relatively static culture is one thing; in a period of very rapid change, it is quite another. The meaning of rapid social change for parent-child relations was emphasized in general terms some years ago by one of our sociologists. "Extremely rapid change in modern civilization," wrote Davis,

> in contrast to most societies, tends to increase parent-youth conflict, for within a fast-changing social order the time-interval between generations, ordinarily but a mere moment in the life of a social system, becomes historically significant, thereby creating a hiatus between one generation and the next. Inevitably, under such a condition, youth is reared in a milieu different from that of the parents; hence the parents become old-fashioned, youth rebellious, and clashes occur which, in the closely confined circle of the immediate family, generate sharp emotion. . . . Not only are parent and child, at any given moment, in different stages of development, but the content which the parent acquired at the stage where the child now is, was a different content from that which the child is now acquiring. Since the parent is supposed to socialize the child, he tends to apply the erstwhile but now inappropriate content. . . . He makes this mistake, and cannot remedy it, because, due to the logic of personality growth, his basic orientation was formed by the experiences of his own childhood. He cannot "modernize" his point of view, because *he* is the product of those experiences. He can change in superficial ways, such as learning a new tune, but he cannot change (or *want* to change) the initial modes of thinking upon which his subsequent social experience has been built. To change the basic conceptions by which he has learned to judge the rightness and reality of all specific situations would be to render subsequent experience meaningless, to make an empty caricature of what had been his life.[11]

This is in marked contrast with what one finds in a slowly changing, static society. Lang, writing of the family in historic China, says: "Another feature that served to strengthen the position of the old man was the fact that imperial China was a static civilization. The old man represented an accumulation of wisdom. The young man wanted to imitate him, not to fight him. For hundreds and

[11] Kingsley Davis, *op. cit.,* pp. 523-25.

thousands of years there was no conflict of generations in China."[12]

Standing aloof, and viewing the study as a whole, one overall conclusion stands out, and it can best be expressed by the single word "exaggeration." Lengthening the time interval between generations exaggerates the problems between them. The basic assumption underlying this is that the problems of parent-youth relationships grow largely out of the time interval that separates them—the different stages they occupy in the unfolding life cycle and the difference in cultural values of the periods in which each generation passed or passes through when in that given stage. When that time interval is lengthened unduly, all problems tend to be exaggerated. Children seem more troublesome to their parents, parents seem less understanding to their children, solicitousness in parents becomes more pathological, and their firmness turns into rigidity. Chronological distance tends to coincide with psychosocial and cultural distance.

SUMMARY

1. An overage parent is one who is older than his child by more than the customary time span that separates successive generations. The dividing line is arbitrarily drawn in this study at twenty-seven years.

2. Overage parental situations may involve overage fathers, overage mothers, or both parents over age.

3. A considerable proportion of children have parents who are over age, by customary measure of time intervals between generations.

4. Overage parenthood is often associated with medical problems, orphange, and child dependency. On the other hand, many overage parents are well situated economically

[12] Olga Lang, *Chinese Family and Society*. New Haven: Yale University Press, 1946, p. 10.

and give their children unusual opportunities for development.

5. The age or time differential between generations measures the difference in place between the two on the life cycle. The greater this differential, the greater the scope and differential between the two.

6. The resultant problems are grouped under three heads: the physical, the psychosocial, and the cultural. Rapid cultural change intensifies the latter, particularly.

CHAPTER XI

Parents' Occupation and Child Development

Every man's work . . . is always a portrait of himself.
—SAMUEL BUTLER

Thou renderest to every man according to his work.
—PSALMS LXII:12

ONE of the first questions we ask about a stranger is: What does he do? On the basis of the answer we obtain, we proceed to place him in the social scheme of things. Obviously, occupation tells us a great deal about a person; logically, its study should constitute a definite segment of the sciences concerned with man's behavior and social relations. This chapter begins, then, with a brief reference to a possible sociology of occupation, but the greater part of it is devoted to one specific aspect of it. How does the occupation of the parent affect the social development of the child? As a beginning step in formulating an answer to this question, a pioneer study, made under the auspices of the William T. Carter Foundation, is presented.

A SOCIOLOGY OF OCCUPATION

Recognition of the role of occupation varies considerably in books on general sociology. Some well-known textbooks of recent vintage do not even mention it; others give it brief but trite reference, such as saying that the occupational group which one joins will determine one's attitudes and interests. Still others confine their treatment to pointing out relationships, chiefly statistical, between occupation and such phenomena as birth, death, divorce, and marriage rates; or magnify its role in some one aspect of social relations, such as its status-conferring significance.

This lack of systematic development is not in keeping with its undoubted importance in the life of the individual and society. Speaking of its significance for the former, Dublin and Lotka write: "The work a man does, the conditions under which his work is done, and the wages he receives for doing it determine in great measure the circumstances of his life, the house he lives in, the clothes he wears, the food he eats, and his recreation."[1] And they might have added that it determines the people with whom he associates, the nature of his relations with them, the area as well as the house in which he lives, and many other aspects of his daily life.

Concerning the sociological significance of occupation, Sorokin writes that "neither individual conduct and psychology, nor group behavior and characteristics, nor social antagonisms and solidarity, nor processes of social reconstruction and revolution, nor almost any important social change or irregularity, can be accounted for satisfactorily without the occupational factor."[2] The same author has emphasized its very great importance in the process of social mobility, i.e., in changes of persons and families in residence and in status.[3] More recently, W. Lloyd Warner and his associates have recognized occupation as a basic factor in the determination of social status, and the operation of the social class system.[4]

If the social role of occupation has not been systemati-

[1] Louis I. Dublin and A. J. Lotka, *The Length of Life*. New York: The Ronald Press, 1936, p. 220.

[2] Pitirim Sorokin, *Contemporary Sociological Theories*. New York: Harper and Brothers, 1928, p. 718.

[3] Pitirim Sorokin, *Social Mobility*. New York: Harper and Brothers, 1927, chaps. VI, X-XIII, XVIII.

[4] W. Lloyd Warner, Marchia Meeker, and Kenneth Eells, *Social Class in America*, chaps. 1 and 2.

cally developed by the sociologists, specific aspects of it have certainly engaged their interest in recent years. From February 1936, when the first issue of the *American Sociological Review*, appeared, to February 1952, a total of sixty articles reporting research studies of occupation appeared in four leading sociological journals: the *American Sociological Review*, the *American Journal of Sociology*, *Social Forces*, and *Sociology and Social Research*. Included in these articles are references to forty other articles and books dealing with sociological aspects of occupation, published during the same or earlier years. Tabulation of the articles in the four sociological journals shows that the war years interrupted their appearance, so that, when these years are omitted, the record of productivity, as indicated by these research articles, becomes still more impressive.[5]

Classified by subject matter, these sixty articles show a high concentration around three topics. These are occupational mobility, the prestige and status of occupations, and the cultural characteristics of specific occupations. A lesser number deal with the relation of occupation to birth, marriage, and divorce rates; intelligence factors and differentials involved; and the relation between occupational behavior and certain forms of nonoccupational behavior. It is to be noted that there are no studies of the effect of parents' occupations upon family life (other than statistics of birth, marriage, and divorce), and none of their impact upon the development of the children in these families. In an initial effort to contribute to this end, the William T. Carter Foundation proceeded several years ago to conduct a pioneering study of the occupations of parents in relation to the development of their children, and it is to a report of this study that the remainder of this chapter is devoted.

[5] Based on a bibliography compiled by Mrs. Bernece W. Shalloo, of the staff of the William T. Carter Foundation.

THE SCOPE OF THE STUDY

The study is based on information gathered from eighty-one persons, sixty-seven of whom were students in a large urban university and fourteen of whom had entered employment following their sixteenth birthday. In age, they ranged from eighteen to thirty years at the time the information was secured. Fifty-nine of them fell in the eighteen to twenty-four age bracket.

This age grouping of the cases is important, for age is a significant determinant of occupational attitudes as well as occupational choice. A recent study points out that occupational choice, for example, is not an act of simple decision but rather the result of a developmental process—a kind of progressive commitment, with compromise always as an essential aspect of that process. Normally, the authors contend, the young person passes through three stages, beginning with a fantasy stage of occupational interest, then passing to a period of tentative choices, and culminating in a third period of realistic attitudes and choices.[6] The last-named stage covers the years of young adulthood, and it is in this age span that our cases fall. They were at an age of realistic thinking about occupation, and yet not too old to have forgotten their earlier attitudes.

The fact that so many of the persons included in the study were students should also be noted. Undoubtedly it weights the study somewhat toward the intellectual viewpoint. On the other hand, as university students they were trained relatively to grasp explanation of a research project, to verbalize, and to express social facts. Also the continuing relationship between teacher and student made possible certain checks on information obtained.[7]

[6] Eli Ginzberg, Sol W. Ginsburg, Sidney Axelrad, and John L. Herma, *Occupational Choice*. New York: Columbia University Press, 1951, chaps. 7-10.

[7] Bossard and Boll, *Ritual in Family Living*, pp. 209-10.

HOW THE MATERIAL WAS GATHERED

The methods utilized in securing the information for this study included free associational writing on a series of stipulated questions, and informal interviews in a selected number of cases. Seventy-six of the eighty-one cases presented written records; five of them preferred to "talk out" their story. Interviews were conducted with eleven persons who had presented written records, by way of supplementing and clarifying their answers.

The questions covered the occupations to date of the informant's father; of the mother, if employed; the attitude of the informant toward the parent's occupation; an explanation of the ways it affected the informant's development while growing up, with an estimate of their importance; and the adjustments made by the informant to these factors. About half of the case records were obtained without the director of the research being aware of the identity of the particular informant.

THE OCCUPATIONS OF THE PARENTS

The occupations of the fathers of eighty cases (one father died when informant was an infant) are distributed as follows:

Occupation	*Number*	*Per Cent*
Proprietor	16	20.0
Executive	4	5.0
University professor or high school teacher	14	17.5
Other professional	12	15.0
Semiprofessional	6	7.5
Salesman	10	12.5
Clerical	2	2.5
Skilled worker	6	7.5
Semiskilled worker	6	7.5
Farmer	2	2.5
Unemployed	2	2.5

Obviously, the occupational distribution of the fathers is heavily slanted toward the higher occupational strata, as would be expected among the parents of university students. Thus, 57.5 per cent are in the proprietary, executive, and professional classes. On the other hand, more than two-fifths (42.5 per cent) are distributed in the lower occupational strata. Twenty-five of the mothers in the families were also employed; twenty to supplement the family income, and five as the sole or chief support of the family. Fifteen of these were in professional or proprietary positions; of the remaining ten, four were occupied in clerical or sales positions, and six in semi- or unskilled occupations.

ATTITUDES TOWARD PARENTS' OCCUPATION

The attitudes held by the informants toward the occupation of the fathers classified themselves quite readily under five heads. Twenty-five (31.2 per cent) were proud of their fathers' occupation, declaring this in uniquivocal terms, and usually with some enthusiasm. Another fifteen (18.7 per cent) used the word "respect," rather than any reference to pride. Uppermost in their expressions were statements concerning the worthwhileness of what their fathers were doing. A third group, consisting of twelve cases (15 per cent) tended to underscore the idea of acceptance chiefly because their fathers were making a good living (economically) for their families. The word "tolerance" came to one's mind in a number of these cases, as perhaps best indicating the attitude. A fourth group, comprising seventeen cases (21 per cent) definitely had feelings of shame, as they were growing up, of their fathers' occupation; and the remaining eleven, while not using the term "shame," indicated their low regard for the types of work in which their fathers were engaged, labeling them as uninteresting, unimportant, or "unworthy of my father's abilities." In regard to the twenty-five mothers who were employed, twelve of the children were proud, and three expressed themselves as being satisfied with their mothers' work. The remaining ten, while not pronounced in their attitudes, spoke of their dislike of what their mothers did by way of employment.

Just as the attitudes group themselves, so also do the occupations which call forth the various attitudes. The occupations of which the children were proud included the traditional professions (doctor, lawyer, university professor), high-level executives, and the proprietorship of businesses with creative or ego-satisfying aspects. Illustrations of the last-named would be the building of fine homes or the manufacture of some nationally advertised product. In the cases where the attitude of respect was emphasized, the occupations ranged from semiprofessional jobs to the management of socially useful projects, as of a social welfare nature. Occupations which were "accepted" by the children, chiefly because of the income they produced, included proprietorship of businesses of little or no social prestige, and salesmen working wholly or largely on a commission basis. The jobs of the parents of which the children were ashamed were chiefly of two kinds: one, to which the parent went in working (nonwhite-collar) clothes and from which he returned with "dirty" clothes and body; and the other, where there were feelings of shame because of the product handled. For example, a man might develop a highly lucrative business devoted to the cleaning of cesspools, but create serious problems for the social life of his adolescent daughter. There are an amazing number of jobs which involve products or services that everyone needs, yet open connection with those jobs "tars one with the brush." Also, some of the "tar" drops on the members of the family, particularly on the children during the socially competitive years of adolescence. Finally, there were the occupations accorded low regard by the children, but where the idea of shame was not included. These included routine clerical positions, termed "uninteresting," and salesmen, where selling did not permit them to retain their integrity.

WHAT FACTORS ARE EMPHASIZED?

How do people in early adulthood think their parents' occupations affected their development as children and as adolescents? This question was asked of the eighty-one persons included in the study, and emphasized as the major item in the inquiry. The answers given, while showing considerable variation in their concrete expressions, tended to group themselves for the most part under seven main headings. These are stated, together with numbers and percentages, in the following table.

Factor	*Number of Persons Mentioning*	*Per Cent*
Resultant home life, other than economic	64	79.0
Social status	57	70.4
Economic aspects	29	35.8
Guests brought to the home	24	29.6
Traits emphasized in the home	19	23.4
Pressures put on children	18	22.2
Selection of child's occupation	16	19.7
Other factors	28	34.5

From this tabular summary, it is evident that the average number of factors mentioned per person is three, and that the emphasis was largely upon the kind of home life that the parental occupation made possible. The analyses of these factors that follow will clarify more adequately their nature and role.

PARENTAL OCCUPATION, FAMILY LIVING, AND CHILD REARING

Reference has been made to the relative lack of studies of the relationship between occupation and family life. It is an amazing omission in the literature of the family. The present study accentuates this omission. The greatest emphasis in the case material is upon the effect of parents' (chiefly fathers') occupation upon family living and child rearing. It was the factor most often referred to, and the one most stressed for importance.

Only a minority of our informants spoke of the occupational factor as a helpful one for family living, in ways other than economic. "Having a long week end," writes one, "my father could spend much time with us. We took many interesting trips together." "My father's leisurely life and his intellectual pursuits," writes another, "made for a rich intellectual atmosphere. We have many interesting table conversations. . . . My father's library of books connected with his work, including some dealing with 'the facts of life' was the source of learning not only for my sister and me but for a good portion of the neighborhood at our age levels. . . . The presence of clear and good books right in the home is a great advantage." What children seem to like is an occupation which allows the parent the time and nervous energy to be a parent. Most of the parents in this study so situated were university professors. Assuredly this is one of the compensations of this particular profession.

Most of the case records (57 out of the 81) include statements of complaint or plaintive regret because of the ways in which the parents' occupations interfered with family life. "My father was always too busy," was the most common comment. Nineteen of the eighty-one informants voiced this criticism. Typical statements follow.

We rarely had meals with my father, and had little opportunity to share experiences with him. He was always so busy, working even on Sundays. When he came home from work he was usually too tired to pay much attention to us.

My father's work took him away from the house early in the morning. He would be gone all day. When he came home he was extremely tired, and mother would be tired, too. He rarely played with us or amused us with stories. The most he did for us was occasionally on Sundays he would read the funnies to us.

My father was too busy developing his business to pay any attention to us. He tried to substitute for this by buying our affection.

Because mother worked, we children were left alone a great deal. As the oldest child, I had to take charge of my younger brother and sister and do most of the household tasks since I was 12 years old. When my parents were home, they were too tired to pay much attention to us.

My father was so busy when I was younger that I never developed any affection for him. It was not until in my teens, and later when I saw how much he had accomplished, that I began to respect him. Now it is too late because my father died from the strain of too much work. One of the things I have learned from my father's occupation is that a man should never allow an occupation to take him away from getting to know his family.

Another frequently found criticism was that "father was away from home so much of the time." Ten case records specify this.

My father left home for work early in the morning; he came home after seven at night. He was always very tired when he came home. I saw little of my father during those years.

My father's job was time-consuming, and as a result he spent little time with his children. I felt very shy in his presence and ill at ease with him.

Father's business took him away over long periods of time. When I did see him, it was over week ends. He was never around when I needed him. What home life we had was without him for the most part.

Father away from home too long, father always tired, father too busy: the inevitable result was that the child-rearing process was left largely or wholly to the mother. Seventeen of the cases emphasize this fact, and the situations described in other cases must have led to similar arrangements. The comments concerning the mothers' assumption of control over the children are usually brief and direct. They identify the mother as aggressive (nine use this word) or the father as ineffective. In several cases where the father was too busy or too tired, the mother was ineffective, with results that were unfortunate. Illustrative excerpts follow.

> Father was away all day. Mother is an aggressive person.

> Mother is an aggressive person and father is ineffective. Mother just took over.

> Because father was away so much, mother assumed all the duties of guiding the family's development.

> The discipline was left to mother, but she was ineffective, and we were packed off to boarding schools. Both parents failed us, and we have developed without their guidance. I blame the business for all this.

Where the mother is employed, several distinctly different attitudes appear. There are those cases where, because of family circumstances, the employment of the mother was necessary, and the fact was accepted with little or no comment. Second, there are the cases where the child is proud of the mother for the work she is doing, or the child is interested, or sees distinct advantages to what the mother is doing. Third are the cases with complaints—of the mother's absence over long hours, of the mother's fatigue and irritability, of confusion in the household, or of the mother's inability to share the young child's activities. In analyzing the material bearing on the employment of the mother, one comes to see the play of many factors, including the age of the children, the demands of the job, the health and energy of the mother, the character of the child and, perhaps most important of all, the extent to which each person involved sees the situation as a whole.

Finally, young people seem to resent any job or business

that intrudes upon the home. In seven of the cases, considerable emphasis is given to this. There seems to be in these cases a strong feeling about the privacy of one's home, and that no occupation should be allowed to invade it beyond a certain point. Three cases are presented briefly.

My father is a clergyman. We live in a relatively new home, bought by my father's congregation. We have little or no privacy in our home life. Everyone seems to think they can come to see the "pastor's home" any time they want. Some of the church officials walk in without knocking or ringing the doorbell. Our telephone is ringing from morning to night. We can seldom finish a meal without interruption. People come to our house for all kinds of reasons: to get married, to tell their troubles, to ask for advice, or to complain about another member of the church. Sometimes it takes us several days to finish a conversation. One thing I am sure of, and that is that I'll never marry a minister.

My mother keeps a store that is a part of our house. Business interrupts everything, especially our meals. Often my mother must leave the table to wait on the trade. The fact that I disliked most was that we never closed the door from the store to the home: the customers thus were able to invade our privacy at all times. It was not unusual to see customers' children playing in our living room.

My father is a doctor, with his office at home. In addition to his office, there is a large waiting room. But his patients early took over the living room across the hall. From there, they come upstairs to the bathroom. When they are on the second floor, they walk around, opening doors and looking into the rooms. There is not a square inch of privacy on the first two floors of our home. Often, patients have come filing into the living room and the dining room while we are still at dinner. I have even met patients on the third floor when I come out of my room.

PARENTAL OCCUPATION AND SOCIAL STATUS

Human folk are given to making comparisons, and the practice begins early in life. "My father is bigger than your father." "My daddy can lick your daddy." "My father drives a truck, what does *your* father do?" "*My* father is a doctor." Comparisons like these have to do with status: they are, in fact, the essence of status. Status comes early in one's life from what parents do, just as Warner and his associates have shown it determines the status of adults. It is not surprising, therefore, that the status implications of parental occupations come second in frequency and emphasis in the present study. A total of 57 out of the 81 cases (seven out of every ten) touched on this phase of the significance of their parents' occupation, and the reactions grouped themselves under three main headings.

First were those who were conscious of a relatively high or satisfactory (to the informant) status of the parents' occupation. One gets from a perusal of this material a clear sense of feelings of family pride, emotional security, social assurance, smugness, and snobbery of the informants. The tone of these attitudes may be gathered from the following selected excerpts.

I was conscious always of my father's position. I was proud to tell people who he was. I learned early in life, too, that the men in my father's family had all been prominent in the business or professional world.

Father was a well-to-do businessman. He was generally regarded as the wealthiest man in our community. The teacher would refer to this fact sometimes in our school work, and the other children were much impressed. I can still remember this although I was only nine years old when it first happened.

Knowing my father was so well known and realizing that our actions were always noticed, made me feel quite superior to the other people in the neighborhood. The things we did and the trips we took were always noticed. Any new item we purchased was thoroughly discussed in the neighborhood.

From childhood on, I was impressed by the fact that my father had his own business and his own office. The nature of his business, and the contacts he made, were such as to emphasize the high social status of the family. Our family also has a history filled with persons in the professions.

Most frequent among the status reactions were those which revealed feelings of shame, embarrassment, disappointment, or other forms of social inadequacy. It should be noted that these comments were directed, as a rule, not at the difficulties, burdensomeness, or economic compensations of the occupation, but at how it compared with those of other parents. Four brief quotations from the case material will reveal the nature of these attitudes.

When I was in the sixth grade a neighboring woman told me that she considered my father's occupation rather scummy and that she did not want her children to be contaminated by association with me. It dawned on me then that not everybody regarded my father like I did when I was a child, so that I came not to tell what my father did.

I learned about social distinctions early in life and in a peculiar way. Mother hung out her weekly wash to dry, and her next-door neighbor said: "You don't have such hard washes. Your husband wears no starched shirts and they are not so hard to iron as my husband's white starched ones." Then she laughed in a snooty way and added: "Of course, I shouldn't complain. That's the inconvenience of having a husband who is a white-collar worker."

With increasing age and education, I seem to have gotten an increasing awareness of the lack of prestige that was associated with my father's occupation. It came to a point where, if I could avoid it, I never mentioned him. Still later on, while I was in a school of another type, I saw that I was not in the same social strata as my classmates. Like all children, I wanted to be proud of my father, but often I felt inadequate and insecure among my pals because of my father's occupation. At times, I was made to feel very inferior.

I came to feel a sense of shame and embarrassment about my father's job, not because of the lack of money, but because of the lack of status. I recall being very impressed with the status of occupations of other parents and secretly wishing that my father could achieve that status so that I could impress other boys and girls.

Much has been written of the importance of the concept

of the self in the determination of the behavior of the individual. Obviously this applies to boys and girls of the ages included in this study. This concept, it should be emphasized, is largely a family concept, i.e., one derives one's concept of himself and his status from his family, on the basis of its status and role in the community. In other words, one grows up to the realization that he is a Vanderbilt or a Capone, a Lowell or a Kallikak. Robert Taylor, in his delightful study of Winston Churchill, makes it quite clear that one of the keys to that many-faceted public figure is the fact that he conceives of himself as a Marlborough, and apparently identifies himself with the historic duke of that famous line.[7a] Moreover, this identification process is a two-edged sword. The young boy or girl not only conceives of himself or herself in terms of the family status, but also tends to be treated by other persons in such a way as to confirm this concept. You not only conceive of yourself as a Roosevelt, but you also are treated as such.

All this, of course, has a distinct bearing upon the role of the occupational factor. Occupation is one of the major factors in the determination of the status of the family; the child is a member of that family; the child identifies himself, happily or reluctantly, with that status; and other persons accord that status to the child. Because some children resist such identification, or seek to escape it, or drive themselves to rise above it, does not minimize in any way the importance of the central principle involved.

A third group of reactions to the status of parents' occupations emphasized the ambition and drive they created to achieve a status higher than that of the parents. Implicit in these fifteen cases is an awareness of the lack of status of parents' occupations, but the response is defined not in

[7a] Robert L. Taylor, *Winston Churchill: An Informal Study of Greatness.* Garden City: Doubleday and Co., 1952.

terms of humiliation, but rather of a determination to rise above the family level.

Seeing what my father did gave me a great incentive to make something out of myself. My father did the best he could, but I decided I would do better, and rear my family on a higher level. Father's occupation has given me greater incentive to qualify myself for a more secure position. This has been in my mind all through my college career.

My father's occupational experience has made me seek security in jobs for myself. I am now working part time, and I do everything I can to work myself ahead so that I shall never have to go through what my parents went through while I was growing up. As I grew older and realized the wrong phases of our home life, I vowed that my life and my marriage would be different. In fact, fear of an unhappy marriage has made me so cautious that I haven't married at all.

My father's low-paying job has made me want to get above him, to earn a decent income, and to live life the way I want to. I want to have a beautiful, elaborate home, a car, and money to spend for pleasures. His position has made me strive for prestige and to be considered one of Warner's upper classes. I want to reach the uppermost rungs of the social ladder by the usual standards—money and prestige. My observation and experience with the present lack of these things has given me my impetus.

ECONOMIC ASPECTS OF PARENTS' OCCUPATIONS

The purely economic aspects of parents' occupations were mentioned in twenty-nine of the case records. This is somewhat less emphasis than one might expect. It may have been due, in part, to the fact that many of the occupations were of middle- or upper-class status, but even in those below those levels, it was other than economic aspects that were often given primary emphasis.

Ten of the twenty-nine cases emphasized the fact of economic adequacy, pointing out that the father's earnings permitted a good life for the family.

Father's position made family life possible at a satisfactory level. We always went to summer camps, our home was one to be proud of, and my brother and I have gone through college in comfort.

My father's occupation made possible every advantage for us. All of us have gone to private schools, with summer camps and long vacations. We have had the best medical care, and have been surrounded with books, magazines, and various other educational advantages. We have also traveled a good deal.

Twelve persons emphasized economic inadequacy as a result of the parents' occupation. Several of these described situations where income apparently was not sufficient to meet the customary standards of the communities in which they lived. In most of the cases, however, the reference is principally to the fact that the nature of the occupation requires the maintenance of certain appearances, which the income derived from it did not permit. Finally, there were families in which the economic problem grew, not out of the amount, but out of the irregularity, of the income. The following three excerpts identify these respective situations.

Father was unemployed for several years, during which time we received food and clothing from religious and public relief agencies. Later on, father found employment, but it was second-rate work in a mill, he came home dirty, and he did not make enough to meet the needs of our family.

Father was a white-collar worker, in the employ of the city. His occupation made living among upper-class people necessary, but we never had the material means which the other children had.

My father makes about $15,000 a year, but with us it is either feast or famine. Some days I can go out and buy three dresses, other times there isn't even money to go to the movies. As we grew up, we came to understand all this, and have developed a come-what-may attitude. The emphasis has been to make the best of whatever the situation is at present.

A third economic aspect is the emphasis upon money. This appears in fifteen case records, with varying degrees of attention given to it. And there is a striking similarity in these case references. They point out that, because of the parents' occupation, the inadequacy of the income it yielded, or the irregularity of that income or the struggle to maintain appearances, money came to be stressed unduly in the everyday life of the family. The family regime might compel the accounting of every penny, the philosophy of the home made it a foremost topic of conversation, or the need for "front" necessitated the weighing in the balance of every expenditure. Nine "penny pinchers" identified themselves with relative frankness, each, according to self-analysis, the product of a constant emphasis upon money in the family life.

PARENTAL OCCUPATION AND FAMILY GUESTS

The reader may be surprised to find that the fourth most frequently mentioned way in which parents' occupations were thought to affect the development of child members was through the guests who came to the home. Three out of every ten cases mention it. Possibly this factor should have been included under the head of family-life effects, thus still further increasing the relative importance of family consequences. However, the choice has been to give it separate consideration.

Most of the comments about guests coming to the home emphasized the constructive contributions they made. They are identified either as being well known and influential or cultured and intellectual. Typical of these references is the following:

> My father's friends, many of whom are also professors, are similarly of higher than average intelligence. When they visited, the talk was often over my head, but I picked up vocabulary rapidly, and always tried to comprehend. I think the tenor of conversation, and especially the type of humor, one hears between one's parents and guests has much to do with the development of one's tastes.

Not all guests, however, were helpful. One of our more mature informants, whose parents were in a business which required more or less constant promoting, spoke disparagingly of the seemingly endless stream of "manipulators, promoters, self-seekers and parasitic fringe" who passed through the family home. Or there is the son of an innkeeper who spoke of the people who passed through the family portals. Perhaps it is a questionable classification to refer to these as guests, but the identification of their role certainly is unmistakable:

I early learned that alcohol reduces all persons to a common level. I also learned early what a hard person a drunken woman can be. The revulsion of this kind of scene still persists. . . . The real outstanding memory is of the violence that broke out so frequently. I also saw much of unhappiness and unfaithfulness between married persons. Subconsciously, I am still surprised if I happen to meet a happily married couple.

OCCUPATION AND PARENTAL EMPHASIS UPON TRAITS

A good deal of work has been done in recent years on the identification of occupational types. These studies show that persons in the same occupations tend to have in common many personality characteristics or traits. This is due in part to the process which selects persons with certain traits for particular occupations but, beyond this, results from the fact that occupational demands tend to develop certain patterns of behavior. In addition, there are socially stereotyped conceptions of different occupations, and this becomes a factor, too, in the crystallization of occupational types. These common traits exist in spite of the fact that each worker in that particular job is a unique person.[8]

Illustrations of all kinds are readily available. Henry has shown that the successful executive represents a crystallization of many of the attitudes and values generally

[8] William E. Henry, "The Business Executive," *American Journal of Sociology*, January 1949, pp. 286-91.

accepted by middle-class American society. These include a strong drive for achievement, the acceptance of authority, decisiveness, aggressiveness, and a strong orientation to immediate realities.[9] Also, when executives give an order, they expect it to be obeyed. Wray has pictured the foreman as a marginal man, a poor fellow in the middle, "in the sense that a person may be the middle one of three in a bed." The workers consider him a part of management, but management does not. He is in a dilemma, with a good deal of personal conflict.[10] Whyte emphasizes the emotional tensions of the waitress.[11] Cottrell's study of the railroader shows a person with an intense time consciousness in all his social relations, yet a man who cannot predict when he will be at home to spend time with his family.[12] Wilson has given us a picture of what the academic life calls forth in a man.[13]

That the traits emphasized in the parents' occupation are manifest in the home and in the child-rearing process is fully attested in the materials of this study. Roughly one out of every four emphasize the fact.

My father was an executive in a large corporation. The qualities exhibited in his work have made quite an impression upon me and brought about an attempt to make them a part of my own life. These qualities are: reliability, ability to maintain the strictest confidence about business matters, an untiring effort to accomplish tasks, no matter how much extra time they require. The

[9] *Ibid.*

[10] Donald E. Wray, "Marginal Men of Industry: The Foremen," *American Journal of Sociology*, January 1949, pp. 298-301.

[11] William F. Whyte, "The Social Structure of the Restaurant," *American Journal of Sociology*, January 1949, pp. 302-10; see also, in the same issue, an article on "Occupational Career Pattern as a Sociological Instrument," by William H. Form and Delbert C. Miller, pp. 317-29.

[12] W. F. Cottrell, *The Railroader*. Palo Alto: Stanford University Press, 1940.

[13] Logan Wilson, *The Academic Man*. New York: Oxford University Press, 1942. See also, F. R. Donovan, *The Schoolma'am*. New York: F. A. Stokes Co., 1938.

whole emphasis in our home has been upon practicality, thriftiness, self-discipline, and devotion to tasks.

After being ashamed of my father's occupation when I was younger, I was taught the value of being able to do something particularly well. Because my father was so good in his job, he was called upon at odd hours and during vacation to come and help straighten things out.

My father was in the seaside resort business. The weather is very important in this business, and the weather often is uncertain. I early learned to take chances, to gamble on the weather, to work long hours, to think and plan ahead in all kinds of details of the business.

My father's methods of preparation are very methodical and always done in plenty of time. I generally wait until the last minute. He makes sarcastic remarks, which annoy me.

OCCUPATION AND PARENTAL PRESSURES

Akin to the emphasis upon the traits which are characteristic of the parents' occupations is the pressure upon the child to measure up to the level of family expectations and family performance. Approximately one out of five of our cases stressed this fact.

Families where these pressures were most manifest were those in which the parents were engaged in occupations of high status, chiefly professional. The pressures mentioned are chiefly these: to measure up to a high level of scholastic performance in order to get ahead in the world, and to conform to a code of social behavior expected of families of the given status. These pressures are particularly strong in those cases where the parent is highly conscious of his position; where the child is of the male sex and is expected to carry on; or where the family lives in an area, usually for professional reasons, where most of the families are of a lower status. They are also very strong in selected professions, such as the ministry and teaching. On the whole, the more conspicuous the occupation, the more exposed the family is to public view and, possibly, the less secure the family feels, the greater is the pressure upon the children.

DETERMINATION OF SIBLING OCCUPATION

Eighteen of the eighty-one cases stated definitely that their choice of an occupation was determined by their parents' occupation. Since most of the informants were still in college or university, the actual number of cases where the occupation of the child *is* determined by the occupation of the parent may be larger or smaller than the above figure indicates. It will be remembered, too, that forty-five of the cases are women, and, since in the majority of homes it was the father that was employed, our findings must be viewed in that light. The following excerpts will reveal the nature of the parental influences.

My father's occupation as a builder of fine homes has given me my interest in furniture and interior decorating.

I have chosen an occupation which requires the same traits that are necessary in my father's work.

My father's work has prejudiced me against that field but my mother's occupation has interested me so much that I am going to follow in her footsteps.

Anything, any job, so long as it avoids doing the kind of work that my father did. Nor will any child of mine ever follow that line of work.

I am not following in my father's footsteps, but it certainly is true that the people who came to our house as a result of my father's occupation have become the "key" people in determining my selection of an occupation.[14]

MISCELLANEOUS EFFECTS

A third of the case records (twenty-eight out of eighty-one) mentioned consequences of parents' occupations which

[14] For a discussion of the role of "key" people in occupational choice, see Ginzberg, *et al.*, *Occupational Choice*, pp. 36, 38, 52, 64, 92.

did not fall in any of the categories presented thus far, nor did they cluster to any marked extent about central ideas. Space does not permit a detailed presentation of these, despite the fact that they seemed important in the families involved. Selected factors will be presented briefly.

Mobility of residence, due to the nature of the father's employment, was mentioned by several informants. One young man writes: "We have moved fourteen times and have lived in all kinds of places and with all kinds of people." Other cases, while reporting fewer moves, stress change of residence as an important factor.[15]

Several persons referred to the ways in which their parents' occupations contributed to their sex education. Three young women, whose mothers were registered nurses, found this a happy situation because they felt free to talk "the facts of life" over with them. Two found their father's professional library of distinct value. A young man writes that, because of his father's occupation, he was exposed to sex experience at an early age, with effects that were traumatic and created marked difficulties in his sexual development.

Three persons refer to the fact that their fathers' experience in public service made them realize the problems of persons in public life, and the need to be tolerant of them. Four other cases reported a greater understanding of life problems in the areas in which their parents were occupied, and a greater respect or tolerance for people who were dealing with those problems. A number of others spoke in general terms of a greater understanding of life as a result of their parents' occupations.

Seven persons wrote of their parents in a detached and critical vein, emphasizing that their occupations led to the

[15] For a general discussion of the effects of residential mobility upon child development, consult the author's *The Sociology of Child Development*, pp. 386-92.

development of compensatory forms of behavior. In four other cases the references to the parents are laudatory, with signs of compensating defensiveness on the part of the case contributor. Both points of view are represented below.

Because my father was not a success in business, he became pompous and tried to hide the fact, even from himself. He would never admit he was wrong about anything, and he became more and more narrow-minded and bigoted. For this reason, I lost respect for him and his opinions.

In each of his jobs, father tried to let us know that he is one of the most important persons working there. I do believe that he is not just an average office worker, but he is certainly not the V.I.P. he leads people to think he is.

My father has a menial position. But it is just as honorable as anyone else's. My father's work is hard, but he is a very honest person. I think he is just as good a citizen as the parents of other students whose fathers wear white collars and go to work in their own offices, and have their own secretaries. Besides, I guess plenty goes on in those offices that would not bear the light of day.

At least two informants found their school and social relations complicated by the fact that the fathers had business enemies whose children went to the same school they did. In a third case where this relation prevailed between the fathers, the children faced the situation, talked out their mutual problems, and became good friends.

Finally, nine case histories reveal the development of strong resolutions to avoid aspects of the parents' occupational history and to achieve the opposite. One father was lazy: his son was steeled in a determination to be busy and apply himself. One boy and one girl saw that their parents had menial jobs: they were fired with ambition to avoid work of that kind. Three more, aware of family problems which resulted from inadequate income, were fortified in their determination to make a good living for themselves. Another had one ambition: to attain to a job which would give a prestige which his father's occupation was never accorded. Two more, annoyed because their father's jobs made home life impossible, decided that they would never accept any position which presented the same problem. Undoubtedly others had reactions similar to the foregoing: we are recording here definite comments of this kind.

THE RELATIVE IMPORTANCE OF OCCUPATION FACTORS

Each participant in the study was asked to rate, on a five-degree scale, the relative importance of parents' occupation in their development during the years of childhood and adolescence. The accompanying table summarizes the answers that were given.

TABLE IV. THE RELATIVE IMPORTANCE OF PARENTAL OCCUPATION FACTORS

Rating	*Number*	*Per Cent*
Great importance	60	74.1
Important	8	9.9
Medium	10	12.3
Minor	3	3.7
No importance	0	0.0
	81	100.0

The information on this point was not confined to a mere check rating, but the participants were asked to write, or, if the data were obtained orally, state supplementary information, so as to clarify the rating given and to give insight into the "feeling tones" that accompanied the ratings. On the basis of this material, several additional facts may be noted.

First, eighteen of those who stressed the high importance of parents' occupation added that it had not only affected their own development but that it would affect the life of the families they would form and the ways they would rear their children. Most of these were statements emphasizing their plan to avoid in their prospective families conditions which existed in the families in which they had been reared.

Eight of those who gave a medium rating for the occupational factor appeared to be rather self-centered individuals. In each case, they were living in homes where the father's income was indicated as ample for good living, and the nature of the occupation was such as to keep the father away from home a good deal of the time. These were families, in other words, where the father was a sort of silent check-writing agency, with the children living a comfortable life, engrossed in their own development. To them, it seemed that the fathers' occupation was of minor importance. Somewhat similarly, in the cases who rated parents' occupations as of minor importance, each of the three persons were living under substitute home conditions (such as with grandparents), such arrangements being necessitated by the nature of the parents' occupations.

PATTERNS OF ADJUSTMENT TO PARENTAL OCCUPATIONS

The final question asked of all the participants concerned the adjustments they thought they had made to their parents' occupation. This question was explained at some length, attention being called to the interest of the study in finding out what might be called the patterns of adjustment rather than isolated or specific responses. In other words, how did the participants think they reacted habitually to the situations and factors in the parents' occupations?

The answers that were obtained duplicated in part the answers given to question No. 3, i.e., How did your parents' occupation affect your development? This had been foreseen; in fact, the question on patterns of adjustment was intended in part as a check on answer No. 3. But, in addition, the answers did furnish additional information which revealed patterns of adjustment, and this information will next be summarized.

1. Out of the total of eighty-one cases, twenty-two said that no adjustment on their part was necessary. Their replies emphasized the idea of acceptance rather than adjustment. In other words, they felt that they had been born into a good situation, their home lives were happy, and their parents' occupations were satisfactory, either in economic or other ways. The following quotation presents a viewpoint that is representative:

I really cannot say much on this point because I have not been conscious of having to make any adjustments. When you are born into a good situation, you naturally have little adjusting to do. If my father were a coal miner, I would probably have to do a lot of adjusting. Or, if he were a dockhand, for example. Well, thank heavens. The only real adjustment has been that of living up to a high intellectual standard.

2. In twelve additional cases, some degree of father fixation seemed obvious. Here the type attitude was something like this. What father did was fine. He was accepted as a model. Father's role was not to be questioned. In other words, the father's occupation was a good one, and not to be questioned—because it was father's. Not that this attitude was ever expressed in that many words: the meaning, however, was implicit in all that was said.

3. Another twelve cases emphasized patterns of conformity, and without much, if any, additional comment. Such was the situation, they implied, and all that one could do was to adjust to it. Here is a typical comment:

Viewed in retrospect, my adjustments consisted of facing the facts realistically and accepting them. That most things happen for the best, I have always tried to believe, for I have learned that every experience, whether a pleasant one or a disappointment, is a profit to the individual. My parents' occupations have been viewed and accepted as part of everyday living, and adjustments to them have been largely unconscious.

4. Another thirty cases reported patterns of conformity, but apparently accompanied by feelings of resentment. These resentments were chiefly against the father, twenty out of the thirty so indicating. These resentments took a variety of forms. "I thought, until the last year or two, that my father was lazy and incompetent, and I felt that the rest of the family were deprived of things because of it." "As I grew older, I found that my father did not have the energy or interests that I did." "I have grown to dislike any mention of the things that remind me of my father's occupation, although I respect what he is doing." "I had a nervous breakdown, which I attribute to my father's occupation."

5. By far the largest number, fifty-four out of the eighty-one, identified characteristic attitudes, traits, or values which they thought they had developed as a part of the pattern of adjustment. Twelve of them, for example, stressed the formation of realistic attitudes. "My father's occupation helped me to see people and the world as it really is." "I just had to adjust to the things I've mentioned. It was a matter of facing the situation realistically and accepting the fact that no change could be made. . . . The things which seemed so cruel had to be faced and overlooked."

6. Ten of our participants emphasized chiefly the development of independence and self-reliance in their patterns of adjustment. "I developed a very independent, I'll-take-care-of-myself attitude. My parents now seemed two old people, whom I loved, but who lived in a world of their own." "Because my mother's business engrossed all her time, I was early forced to take care of myself and look out for my own interests. I was often lonely and hurt earlier in life, but it is now no longer a problem because I have become hard and self-sufficient." "I am not dependent on my parents because I have learned to do all things for myself."

7. Sixteen of the participants reported themselves as having developed compensatory or consoling values as a part of their pattern of adjustment. Some of these were religious in nature, others involved some form of comforting personal philosophy. "I came gradually to develop a less materialistic view of life." "My adjustment has forced me to develop a stronger faith in God and in myself. I feel that I would be a much different person if my father were a skilled or professional worker." "As a child, I learned to entertain myself in inexpensive ways, i.e., reading, painting, or helping my mother. I am always amazed at the number of expensive toys some parents feel they must provide for their children. I now think there is a need for the real beauties of life aside from the material things. Money is important but it just doesn't fill the entire bill for living."

8. In rather striking contrast to the preceding comment is the fact that eighteen of our informants identified themselves as penny pinchers, and stressed this as a part of the adjustment pattern. Nor did this emphasis on money grow entirely out of the lack of earnings of the parents. In some cases, it was due to the nature of the father's occupation, which emphasized money or involved a constant awareness of it; in others, it was the irregularity of income, with its "famine or feast" fluctuation, which led to an unusual interest in financial problems; and in still others, money came to be valued as the means necessary to secure compensations for deficiencies in life (like lack of social status) resulting from fathers' occupations. Most of these persons wrote with marked frankness and somewhat cynical appraisal of life, indicating an early and strong worship of Mammon.

9. Ten of the fifty-four mentioned other or additional traits as aspects of the adjustment pattern. This included such traits as tolerance of persons in occupations identical or similar to those of their parents; caution; the habit of

reading, as a part of a pattern of seclusion; and strong devotion to the mother to compensate her for the unhappiness and unpleasantness that resulted from the father's occupation. Finally, there was one daughter who just went to bed and stayed there until her father returned home from occasional business trips.

A Suggestion for Adjustment. The analysis of the material on adjustment patterns would not be complete without reference to one particular case history, which suggests an interesting possibility in the adjustment of children to the occupation of their parents. The history was contributed by a person whose father was a machinist. The case record follows in part.

I don't remember much of my pre-school attitudes towards the occupation itself. I do remember that much of the dirt and grease he acquired in his job was still with him on his return home, and that I didn't like. When I started going to school, my attitudes changed as I became acquainted with other children and their families. I found that not all fathers worked for the railroad. Some were doctors, lawyers, or businessmen. They arrived home clean, and seemed to be in a different category from my own father. I finally developed the attitude that their occupation was much more desirable than my own father's. This attitude grew with me until I finally wished that he were engaged in something that seemed more important.

As I grew a little older, I became more curious about my father's occupation. Some of my classmates would brag about their fathers' occupations and of how important they were. When they asked me about mine, I tried to put on a brave front, but I didn't have anything to really brag about. Finally I decided to get to the bottom of this business of occupations. I asked both my father and mother about it. They were very obliging, and I was told all about the shops, the particular work my father did, how he had to apprentice when he first worked there, how he was finally promoted to gangleader, and of the many extra things he had to do in connection with this job. My father even took me on a tour of the shops, and showed me where he worked. He let me look in his desk, showed me his tools, and the blueprints he used, and in general gave me a good tour of the entire shop. Although I was too young to actually understand the workings of this huge repair shop, I still remember the feeling of pride I carried around with me. It wasn't every child that had a chance to go through the shops. It was then I began to see my father's occupation in a different light. I realized that he was just as important in what he was doing, as some of the other people were in their respective occupations. I was able now to brag as much as any of the other children, and I did, too.

My attitude changed even more when I would listen to my father and some of his friends talk. They all respected him, and often referred to his ability as a machinist. The high point came one day when my father was taking his vacation. The doorbell rang, and there stood one of the men from the shop. We had no phone at the time, and he had been sent to ask my father if he would come to the shop and help them work out a problem that had arisen. Well, that was really something to be proud of. To think that my father was so important that they had to send someone to get him to help them out. From there on, I regarded my father's occupation from a new perspective. I admitted that he wasn't receiving the salary that others were, but we had as happy a family and had enough of everything. Maybe he did get a little dirty, but he was well liked, and respected, and I had nothing to be ashamed of.

PROBLEMS FOR FURTHER STUDY

It is both the reward and the challenge of any research study that it suggests more questions than it answers. Obviously, the foregoing analysis is of this kind, serving to frame a number of problems for further study. A few of these will be presented in brief form.

1. How is the age of the parent related to the occupational factor? It is highly probable, for example, that professional men become parents at a later date than do those engaged in unskilled occupations. It is not unlikely that professional men frequently marry women somewhat younger than themselves. If both of these facts are true, then age of father, disparity between ages of parents, and the occupation of the father are associated with each other

in their significance for child development. Can they be disentangled in a future research project? How much of the child's attitude of respect for a professional father, for example, is due to the profession, and how much to his age?

2. A very fruitful field of investigation would be the conduct of studies in the relationship between the traits and values emphasized in specific occupations, family life of persons engaged in those occupations, and the nature of child-rearing in such families. Reference has already been made to the identification of a few occupational types, and the attendant attitudes and values stressed. How do these affect family life and child rearing? The number of studies that could be made here is almost endless, and the insight they could contribute is almost limitless. This is perhaps the most neglected area in the study of family relations and child development.

3. The occupation of the parents determines in large measure the stream of words that flow through a household, and thus is very important in determining the child's linguistic equipment. This has been explored in another study by the author,[16] but not to the extent that the importance of the subject warrants. Moreover, it is not simply the words but the mental imagery that is associated with words which the child acquires, and the connotations that go with words. The word "machine" has a quite different connotation for the son of a machinist than for the child of a corporation lawyer; obviously, so does the word "corporation." Many (some semanticists say all) words are "loaded," that is, their meanings are tinged with emotion. Parental occupations, the minutiae of family conversations, these are important factors in the "word-loading" process.

4. The relationship between the occupational world of the family and the ideological equipment of its members

[16] James H. S. Bossard, "Family Modes of Expression," *American Sociological Review*, April 1945, pp. 226-37.

is another relatively unexplored field. Consider an illustration. John Forman is a mechanic, working in a large plant of a large corporation. He is employee No. 16,482 on the rolls of the corporation. On the basis of his everyday work life, he develops: (a) conception of employer, employee, labor, management, labor organization, and the like; (b) a conception of himself in relation to all of these; (c) a series of values he has developed on the basis of his occupational experience; (d) a number of rationalizations, centering around the successes and failures he has had; and (e) versions of the large economic, political, and social ideologies he has obtained from his associates. But John Forman is also a husband, and the father of two sons. Now it is exactly at this point that research studies in this area usually cease. John Forman as a worker is not tied up with John Forman as husband and father, in spite of the fact that his experiences and mental orientation constitute a large part of the cultural milieu of the Forman household. It would be the essence of an understanding of the child-rearing, i.e., personality formation, process to compare such a family with that where the father is a noted surgeon, an investment broker, or a Supreme Court justice.

SUMMARY

1. A sociology of occupations is in process of formation, although it is still confined largely to the periodical rather than the textbook literature.

2. As a contribution to this literature, this chapter presents the results of a study of eighty-one case records, dealing with the relation between parental occupations and child development.

3. Attitudes of the children toward the occupations of their parents range from obvious pride to deep shame. The professions seem to be most respected by the children; and unskilled, "dirt and grime" jobs, the least.

4. Children seem to be most concerned with the home life and the social status that are associated with their parents' occupations. Economic implications are apparently of lesser importance.

5. The occupational pursuits of the parents are rated as of very great importance by most informants, as a factor in their development during the growing-up process.

6. Patterns of adjustment to parents' occupations cover a wide range, from quiet submission to bitter resentment; and from a complete absence of resultant problems to anguish and trials which may have left permanent trauma.

CHAPTER XII

Domestic Animals

Their Role in Family Life and Child Development

There are times when only a dog will do for a friend.
—DON BLANDING

THE dog population of the United States exceeds twenty million. One in every four big-city families has a dog, and among farm families the proportion is three out of four. Families with children are more prone to have dogs than families with none. Dogs, of course, are not the only domestic animals that serve as family pets, but they are twice as popular as cats, their nearest rival. Other animals thus utilized include a wide variety, ranging from geese to lizards and white mice and hamsters.[1]

Despite their age-old and widespread popularity as household pets, very little serious attention has been given to the role of such animals in family life and child development, and yet the most superficial observer of family life cannot but see what an important role they do play. The present chapter seeks to contribute to this end by presenting (1) the results of an original study of the role of the dog, based on thirty-seven case studies of families who had dogs as household pets, (2) a summary of responses to a published article summarizing this study, and (3) a statement of the need for more serious consideration and research in this area of family life and child development.

[1] Dickson Hartwell and Leon F. Whitney, "Dogs Are Big Business," *Collier's*, December 25, 1948, p. 22.

THE ROLE OF THE DOG AS A FAMILY PET

In order to determine the attitude of family members toward dogs as household pets, and to assess inductively their role in family life, a series of case studies (thirty-seven) was gathered over a period of three years, in which family members were encouraged to state their experiences as dog owners. The material was gathered by the interview method. Observations of these, and an additional eighteen families, were made over a number of years, to supplement the case records. The conclusions of this study, as published in *Mental Hygiene*, a quarterly publication of the National Association for Mental Health, follow.

1. The dog is an outlet for our affection. This is its basic service and the chief reason for its presence in most homes. Repressed persons tend to disguise or to deny this interest, or to explain it on other than affectional grounds. "I'm afraid to be without a dog." "It's lonely without a dog." "He eats the scraps." Again, the manifestations of this interest in the dog vary from an occasional kindly cuff to the most tender solicitude, dependent upon the nature and needs of the person involved. In most families, however, affection for the dog is open and frank, with general agreement that the dog receives more attention and affection than any other member of the family. The therapeutic significance of this seems very obvious and very great, and the growing conventionality and impersonality of contemporary life make it of increasing rather than of decreasing importance.

2. Moreover, the dog serves each of us according to our respective affectional needs. Not being able to speak or to argue, the dog will not say the wrong thing to dampen our ardor or to spoil the rapport of the moment. Little Jane, out of sorts because her friend Mary will not play her way today, finds solace with her Scottie. Jack hates girls,

mother is busy, and father gives him no affection, but his Airedale gives to him just what he needs. Mother is spending a long winter evening alone, while father is entertaining the out-of-town buyer. She overcomes or forgets her doubts because of the friendly collie that lies before her on the living-room rug. Cousin Edna, who is not quite welcome at the relative's home where she is now living, is at least confident of the genuineness of the affection with which the family's energetic Boston pup greets her. Father, returning late at night after a long and discouraging day, is met at the door by a wagging tail and a pair of adoring eyes. Each to his needs, regardless of what they are, no matter how they vary, ready to give, asking nothing even when expecting much, stands the family dog.

Furthermore, there are none of the customary inhibitions to limit or restrain our affectional relations with the dog. Few of us are wholly free of these inhibitions in our relations with humans; often they operate to some extent even with those who are most close. We leave unsaid the word of endearment or unexpressed the physical signs of our feelings because of the inhibiting shadow of some word or aspect in our relationship. None of this is true with our domestic pets, like the dog. We can love them, we can express our affection, and there are no inhibiting handicaps.

3. There is often a deep and abiding quality about the relationship between a human and a dog. One is struck repeatedly with the mellow tribute of the older person to the canine companions of his youth. Such tributes appear constantly in conversation or in autobiographies. Writes a Congressman from Iowa:

> After much begging for it, I was given a silver dollar one Saturday morning with which to buy a black collie puppy that I coveted. With the piece of silver clasped tightly in my hand, I ran all the way to town, fearing some other boy might get what

I wanted. With the puppy clasped tightly in my arms, I hastened back home. I bestowed the name of Prince on the tiny creature. After that we all made so much ado over that little dog that the old dog on the place . . . died of envy and grief—or was it merely old age?

Prince and I grew up together. We became inseparable companions. I might have taken him to bed with me had my mother been less particular about sheets and pillows. I was very fond of Prince and he was fond of me. He would never play with any one else or at least not in the same way he played with me. He would growl and snap his teeth at any one who made so much as a motion of striking me. He must have thought of me as the particular lamb that he had to look after. Every morning I found him waiting for me at the door, and if I did not hasten my steps he would whine and yelp. He always greeted me by jumping almost all over me. One of his favorite tricks was to pick up a stick and dare me to take it away from him. In time I taught him to play many of my games, such as hide-and-seek and ante-over. And he taught me many of his tricks. I am still sure that I learned as much from him as he learned from me. And I am equally certain that if it had not been for Prince, I might have grown up a different kind of boy and even have been a different man.[2]

4. The dog contributes to the development of many a human being the challenge of a continuing responsibility. This matter of a continuing responsibility is one of life's major experiences—sobering, exacting, maturing, character-forming. Not all of us have it. Many persons go through life without it; others find it first when parenthood comes to them. This experience may come early in life, to a growing child, when a pet is consigned to his care. Walking the dog each morning and night, feeding him, finding him when lost, looking after his water supply, protecting him from the neighbor's bullying bigger dog, making his bed; if it is a female, keeping dogs away when she is in season—in these ways, children may profit early in life from a continuing

[2] From *I Remember, I Remember,* by Cyrenus Cole. Proceedings, Iowa State Historical Society, 1936, pp. 20-21.

experience with a personal responsibility. Thus the dog may become a very valuable factor in the training and character formation of a growing boy or girl.

5. The dog is one of the best vehicles for parents to use in training children in toilet habits. Josephine, the pup, must be housebroken. Mother, father, brother, sister, are all engaged in the process. They take Josephine out; they chastise her for her making a puddle; there is constant talk about Josey's toilet habits. Small wonder, then, that little Helen presents no problem in her own habits, for she too joins the family circle in the training of Josephine. Here, again, self-discipline evolves as an accessory before the fact of imposing a discipline upon someone else.

6. Again, the dog is possibly the best available vehicle for parents to use in the sex education of children. First, the external physical differences of sex can be seen, identified, and discussed, without hesitation or inhibition on the part of either parent or child. Then certain habits peculiar to each sex may be discussed, so that sex is a difference not just in physical structure, but also in function and in ways of living. If the dog is a female, the alternation of periods has to be faced, and this becomes the medium through which various problems are discussed, including periodicity in the human female. The female may have been spayed or she may be serviced by a male. The ensuing pregnancy and birth of the pups are a demonstration of that which it is perhaps most difficult to teach the younger child. With a dog, they are demonstrated to the eye as they are told to the ear. Such physical demonstration can be made a corrective of a most effective kind of the misinformation on sex that children pick up at various times and places.

7. The dog is a satisfactory victim of personal needs for ego satisfaction and ego gratification. If things have gone wrong, and you feel like kicking someone, there is Waldo,

waiting for you. If you have been ordered about by the boss all day, you can go home and order the dog about. If mother has made you do what you did not want to, you can now work on the dog. Long observation of children's behavior with domestic animals convinces me that this is a very important function. Often the child has been the victim of commands, "directives," shouts, orders, all day long. How soul-satisfying now to take the dog for a walk and order him about! This is a most effective therapeutic procedure.

8. Akin to what has just been said is the fact that the dog satisfies the very human longing or desire for power. The wish to dominate someone seems most fundamental. Wife, husband, child, each finds in the dog an outlet for such conflicting desires. Sometimes this demand for power finds expression in a persistent habit pattern, and the dog, in satisfying it, thereby saves some other member of the family from being its victim. Sometimes it is a sporadic need, growing out of a background of fluctuating experience. At times, it is the chronic need of a Caspar Milquetoast who finds only in the dog what he fears to seek in any other human. Here, again, the dog may serve a useful role in the mental hygiene of the child, training the child in the art of command, satisfying the ego in the experience of control, and draining off a resentment at being controlled by some parent or other adult.

9. A dog accustoms one to the idea of the normality of physical processes. We humans are apt to become so civilized that we forget that we are human; the conventions of life lead us to refrain from certain physical processes when we are in the company of our fellows; reference to some of them is even taboo in conversation. The net result is that there is apt to arise an unconscious conviction that these things are unusual and unnatural. This is particularly true of city folk, who lead an artificial life in many respects, often without contact with other forms of life. To live with

domestic animals is to see another animal engage in the same processes you do; the effect upon the observer, and particularly the child, is to gain a net impression of the "naturalness of it all."

10. A dog serves as an effective social aid. By the time one has walked a dog a few months, one is sure to have increased markedly the range of one's acquaintances, even in the most impersonal city neighborhood. The genial old man stops to chat; the buxom mistress smiles, first at the dog, and then at you; the neighborhood children make friends with the dog and incidentally notice you. Finally, on the dreariest day, when you were least inclined to take him on his outing, fate obliges by having your favorite blonde happen along, and the dog obliges by making up to her, to the end that another "contact" has been made.

The child, again, is the special gainer from all this. He or she makes many contacts in the neighborhood because of the dog. It is a sure way to meet the new children in the block. And you can do them the first favor by letting them hold the leash. You can make that little girl with a turned-up nose jealous because you have a dog. You learn about Mr. Davis; he is a friendly man and likes dogs. You learn about Mr. Meyers; he barks at you if the dog nears his least favorite shrub. Mrs. Jones feeds a dog, even under war rationing. Mrs. Bird growls at you because she hates "animals of all kinds."

11. A dog often reveals the underlying feelings in the neighborhood, and by bringing them out into the open serves a useful mental-hygiene purpose. Mr. Smith does not like you, and as a result he chases your dog. You think the Goldsteins, coming into the neighborhood, have depreciated your property, and you threaten their hound. Mr. Kline is a splendid man, and you throw his dog a bone. Even as you do it unto a man's dog, so you do it unto him.

This serves often to bring the unconscious likes and dislikes of a neighborhood out into the open. Dogs do not create neighborhood feuds—they reveal them. In so doing, they may serve to heal them.

12. A dog is an effective and continuing object of conversation in the family. Particularly is this true because he stands mute. If relations between husband and wife are strained, the dog becomes the needed excuse for a renewal of conversation. Compliments may be paid to another member of the family through the dog. The dog serves as an excellent butt for jokes; you may poke fun at him with safety; you may show off your best humor on him. You may compose a poem about him. Also, a dog is an excellent excuse for saying certain things for the benefit of the children.

13. Finally, a dog offers companionship. He stays with you when you are alone. He serves as solace when you are lonely. And what excellent company he can be. You can talk to him, you can sing to him. He does not argue concerning the propriety of your remarks or the pertinence of your observations. If you sing, he will not, as a rule, embarrass you with comments on your voice, your enunciation, or the lyrical quality of your performance. A dog is a silent, yet responsive companion, a long-suffering, patient, satisfying, uncritical, seemingly appreciative, constant, faithful companion, more affectionate than you deserve and appreciative far beyond what anyone could expect from a human rival.

To the lonely child and the shy adolescent, to the unhappy wife or the misunderstood husband, to men on far-off military locations or on distant construction jobs, innumerable dogs make their contribution to mental hygiene. And they cannot even say the words. Humans are more verbal.

RESPONSES TO THE FOREGOING STUDY

The responses to the foregoing study were of such a nature that it seemed desirable to summarize them. This was done covering a five-year period from July 1944, when the original article appeared, to July 1949. The results of this summary are presented here as an indication to students of human relations of the importance which a representative segment of the population attached to household pets.

The story begins on Saturday, August 12, 1944, when the *New York Sun* devoted its leading editorial to the original article, praising it as a "piece of factual reporting," and pointing out that "among the great needs in the complexities of modern civilization are those of conquering inhibitions, of blowing off steam without damage, of getting away from larger problems to such simple things as the care and feeding of pets." The caption of the editorial read, *Towser, M.D.*

Next the article fell under the eye of Mr. Arthur E. Patterson. In the *New York Herald Tribune*, of August 14, 1944—writing appreciatively, but with tongue deep in cheek—Mr. Patterson, after following the Brooklyn Dodgers for the greater part of the summer, recommended the article for Brooklyn baseball writers, as well as "to other persons interested in mental problems."

In due course of time, four veterinary journals republished the article as it had appeared in *Mental Hygiene*, and at least one result of these printings proved to be of direct advantage to the author. The incident involved one of my students, an attractive young woman married to a budding veterinarian. Her husband had not taken kindly to her choice of a course in sociology to meet her university requirements, counseling rather courses in chemistry and Latin. There had been several domestic arguments about the sociology course when the husband read the article in his professional journal, and saw in its emphasis upon domestic pets an aid to his professional practice. Shortly afterwards his wife enrolled in a second course in sociology with me—at her husband's earnest suggestion. Obviously academic recognition of various disciplines comes about in devious ways.

Almost simultaneously with the republication of the article in the veterinary journals, permission was granted for its use as a tract by several organizations interested in the prevention of cruelty to animals. Ultimately, more than 125,000 copies were printed for this purpose. This was a utilization that I had not foreseen, but one in which it was a pleasure to coöperate.

Meanwhile, a leading Philadelphia newspaper reproduced the article in its daily columns, accompanied by a photograph of "me and my dog," the photograph alone covering one-eighth of a newspaper page. One incidental feature of this incident warrants comment. The appearance of the photograph was remarked upon by all the neighborhood children who came to our home habitually, and the references were all to the fact that "Josey Bossard [my dog] had her picture in the paper." Such references—and omissions—aid mental hygiene in placing one in one's proper proportions.

Finally, there has been the distribution of reprints. Several hundred of my own were quickly exhausted. From the National Committee for Mental Hygiene comes the following information, as summarized in a letter dated August 4, 1949, from Nina Ridenour, Director of the Committee's Division of Education. She writes:

> Since the article first appeared, we have sold approximately 1,500 copies. The member of our staff who is in charge of the distribution of literature at conferences tells me that she often has had people come up to her table who were looking for that par-

ticular article and ask, "Is this where I can find the pamphlet about a dog?" She says they often buy an additional copy for a friend or if perhaps they are accompanied by friends, the friends will buy several for other friends. In view of the fact that this has not had wide distribution among homogeneous groups as do some of our pamphlets, I think the number of 1,500 is quite a large one to have been purchased by individuals, usually in single copies or quantities of not more than a few. It still seems to have a steady sale and, like you, we find that scarcely a week passes when someone does not write to us concerning it.

These published comments and republications served to bring the article to a relatively extended reading public, and within a comparatively short period of time. Probably they explain in large measure the next phase of the author's experience, as involved in a deluge of personal mail regarding the article. Between August 1, 1944, and August 1, 1949, a total of 1,033 letters relating to this article, or to the general subject of dogs as domestic pets, have been received. The number of these letters is imposing, especially when compared with the experience resulting from other articles I have published. Although I have contributed more than a hundred articles to a variety of journals, many of them dealing with controversial issues and all of them confined to the field of human relations, no other article has brought forth such a flood of letters. The nearest approach was an article on family table talk, which yielded exactly twenty-five letters from readers.

More striking than the number is the variety of the correspondents. These range from a high-ranking official in the executive branch of the federal government and a noted New York banker, on the one hand, to a farm boy in Delaware, who wrote just to say that he, too, loved dogs, and a fourteen-year-old lassie who wrote to ask for help for a pet poodle whose bowels yearned constantly, but not with compassion. One specific group consists of letters from thirty-one medical men, mostly psychiatrists and neurologists. These letters were mostly brief and businesslike, asking if reprints were available and in what number. Eight physicians, serving as faculty members in medical schools, wrote and asked for duplicate reprints. It seems a reasonable assumption that this material was utilized in professional treatment or education.

Taken as a whole, these 1,033 letters seem to have come from a typical cross-section of the American reading public. Selected excerpts will serve to illustrate this fact.

"I have just read your pamphlet on the mental-hygiene of owning a dog, and I loved it. We are a dogey family and have brought up thousands (?) of pups and many other families of all sorts of animals. I wish that I could have written it because it expresses just the ideas that are in my mind. It should be sent to many people that I know." This from a letter by the wife of a prominent clergyman.

"My family," writes a well-known social scientist, "has been talking over your article, *The Mental Hygiene of Owning a Dog*. We have a loveable setter. If only human beings could be as understanding."

"To a psychiatrist," writes a member of that guild, "your article is good mental hygiene, and to dog lovers, it is good sense."

Finally came a letter from an official of a civil rights commission who wrote so scathingly that good taste and the accepted rules of scientific publications forbid the reproduction of the letter. His complaint was that the article was anti-Semitic. The basis for this charge was as follows: In the article, reference was made to the fact that a dog often reveals the underlying feelings in a neighborhood, and that persons treat neighbors' dogs in ways that indicate their attitudes toward the neighbors themselves. One of the specific instances cited from the case studies upon which the article was based was that of a case in which a dog was threatened because he belonged to a Jewish family that had recently moved into the area, and whose presence was resented as a threat to property values. This letter obviously reveals a distinct mental hygiene problem in itself.

Next to the letters were the callers whom the article brought to my door. These visitors were mainly dog lovers. Some of them called to show me their dogs and to tell me of their pedigrees; others sought advice on the breed of dog to buy, as exemplifying the dog traits of which I had written. Several men called to tell me how their wives, grieving over the absence of sons in the armed forces, found comfort in dogs as substitutes. One caller was profuse in his appreciation of the improvement in his wife's disposition after the adoption of a cocker spaniel. Another noted a vast change in his wife's health following the purchase of a Scottie. (Two years later, he called to present his second wife, and a new dog.) Still another had developed a patented equipment for a dog in the home which he attributed to an interest growing out of the article. (I have received no share in the royalties to date.)

Perhaps the most dramatic memory of these callers centers around the best dog fight that I have seen. It came about as follows: An elderly gentleman came to call in the cool of a July evening, to tell that he had read the article and wanted to show me his pedigreed pup. I invited him to sit on the lawn at the rear of the house, and I lifted the canine caller to my lap the better to appraise him. My own dog, a highly possessive female, turned the corner of the house just at the moment when, my examination completed, I was returning the visitor to the ground. What followed in the next few moments was highly hectic, involving two dogs, two middle-aged men, three adolescents, and a friendly neighbor. Peace was established, ultimately, by force of might.

It seems pertinent to include, too, one's experiences with

the article in the teaching of university classes. Contemporary college students, as almost everyone knows, constitute a sophisticated and critical audience. At times I have been tempted to announce to an assemblage of them that I have just returned from the moon and will now summarize the latest football scores from the lunar Ivy League, in the hope that something might pierce the acquired poise of their adolescent maturity. To all this there is one notable exception. Each year, in a course dealing with "Family Relations and Child Development," I summarize the dog study and my experiences with it. This breaks the ice as nothing else can. Beginning by learning of the dog members of the families of my students, I come to learn of the human members. This is particularly true in the case of normal families, and I belong to the school that believes that normal families, and an understanding of them, are also deserving of scientific attention.

The personal element in this rather autobiographical account is entirely incidental. The essential fact is the importance that real people seemingly attach to domestic animals as household pets. The responses to the original publication of the article were so frank, so spontaneous, and from such a large segment of the population, representing such a wide range of social strata, as to leave no doubt that the love of animals by humans is one of the universals in the existence of both.

It would seem proper to add, as a final response, the comment of a member of the editorial staff which published both the original article and the summary of the responses. Speaking of the original article, she wrote:

It has been just about the most successful article we have ever published. I think there is a lesson somewhere in that—I am not quite sure what, but perhaps it is that we have too much of a tendency to present mental hygiene as something unusual and complicated—involving psychiatrists, psychologists, psychiatric social workers and such—while really it is made up of elements as simple and everyday and easily available as the sunshine and fresh air and clean food and water that are the basis of physical hygiene.[3]

To all save the hopelessly esoteric, it should be obvious that household pets are an integral part of many family groups, enriching the range of their activities, broadening the scope of their responsibilities, integrating the relations of their members, and promoting the family hygiene.

THE NEED FOR SERIOUS CONSIDERATION AND RESEARCH

The study presented in this chapter is but a scientific appreciation of the role of domestic animals in family life, which might be utilized to document the need for a more serious consideration of the subject, as well as to indicate problems for more extended research. This double emphasis suggests what we believe to be the next two steps in the adequate development of this area of family and child study. First must come a recognition that household pets do play an important role in this area. In other words, one must take the matter seriously, not as an exhibition of sentimental regard for dumb animals, to be disposed of in pleasing phrases, but as an important phase of life, to be considered with due objective analysis. Second is the setting up of research projects to evaluate how, in what ways, and to what extent this complex of factors operates in the family field. What needs do household pets satisfy? What contributions do they make to family life? To child development? In small families? In sex education? In relations with other boys and girls?

An ounce of imagination may produce pounds of hypotheses in virtually any field of scientific inquiry, and particularly so in this area. Because the field is so new and unexplored, research projects need to be conceived with

[3] Letter to the author from Margaret H. Wagenhals, assistant editor, *Mental Hygiene*, New York, N. Y.

almost daring ingenuity. Some of these might take the form of observed experimentations. Could dogs as pets be of use in the prevention of juvenile delinquency, for example? A case study from our collection suggests the possibility.

Henry, a fourteen-year-old Negro boy, born out of wedlock, was showing signs of developing a delinquent pattern of behavior. His mother, a domestic, is away from home most days, leaving the boy at loose ends except for an infirm grandmother, with defective vision. At this point, the mother's employer presents the boy with a well-bred Belgian police dog, and a stipend to underwrite the cost of his feeding. To this lonely boy, the dog is a godsend. A deep attachment develops between boy and dog. He readily assumes responsibility for his care. Ownership of the dog gives the boy prestige with other boys. His ownership and care open up a new life for the boy. After five and a half years, during which there have been no further signs of delinquent behavior, Henry leaves home to enter the armed forces. At this time, his mother, grandmother, and Henry agree that the coming of the dog was the turning point in his life.

Is this story a fanciful and sentimental tale? Or does it carry the germ of an idea? What is the possible role of dog ownership in a delinquency-prevention program? There may be more to this possibility than meets the eye.

SUMMARY

1. The dog is our most popular household pet. Many other animals also serve in this capacity.

2. The role of domestic animals in family life and child development has been neglected for the most part by serious students, despite their obvious very great importance.

3. A study of thirty-seven families which kept dogs as household pets shows a wide variety of functions which they served. These include: an outlet for affection, the challenge of a continuing responsibility, a vehicle to use in training of children, a satisfaction for the ego, a gratifi-

cation of the desire for power, an education to the normality of physical processes, an effective social aid, and a reliable and faithful companion.

4. The response to the publication of this study has been of such a nature as to reinforce the contention that dogs, and other household pets, are an integral part of family life.

CHAPTER XIII

Process in Social Weaning

A Study of Childhood Visiting

All experience is an arch, to build upon.—HENRY ADAMS

FOUR sets of influences combined to bring about the study of childhood visiting presented in this chapter. One was the frequency with which students in university classes suggested it. In a course dealing with the sociology of child development, in which the role of the guests in the home of the child was emphasized, students were quick to point out that, just as the guest may be of importance, so also is the experience of entering another home in the role of guest. A second factor has been the frequency with which its importance has been referred to in life-history documents. Over and over again, one encounters phrases or sentences like these: "I shall never forget my first visit away from home," or, "I first learned about that when I was a child visiting at my aunt's home," or, "I first saw that on a trip to my grandfather when I was eight." Third, one finds similar references repeatedly in autobiographies. Apparently persons who write the story of their lives deem it important to mention, and actually do recall, experiences gained on childhood visits. Finally, in studying the detailed process of social weaning, it would seem that childhood visiting is the beginning of that process.

The social weaning of children from parents is conceived customarily as occurring between the twelfth and twentieth years, and as characterized by a series of relative crises in the parent-child relationship. This chapter presents an analysis of a series of case studies indicating that this process begins much earlier in life with brief and experimental departures away from home, like the short flights of fledglings away from the nest; and that one of the detailed phases of this process is the child's experience in visiting in other people's homes. Such visits provide a series of experiences which serve as instrumentalities both in the social weaning and in the social learning processes.

Originally, information was gathered from a total of 234 boys and girls, ranging in age from sixteen to twenty-two years, and covering their visiting experiences up to the fifteenth year. Of these 234 cases, 100 records were selected as sufficiently complete to warrant analysis for the purposes of this chapter. Of the total number, sixty-one were girls and thirty-nine were boys; eleven were foreign born and eighty-nine were native born; eighty-six were students at a large urban university and fourteen were students at a suburban senior high school. The methods utilized in the gathering of information consisted of free associational writing, supplemented by personal interviews in twenty-two of the cases.

THOSE WHO DID NOT GO VISITING

It seems feasible to turn first to those who did not go visiting. Sixteen of the hundred cases report little or no visiting away from home as children. This is roughly one out of six. In a few of these cases (five altogether) there were exceptional circumstances, such as illness of a chronic nature, or the recent arrival in this country of the family, or the rejection of a newly arrived child in a neighborhood, which limited social contacts, but in most of the other cases the controlling factor was the attitude of the parent or parents. Many adults have a pathological distrust of human beings and, in their capacity as parents, force this attitude upon their children, or manage their children's social relations on the basis of that distrust. Twelve of the cases, including one of the exceptional circumstance cases referred to above, reveal, in varying degree, the operation of this parental factor. Of these, the following case will serve as an illustration.

My father was completely domineering in our household. And he had very narrow-minded ideas about life and people. There were very few people that he liked, and he believed that a child was greatly influenced by the company he was in. Therefore, since he had one or another reason for disliking most of the people we could possibly visit, I was obliged to spend most of my time at home. Besides, my father criticized everyone and made them look so undesirable that I did not even want to visit them. He criticized most of my friends as "ill-bred," "uncouth," "boy-crazy," and "tramps." "Besides, who knows what homes they come from." As a result, I never entered my friends' homes even in the afternoons, for fear of my father's questions and disapproval afterwards. I grew up as a lonely child, with a complex about my social backwardness that has affected me to this day.

True, several of these parents sought to meet the issue by encouraging persons to come to their homes, but in general, children who did not go visiting to any appreciable extent seemed to show definite resentment against the elders who were responsible for it. It was a known lack in their experience, and usually became a bone of contention between children and parents.

THE EXTENT OF VISITING

The eighty-four who reported visiting away from home as an appreciable part of their remembered experience showed considerable variation in the number and diversity of their visits. Some of them left home the first ten or fifteen years of their lives only on scattered occasions, such as a visit to grandmother in summer time or to Aunt Mary over the Christmas holidays. Others visited extensively, several times a week as a rule, and from an early age, abroad and in this country, in various states, and in the homes of differing social status. Obviously children reach adolescence with marked differences in the amount of social experience they have had, and most of them show, either in resentment or feelings of satisfaction, their awareness of it. This contrast, both in frequency and in attitudes involved, may be gathered from the following two excerpts.

When I went to friends' homes for lunch, [writes one] I felt, and naturally, I think, a bit strange, for everyone has their own way of conducting a meal, what they have for lunch, how they cook and serve it. Besides, one was not in the sanctity of one's own home, but had to be on strict behavior in regard to table manners. This was unnatural to me, and, of course, had its psychological effect on the meal. However, as I grew older, I took visits, eating and meeting other people, more in stride.

The hesitance and lack of social experience herein implied is in striking contrast to the easy confidence reflected in the next statement.

Because of the fact that I had been used to visiting relatives and had spent practically every week-end from the time I was two until I was ten with my grandparents, it is understandable that, when at the age of nine, I began to spend days, evenings, and even nights with friends, it had become quite a habit for me to stay away from home at least one or two nights a week, and, also, it had become a habit for us to have guests in our home practically every week.

THE BASIC PROBLEM OF VISITING

Visiting away from home, whether frequent and happy or the reverse, involved for most of the eighty-four cases a major social experience. Often it seems to have been a social hurdle; at times, a social ordeal. Many facets of experience were involved: the attitude of elders to the visitor, of other children at the place visited, of parents with varying doses of preparatory or post-visit disciplining, of foods encountered, of other family disciplines, of physical distance away from home. Taken as a whole, these experiences constituted a definite phase of growing up; a part of the process of social weaning; an adjustment, now conscious and now unconscious, to other people and other places than those found at home. The basic problem involved in such experience seems to be: how to be happy though not at home. This is one of life's major problems, and success and failure in it, an index of maturity.

THE PATTERN OF CHILDHOOD VISITING

To the young person who tells the story of his childhood visiting, his own case appears highly individual and unique. Most of our informants made it a point to say so. But eighty-four of these supposedly unique and different cases fall into a very definite pattern whose successive stages follow each other with an almost compelling sequence; often with the precision almost of a time table.

Visiting away from home began early in a majority of our cases, meaning as early as memory can push back the limits of recall. Most of these early visits were to the homes of relatives, many of whom were already known through visits to the home of the child. The extent and frequency of these visits to relatives would indicate that kinship ties are neither as vague nor as casual as much of the current writing on the family seems to assume. Not only did sixty-seven out of the eighty-four (roughly four out of five) visit largely with relatives, but such visiting was in most cases both regular and frequent.

It is true that relatives today, except in the cases of more recently arrived foreign-born families who tend to huddle together in settlements of their own group, are more scattered geographically than was true a century ago. But it is also true that modern facilities of communication and transportation have more than kept pace with this fact, as has also the increase in family incomes. The result of all this is that kinship groups, while scattered over a wide area, living often hundreds of miles apart, may visit each other with frequent regularity. A family with an automobile is as near, in terms of convenience and time, to kinfolk living sixty miles away today as to those six miles away two generations ago.

These early visits of children resemble nothing quite as much as fledglings hopping away from the nest on short flights to neighboring friendly spots. One gets the impression, too, that visits which were made with parents, and those made without them, had quite different effects upon children at an early age. The security which came from having parents with you during these first experiences away from home seemed to be the bridge that helped to a happy adjustment. Even visits which included brothers and sisters did not work out as well as when parents were there too.

THE ROLE OF THE GRANDPARENTS

It has been pointed out that in sixty-seven out of the eighty-four cases visiting in the earlier years was mostly in the homes of relatives. Of these sixty-seven, the relatives most frequently mentioned below the junior high school level were the grandparents, fifty-four thus reporting. Moreover, a majority of the children reported that they enjoyed these visits to their grandparents (thirty-eight out of the fifty-four), and the reasons given are both frank and revealing. "I was always the center of attraction," says one. "At home I had to compete with adults and other children, but there I had the stage to myself," writes another. This feeding of the ego is mentioned repeatedly. "I was the only guest and got all the attention," says a third. "I was always treated with great consideration," speaks another. "I enjoyed the freedom from my mother's scolding." "I was the oldest grandson and my visits to my grandparents were the happiest days of my childhood," were other typical comments. But grandparents did more than satisfy the budding ego of their grandchildren. Grandma served as arbitrator in the children's games and disputes; grandfather said family prayers, and his sincerity was impressive; grandparents had large homes, with servants; "their house was warmer than our own." Finally, running through a great deal of the comment is the fact that their grandchildren got from them a sense of the continuity of the family, of life, of many things.

But not all visits to grandparents were pleasant, and some of the comments contrariwise were brutally frank. "My grandparents were out of sympathy with young people." "They seemed to resent our intrusion." "They were always irritable." "Their house smelled." "My grandfather spanked me so hard that my shoes flew on the backseat of the car." "Grandmother always gave me wet kisses." This latter complaint came from several grandchildren.

VISITS TO OTHER RELATIVES

Next to grandparents, in order of frequency, were visits to uncles and aunts. These often were visits engineered by the parents, especially if made in the earlier years, involving travel to some distant place, sleeping away from home for the first time, or staying away from home for a relatively long period of time. One reads between the lines in these accounts, seeing the experimental design of the parents, the trying out of the child with the parents standing poised in the wings, ready to come to the rescue in case of emotional need. The nature of the experiences on these visits to uncles and aunts varied. When the aunts were young and "nice-looking," the results often were quite happy, with trips to interesting places, "sleeping three in a bed," dressing up in "older people's clothes," all against the background of "freedom from mother's scolding." But there is a reverse side emphasized in some of the cases, replete with references to competing cousins with the inevitable petty quarrels and jealousies; homesickness, and the necessity of being taken home the next morning; and foods not prepared in the customary manner.

In addition to the grandparents, uncles, and aunts, seventeen out of the eighty-four reported visiting with nonrelatives. These included courtesy uncles and aunts, i.e., intimate friends of the parents who were accorded these kinship titles as a matter of courtesy; couples who "had no children of their own"; and schoolmates of the children. The practice of visiting overnight at the homes of schoolmates was one that began customarily in this group of cases at the junior high school level.

DISSENSION AMONG RELATIVES

Visiting with relatives, however, was not always a matter of sweetness and light. Dissension among relatives was mentioned or implied as frequently as any other fact about such visits. Going back to the material on visits to grandparents, we find that of the fifty-four children who did so habitually, only five visited grandparents on both sides of the house. Of the other forty-nine cases, twenty-five visited only on the paternal and twenty-four only on the maternal side. Moreover, almost all the children were aware of these discriminations from an early age. Nor did dissensions show themselves only in the choice of grandparents to visit. There seems to have been a great deal of bickering in connection with these visits. "I hated these visits," writes one young man. "There was always a lot of criticism of my parents. Mother dislikes all of father's people and father hates all of mother's people." This statement, with but slight changes, was repeated over and over again by our informants.

One of the cases reveals such dissension, but serves also to indicate what some subsequent results may be.

Why did I not visit my mother's relatives more often? This was because my father's family always told me that they were no good and never gave me anything. At that time I did not know why they told me things like that, because when I visited my mother's family they never told me that my father did anything wrong or that my father's family was no good. They (my mother's family) were kind to me, and today I dread the fact that I did not visit them more often, as my mother did by herself. While I was there I behaved very well, I would sit down in a chair and not move or talk unless spoken to. I ate very little. This was not so at my father's parents' home because there it seemed more like home. This has affected me in such a way that when I now visit my mother's mother's grave, tears roll down my cheeks. Not because I loved her or miss her, but because I did not give her the attention and love that a grandchild should. I have come to ignore my father's family, and sometimes now I even hate them.

ADULTS THROUGH THE EYES OF CHILD VISITORS

Adults who entertain children are apt to think of such occasions as times when the children are on exhibition for their elders to observe and assess them and their behavior. The reverse is equally true: the adults are just as much on trial before their child guests. The comments of child visitors about adults whom they visit might well be required reading for all elders who entertain children, from grandma down to mother's most casual acquaintance. These comments are definite and appear in a majority of the case records. They fall into three categories.

First are references to the oversolicitousness of their hosts, to their attempts to assume the role of parent substitutes. Obvious in these complaints, either by direct reference or by implication, is the fact that much of the interest and pleasure of visits of all but the youngest children is the prospect of slipping away from the routine of parental supervision. To the children included in this study, a visit to another house is an experiment in freedom, an escape from parental control. The following excerpt tells in restrained manner what many others say with more brutal frankness: "Once, when I was about ten, we went to visit a very good friend of my mother's. She had no children of her own and wanted company. She did her best to entertain us and we would have had a good time, if only she had not been so careful of us." Not only did the children resent being disciplined by some one other than their parents, but they expressed dislike of anything resembling oversolicitousness or of the nature of parent-like supervision.

A second series of complaints refer to the adults who parade their own problems. Children not only are not interested but they seem to be annoyed, frightened, or even disgusted, when adults do so. Clearly, too, they do not like adults to show deep emotion. Perhaps this is part of the child's resistance to the idea that adults (including parents) have any life of their own apart from serving the needs of the children. Rosamond Lehmann, in her novel *The Ballad and the Source,* speaks of this. "When we are children," she writes, "we do not see the people close to us as themselves—only as our need for them, our habit of them. When something happens to make us realize that they have an enormous life going on apart from us, we feel rather resentful."[1] Certainly the material in this study bears out her observation.

Third are the references to adults who are queer, who tend to act in a foolish or silly manner. There are several comments, for example, about adults who did not "act their age." Then there was the hostess who always carried on a conversation with an imaginary male companion; another whistled like a bird; another kept a bird which was served

[1] Rosamond Lehmann, *The Ballad and the Source.* New York: Reynal and Hitchcock, 1945, p. 100.

food at a separate table by a maid. Also, there were the two maiden ladies who always told stories, "each telling a different story and constantly interrupting each other and correcting what the other one was saying. We were mystified how, when each one was so busy talking, they could hear what the other was saying." Or the one about the father "who tried to be amusing. His wife tried to laugh, and I felt that I should do so, too. But I felt very silly and foolish. I was ten years old then." Finally, there is the one about the young girl who visited at a home and thought the man was very queer because "he helped with the dishes."

CONTRIBUTIONS TO CHILD DEVELOPMENT

The chief conclusions of this study, however, concern the significance of childhood visiting as a part of the growing-up process, as a phase of the child's education and adjustment to the larger world outside of the family. What does visiting when young mean to boys and girls? The answers which appear quite clearly in their spoken and written words, as recorded by us, will be summarized briefly. Before turning to this summary, two conclusions, not so much inhering in the lines as appearing between them, should be noted.

First, one senses in these records the feeling of achievement that comes from the conquest of distance. This seems to have been a vivid experience and a distinct achievement in the lives of many children. A noticeable fact about the case material is the constancy with which reference is made to the distances traversed on the early-in-life visits, the state lines crossed, changes from one traveling conveyance to another, long trips taken alone, etc. Such accounts invariably begin with words like these: "The one visit that stands out in my mind," "My outstanding visit as a child," "The visit that I remember most clearly," "When I was nine, we really went visiting." The idea of distance is one of the first which the child must assimilate and, as he grows, must gain control of.

A second underlying impression is the fact that for most of the children these early visits away from home were experiments in freedom: experimental flights from the home nest. True, the sweetness of freedom might sour quickly, as witness this case.

I remember my sister and my first visit away from home, without mother and daddy. I was nine years old then. We were to visit these friends of ours at the seashore. We had been planning the visit and looking forward to it for weeks. Then when the first night came, we burst into tantrums of crying for absolutely no reason. We would stop for about ten minutes and then begin all over again. Our hostess kept telling us about all the lovely things she had planned for us, but that didn't seem to make a bit of difference. The next day we had to be taken home.

The freedom craved was always temporary, and temporary might mean anything from half a day to a week or two. It was short when visiting with older people, and longer when visiting with children their own age; it was longer when parents were with them; but sooner or later, the glamour would wear off as hosts began to act like parents, and the children wanted to go home to real, not substitute, parents.

But it is what the children learned, the new ideas and persons they encountered, the new experiences they had, which constitute the heart of the process involved in childhood visiting. Visiting meant contact with life, and because life is so varied and complex, the lessons learned covered a wide range. One boy visited a schoolmate and had his first glimpse of gracious living; another was amazed to discover on a visit that there were people who had no indoor bathroom facilities; one girl sat by the hour listening to older people talk, and thus learned of life's problems; another discovered the ease with which old dietary laws could be broken: "I was abashed to learn that sin was so easy," she wrote.

Perhaps the most important phase of this learning process, as viewed by our informants, was the insight into life which they gained. More than half of them emphasized this —how they learned about other people's frailties, oddities, prejudices, pretenses, and social ambitions; how "people acted bored until their favorite topics were mentioned"; "the ways that other people had of rearing their children." Not everything that was learned was unpleasant; there were broadening contacts which taught of other countries, peoples, customs, and codes of behavior. Evaluated in terms of the learning process, these insights gained on visits away from home were of two kinds. First, there were those that were disillusionizing: experiences where you learned that people, relatives, playmates, were not as you thought they were. The other kind were more constructive in nature. Here the visitor assimilated something to be used later on— ways of dealing with people, of handling difficult situations, of entertaining, the importance of class distinctions, or, what was equally important, how not to do certain things.

One feature about these experiences seems to have been what they did to the ego of the visitors. Adults are prone to forget how self-centered the child is, and how vital the expansion and satisfaction of the ego are in the earlier years. One of the most frequently mentioned types of comment in the records relates to experiences of this kind. "I was the only guest and was the center of attention." "These visits to ——— (a couple with no children of their own) meant everything to me. They made so much of me." "I was praised because I ate everything on my plate." "I enjoyed my visits to my aunt. She was old and depended on me, and this responsibility meant a great deal to me."

But an almost equal number of personal experiences were embarrassing, resulting in feelings of humiliation and shame. A goodly third of the cases emphasized this, and it is important to consider them. The psychology of shame remains largely an unexplored area, yet its role in human development must be enormous. "I wet my panties the first time I visited there," writes one. "I fell out of bed when I slept at their house," says another. " 'Oh, you are just a bunch of spongers,' I heard her say to mother." "I spilled soup on their clean tablecloths." "The children where we visited would not play with me." "I was called a poor orphan." Reading and hearing young people recall experiences of this kind, after a lapse of five or ten years, leads one to speculate on how deeply they had seared into the consciousness and how much they may have festered through the years.

Readers who are parents will be interested to note that the majority of the persons included in the study had experiences, still fresh in their memories, which led them to appreciate their own homes and parents more than they did before they went visiting. We humans early learn to make comparisons, and when young children go visiting they see how "the other half" lives, metaphorically speaking; and most of them like their own way best. "We had a nicer life at home." "In our family we have better manners." "My parents were more intelligent in dealing with their children." Particularly interesting is the feature of home life which is emphasized most, and that is food and mother's cooking. Diet is so stressed in present-day pediatric care that a strong emotional complex about food and meals is an inevitable result in the succeeding years. Our own material shows this very clearly. One young woman, writing of a visit when she was nine, speaks for most of them. "We had a miserable week and I got quite homesick. By the end of the week, I was never so glad to get home to my mother and her cooking and her love."

Not all comparisons were favorable to the home base. By no means. The following quotations from the case material speak for themselves. "I noticed that other parents had more time for their children than mine." "Life in that family was completely different from my own. The parents there were not so oversolicitous. The parents and children were like friends and pals. The girls took their mother into their confidence." "I was impressed with the freedom that was allowed us in that home, in contrast with my mother's constant scolding." "I could see that these parents paid much more attention to the intellectual development of their children, and, by comparison, I was much embarrassed." All of these particular comments refer to visits made before the age of twelve, and it is noteworthy what it was that these children saw, and remembered.

One final phase of childhood visiting calls for frank and separate treatment. This has to do with the child's sex education. Perhaps the best thing to do here is to let the record speak for itself. Twenty out of the eighty-four cases reported experiences that were classified under this heading, and the following references will indicate their nature and variety. "The visit that I shall never forget," writes one, "was to a woman who I found out later was the mistress of a prominent man in town. She had an elegant home on a quiet street, with a great many luxuries. She was sophisticated, and what meant so much to a child of eight, she had two beautiful dogs. It was here that I first broke the Jewish dietary laws. It was so beguiling to think that the meat was not ham." One young girl tells how she went visiting and saw a small boy undressed for the first time. "The sight did not disturb me, but the overall impression surprised me," she writes. Another tells of visiting a relative and learning that she was not married to the man she was living with, "and all the while was married to another man. I was told not to speak of it, yet nothing was explained to me. I remember that for a long time this mystified me very much." Four of the girls included in the study reported sexual advances by older boys or adult males in the homes visited, and in at least two of the cases, sex relationships occurred or were attempted. In both instances, such experience took place between the twelfth and thirteenth birthdays of the girls, and were followed by much secret worry and unhappiness. Four of the boys spoke of learning to masturbate on visits overnight to friends' homes. Finally, one boy reports seeing his host and hostess copulate while on a visit to their home. These experiences involving sex occurred in all cases before the thirteenth birthday, in some cases at ages eight and nine, and one gathers that in all cases there were difficulties in assimilating them.

In conclusion, one comes from an analysis of these case records with a conviction that this is the kind of concrete material that constitutes the substance of such terms as child development, formation of personality, cultural conditioning, social learning, and the like. The processes of growing up, becoming a person, being weaned from the parents, consist of a continuing accumulation of the minutiae of experience in living. Visiting away from home involves some of the child's first social steps.

SUMMARY

An analysis of a hundred case records of childhood visiting warrants ten conclusions.

1. Approximately one out of six do little or no visiting during childhood.

2. The chief reason for this is the parents', usually the father's, pathological distrust of people.

3. The extent of visiting by the other five out of every

six varies a good deal in frequency and in attitudes involved.

4. In most cases, childhood visiting ranks as a major social experience. Such experiences obviously are a definite phase of growing up.

5. Visits away from home generally follow a definite pattern: first, to near relatives, then to more distant kin, then to friends of the family, and, finally, to friends of your own.

6. Visits to grandparents are the most frequent. Some of these are pleasant, others are not.

7. Dissension among relatives was mentioned as frequently as any other fact about childhood visits.

8. Children evaluate adults whom they visit just as much as the adults observe and judge the children.

9. Among the specific contributions of childhood visiting to child development are: the conquest of distance, experiments with freedom from parental control, new insights into life, disillusionment with people, and a comparative evaluation of one's own home.

10. One particular phase of such visits involved early sex experiences of one kind or another. Apparently these loomed large in the memory of about one-fourth of the children who went visiting.

CHAPTER XIV

Rites of Passage

A Contemporary Study*

Youth is wholly experimental.—ROBERT LOUIS STEVENSON

THE social development of the individual involves, in all societies, a series of well-defined stages, each of which is characterized by its own pattern of obligations, privileges, and types of relationships with his fellows. Passage from one stage to another involves corresponding changes in the individual's habitual interaction system. To facilitate such passages and to restore equilibrium after the more critical ones, various peoples develop group techniques which take the form of commemorative ceremonial rites. Such rites are commonly designated as *Rites of Passage*, a term first introduced by Van Gennep.[1] He states that these rites have a common purpose, whether they be ceremonies surrounding birth, social puberty, engagement, marriage, or death. They are vehicles to "allow the individual to pass from one fixed situation to another equally fixed."[2] And, he continues, since they have a common purpose, they also have common techniques and stages, though their details vary considerably. The stages into which all rites of passage are divided are three: rites of separation (from the old

* Author's Note—In the research project reported in this chapter, I have had the assistance of Dr. Eleanor S. Boll. She should be noted as co-author of this chapter. An earlier draft of the chapter was read by Professor W. Lloyd Warner, of the University of Chicago, and suggestions made by him have been incorporated in its final form.

[1] Arnold Van Gennep, *Les rites de passage.* Paris, 1909.

[2] *Ibid.*, p. 14.

situation); rites of transition; and rites of assimilation (into the new situation).

As an addition to other studies, made in more primitive cultures, and conceived as operating on a general social basis, this chapter presents the study of a rite of passage in contemporary America, and one limited to the upper part of the class structure. It is a study of the formal début, marking the introduction of young girls into society. Many of the details attendant to this rite vary from one region to another in the United States. For this reason, it should be stated that what is herein presented is for the most part representative of introduction into Philadelphia society.[3]

THE FORMAL DÉBUT AS A RITE OF PASSAGE

The début is a ceremony observed among certain elements of the upper classes for the purpose of introducing young girls into society. This is a formal sign that a girl has ceased to be considered as a child whose prime duties are to "play" with her playmates, to be obedient to her parents, and to attend school. She is now to be considered as a young adult who will take her place in adult society, begin to assume responsibility for her own behavior and decisions, and be ready for a career, for college, or for marriage. This rite occurs, logically, when the average American girl is at the age of ripening physical and intellectual maturity; when she has passed the age set by law for her compulsory attendance at school, and when she is close upon the legal age of consent for marriage and employment. Thus the début comes at a time when she is physically and socially fitted, and legally permitted, to pass

[3] The authors are indebted to Mrs. Edward J. MacMullan, Director of Débutante Parties and Weddings, and Mrs. Richard C. Hughes, Wedding Consultant, both of Philadelphia, for specific material on débutante ritual. They are not responsible for interpretations and evaluations of the ritual found in this chapter.

from a childhood situation into one of adulthood. At least two important meanings attach to her introduction. (a) The girl is now ready for her specific place in society and is recognized as a *functioning* member of an adult group. She may marry, pursue a career or higher education, but she functions socially at the adult level. (b) Her group is a restricted and exclusive one. To gain admittance means that she fulfills certain necessary requirements of membership. The début is a public announcement of this accomplishment. With the recognition, she acquires all the privileges and responsibilities that are entailed in membership. Actually, parents "introduce" a daughter to their own contemporaries in their set. They "present" the product of their careful rearing to their approved friends with the unspoken sentiment: "This is my daughter, now prepared to enter into, and take her part in, our own social set. She is up for your inspection, and may she be acceptable."

RECENT CHANGES IN THE RITUAL OF THE DÉBUT

During the twentieth century, two significant changes have taken place in the ritual of the début, and these run parallel to two changes in modern American life: (a) a liberalized attitude toward young girls, their rights and their activities; and (b) a modifying of upper social class barriers.

(a) First, at the turn of the twentieth century, the début quite precisely delimited two life situations. Before her introduction, a girl of the upper classes was not permitted to attend public social functions alone with a young man or to mingle socially, in terms of equality, with young married couples or with her parents' contemporaries. Her introduction marked the time at which she had completed her education, left her socially restricted little girlhood, was permitted to join adult public social groups, and was eligible to be escorted and courted. Marriage to a socially approved young man was a definite end at a time when marriage was almost exclusively the only career open to girls of their class and when very few of them pursued higher education. A woman who made her début thirty years ago described her situation at that time. Before her début, she says, she never had had a "date." She never had gone out on the street unless escorted by her elders, or in the company of a maidservant. Her introduction was a definite and exciting crisis which, overnight, brought a drastic change in her relationships with her whole social group and immediately gave her new privileges, responsibilities, and a new status. At this time, separation from a subordinate childhood situation was abrupt; transition was a period of intensified and concentrated social participation during the whole of the "season"; and assimilation into the adult group was rather complete upon the assumption of marriage or other adult social responsibilities.

For the present generation of American débutantes there is no such sudden change. The life of a pre-débutante has altered greatly since 1900. Most of these girls today have been escorted and mildly courted from very early teen age and have been welcomed at many public social functions. Many of them have learned the techniques and manners of adult social life by a limited participation in them for years before they become recognized members of it. This means that the preparation for the début has become less a conscious program of indoctrination in the techniques of social life at a certain class level, and more a matter of imitating and assimilating them, in the process of being habitually exposed to them. The period of separation from childhood in the modern début is less abrupt; the transition period less formal and critical for the individual; the assimilation more gradual.

A result is that the conscious dominating role of the parent generation during the débutante season has diminished. One aspect of this is that the season has become less of a period during which the girl is looked upon by the parent generation to see how she has "learned her lessons" and where she will fit into the restricted social circle, since the social aptitudes of the modern girl are already relatively visible before she becomes a débutante. Another aspect is that these "experienced" young girls are considered more capable of making their own rules and arrangements, their own decisions as to their choices of friends, mates, and careers. The season thus becomes a peroid of time during which the members of the younger set are permitted to put their aptitudes to use freely and intensively with each other, with relatively little interference from the older group, although always according to procedures established by them and under their formal supervision. To quote a woman whose lifetime career has been closely related to débutantes and their activities, this is the general purpose of the début in terms of the generation that has preserved it: "This period of life is the time at which young girls and boys are naturally going to intensify their social relations. The rite of the début with its subsequent season is a constructed framework within which they may do so under favorable, prescribed conditions. Since youth must have its fling, it is appropriate to offer them a certain setup, so that they may get it out of their systems in a right way." The "right way,"of course, is what determines the forms and rules of the ritual, which have been established according to the ideals and values of the group and passed down from generation to generation, varying from time to time to make for more specific appropriateness. This presenting of a framework, within which the initiates are permitted to make their own way together, is a far cry from the primitive puberty rituals described by Van Gennep, which were presided over by the elders who, by the process of indoctrination and ordeal, determined the future usefulness of the youths to the adult group. It is considerably changed in detail, also, from the débutante ritual of several generations ago, at which time children were still dominated by the presiding elders of their society. But it holds to the original purpose of a rite of passage: to present a socially approved vehicle for transporting the individual from one marked situation to another.

(b) A second change in the introduction into society that has come about recently is its extension to include members of social divisions formerly excluded. Even after the First World War, the débutante list was almost completely composed of girls from "Assembly" families.[4] In terms of American class structure, this means families of the upper-upper class, or "old families." But before that time, many families in America began to adopt habits of living approximating those of the Assembly members. The inital stimulus was the acquisition of enough income to live in a certain way, to frequent certain places, to send their children to private schools, and to train them for the more socially approved professions. The accumulating of wealth in itself was no entrée into débutante circles. But what the wealth could buy, in terms of a way of living, modified the class barriers as one generation followed another. Children of the

[4] An article from the *Evening Bulletin*, Philadelphia, December 27, 1946, describes the social tone of the Assembly: "A singular survival of the traditions dating back to Colonial aristocracy is the Assembly Ball. . . . The ball room will form the setting for the gathering, which represents the inner ranks of Quaker City society, in the full sense of the word.

"Much water has flowed down the Delaware since the Assembly started, with a small selected company of Colonial belles and their escorts at a meeting held on New Year's Night in 1748, in what was known then as 'Hamilton's Wharf,' a modest warehouse located on the banks of the river.

"Many of the original rules are still observed, with the managements of the ball still in the hands of six men, each of whom serves three years and then selects his successor. . . .

"The flavor of the Ball remains unchanged, in that eligibility for the most part is a matter of heritage, so this evening will see a distinguished company of descendants of the founders meeting on an occasion that has become an institution in Penn's City."

early twentieth century who, because of their parents' increased income, gained private schooling, professional training, a cultivated and leisurely atmosphere in the home, and possibly a sizable inheritance, now have grown children of their own who have been accustomed all their lives to this atmosphere. Thus, about ten years ago, in Philadelphia, the débutante list began to grow markedly, increased by the names of girls who were not from Assembly families nor from a long line of débutantes, but from "new families" of the lower-upper class-girls whose mothers were not themselves débutantes, but whose daughters had grown up with classmates whose destiny it was to "come out." It seems obvious that this change in the personnel of the season should be another factor in the lessened role of adults in the ritual. These new-family girls have increasingly participated in the débutante ritual along with their childhood classmates, until in the year 1947 the débutante list had reached a size unparalleled in the city's social history.

The mere fact of large numbers may create more changes in the ritual. For example, it seems to be causing the establishment of groups within groups; the normal process of group life being that, once it passes a certain number intensity, the group subdivides. There is a hint, at the present time, that this subdividing may again be based upon social class levels, for reasons which will be discussed later. More important, however, a continuing increase in numbers tends to make further changes in the meaning and forms of ritual, for its meaning must come to cover more widely varying needs, and its forms become differentiated from subgroup to subgroup.

THE RITUAL

I. Becoming a Débutante

Preparation. Although the training of a pre-débutante is no longer a conscious discipline of learning the skills of ladyhood from governess, tutor, dancing master, and Mademoiselle, the ceremony of the début is nevertheless a rite which involves long preparation according to a fairly well-defined system. It is not an "event" which parents suddenly decide to "give." The preparation for the introduction into society is a way of living and begins almost with the birth of the child. The pre-débutante must grow up in a débutante-producing environment.

If her parents have assured social standing, she will form her friendships with the children of her parents' friends and do the same things they do. She will go to the private kindergartens, pre-schools, and schools where they go. If her parents' standing is doubtful, but they are financially able to compete, she may be sent to those same kindergartens and schools, where the establishment of early and continued friendships with the accepted children will tend to make her an integral part of the whole pre-débutante group and inseparable from them when the time for their common introduction season arrives. They grow up together "knowing the ropes" and accepted as débutante material.

A large part of the necessity for early association with the group lies in the learning of the tools, techniques, customs, and manners of that group so intimately that they are worn becomingly and naturally. The manner of a group is largely intangible and indescribable, but certain characteristics are marked and obvious. This is the world of careful attention to "correct" dress (even though in certain groups that may mean carefully looking a little careless), of familiarity with certain forms of etiquette and social custom, of being on speaking terms with sailing, swimming, tennis, bridge, horseback riding, ballroom dancing, pedigreed animal breeding, and of facile social conversation. Easy familiarity with the ways of the group marks the wholly acceptable girl, and this is seldom acquired except in a process of slow and continuous living with them. Though Kitty Foyle studied the Social Register and followed the doings of the Main Line with some passion, she could not even speak their language when she gained entrée into one of these homes.

It is partly for this reason that the selection of a neighborhood in which to live is an important item in the value scheme of parents who wish to launch a daughter socially. If funds are restricted, it is better by far to live in the gate house of an estate in a "good" neighborhood than to remain in a middle-class district. This is not so consciously class-conscious as it appears at first sight. The fact is that there must be freedom of interaction between girls who are to be friends together. Proximity of homes is important, but reasonable similarity is more important. If the difference is too great, there is apt to be self-consciousness in the interaction process. Actually, if a youngster accepts invitations freely, but hesitates to return them, she has already broken the most stringent rule of upper-class society and has cut herself off from the most natural channel of preparation.

Eligibility. Theoretically, any girl may become a débutante. This is accomplished by sending in her name to be put in Dreka's Book, the débutante list for her specific season, by selecting a date for the introduction party and sending out invitations. Actually, this is theory in its most abstract form. If the débutante crowd should not attend her party or extend invitations to the young bud for their own parties, the girl may have "come out" but she is a débutante in name only. For, as has been stated, being a débutante means being a *functioning* member of a special social group. Failure is heartbreak, for it is very public, and it has occurred. Therefore the parents of a girl who is not fairly sure of minimum acceptance must weigh the risks. They will very probably receive good advice from a Director of Débutante Parties not to attempt the début, or a flat refusal from her to take charge of the party.

Family background is of prime importance, both as to family history and occupation. Financial standing has great significance. Conduct and character are factors also. But all these values are weighted and dependent upon each other. A girl whose family is in the Social Register will be an accepted and feted débutante though she indulge in behavior which would automatically cut off her less fortunate competitors. Money has earned for many girls what their parents' dubious social status could not, but it does not win acceptability in the face of ignominious behavior. Private school attendance is essential. Should the parents of a young girl suddenly find their financial status and social prestige improving and wish to enter their child late in the desired circle, their first step would be to send her to a select private school. Once there, if the other factors are favorable, she is on her own to win the acceptance of her classmates. This game, again, reduces itself to how quickly she is able, without the long association-preparation, to adopt their form of group life convincingly. On the other hand, should a family with a daughter already accepted as a potential débutante suffer financial reverses and be forced to take their girl out of the private school, she may still make her début with her clique, provided she maintains her contacts with it. To lose touch with them in favor of her new group spells defeat.[5]

Obviously, then, *any* girl cannot become a débutante in the full meaning of the term. The girls who gain entrée to this guarded social circle must know the prerequisites and fulfill them, just as definitely as does a pledge of a Greek

[5] For an interesting study of factors in upper-class eligibility, see David L. and Mary A. Hatch, "Criteria of Social Status as Derived from Marriage Announcements in the *New York Times*," *American Sociological Review*, August 1947, pp. 396-403.

letter fraternity or a petitioning member of a restricted club.

The Final Stages. In the last years of high school there emerges a fairly definite sub-deb group, currently known in Philadelphia as "the soda-pop set." These young girls are spotted as the potential débutantes of their graduation year. In a less organized, but mimicking fashion, they commence their own little social whirl similar to the back-and-forth entertaining of their already introduced sisters. They are trying out their wings, and they feel the first flutterings of accomplishment as their names begin to appear in the society columns of the local newspapers. From this group will come the initiates for the ritual of the introduction.

II. The Introduction: Separation

During the spring vacation from school in the senior year, the first formal ceremony of separation occurs for the girls about to become débutantes. This is the Junior Bal Masqué, given each year for charity, the symbol that a new season has begun. Tickets are issued by invitation only, thus restricting participation to the débutantes of the new season, to those of the two past seasons, and to young men congenial to these girls. A list of the girls who have entered their names in Dreka's Book (a book compiled and in the keeping of a respected Philadelphia stationery firm) is printed in the newspaper as a public sign that this season belongs to them exclusively. Thus they are officially set apart as a new group: an age and social-class separation.

The second ceremony, one that marks the separation from their childhood situation, is an individual ceremony, the formal introduction party. This occurs after the girls have graduated from high school, several months after the Junior Bal Masqué, and when they are about seventeen or eighteen years old. Although a whole year is offered them in which to give the introduction party, June is by far the most popular month. The desire to attain this social and chronological separation at the symbolic moment enters into this choice, as well as does the fact that many of the girls go away from the city during the summer months, and about nine out of ten now go to college in the fall. A second clustering of parties occurs at Christmas vacation, and others are scattered over week-ends during the college year.

The introduction ceremony formerly consisted of two parties: a tea, at which the girl's parents presented her to their friends, and a dance or dinner dance for presentation to the girl's contemporaries. This form is still kept when advisable. But, with the extension of the débutante list, the custom has come to be changed frequently to a choice of one of these parties. If finances are limited, it is better to give one successful party than two less significant ones. The parent generation has a preference for the tea, while the girls usually prefer the greater fun of the dance. The parties vary considerably in size and quality, depending upon both the tastes of the individual families and their financial affluence. The differences range from one small and modest tea to a large and magnificent tea and ball. But these differences, which occur for the most part on a financial-class basis, are differences in degree only. The form of party given, the procedures and techniques for making it a success are set and the same for all girls of all families.

The date for a girl's introduction party may be selected years before her graduation or close upon it. The services of a Director of Débutante Parties are needed to help choose these dates, so that there may not be conflicts during the season. Her further services, as the party date approaches, are indispensable. In a sense, her role in this rite of passage is the closest modern counterpart of the role of the tribal elder or high priest in more primitive sacred ceremonies, for she holds the key to the ritual book of knowledge and is the coördinator for the group. She and her staff take over all the essential, rigid details of the ceremonies, and she acts as personal counselor when she deems it necessary. Débutantes have described the relationship between them and the Director of their party at this time as rather close, permeating, and dependent. One of them remarked confidently, "If Mrs. X. once takes hold of you, you are made."

Whatever size and form of party is chosen, it is a spectacular celebration of its kind. It is announced beforehand in the society columns of the press and, if worthy of such attention, is described therein the day following it. The parents "receive" and introduce their daughter to the guests, who are carefully chosen with the help of the Director. The stage is set for the girl to appear dressed in her most formal best, looking her loveliest, and surrounded by flowers, family, friends, and young men. Often she is pictured in the newspapers in her finery amidst the flowers. She herself is the center of attention during this ceremony, which impresses upon her elders and friends that she is no longer a little high school girl but a young member of adult, select society and is now individually marked as one of the girls to whom this season belongs.

One of the more important parts of the introduction ball is the selection of guests, and particularly of the young men guests. In order for such a dance to be successful, there should be an ample excess of boys over girls—two boys for every girl being a safe ratio. These boys must be conscientious in fulfilling their obligations, for a successful dance is one at which every girl can enjoy herself and no girl becomes a wallflower. The débutante herself must be permitted a real show of popularity. This means, of course, that the boys must understand this sort of party and assume a responsibility for its success, rather than merely coming to have a good time with the girls of their choice. They must also be "nice" boys, in that, if they behave themselves unbecomingly, they reflect upon their hostess at an extremely critical and public period of her social life. Furthermore, they must be eligible boys, for they are the prospective escorts for this season of intensive social interaction, and therefore possible suitors or husbands. Since, at some of the débutante balls as many as two hundred and fifty boy guests are needed, it becomes impossible for a girl and her family to select them alone, for the simple reason that they are not acquainted with so many, of such a caliber. Here the Director of Débutante Parties fills an extremely important need. In her office there is kept a "boys' list," from which the girl may select her guests, with the aid of the Director. To keep this list up to date, cards are sent out from her office each year to prospective members of it. They must be boys who went to good schools, have good families, and are themselves respectable. The ones who are invited to the parties are carefully observed. If they drink too much, or do not dance with their hostesses, or accept invitations but do not come, or engage in unseemly behavior, or shirk their normal social responsibilities, they are taken off the boys' list. In this way a girl's parent may be reasonably sure that the goal of letting youth have its fling in a right way is protected. The emphasis upon this list and the care with which it is restricted is extremely significant as a tool in restrictive class separation.

III. The Season: Transition

Though the introduction party is the greatest single event for the individual girl, it is but a part of her débutante career. A whole year is given to her for her season, a definitely time-delimited period of transition between childhood and young adulthood. This season consists of a highly publicized year of intensive and exaggerated interaction within the débutante group, and one which accentuates the ways in which this group will live in times of subsequent equilibrium. The crowd runs around together to sports activities, public functions, charity events, and exchanges parties in honor of one another. The press follows them, and the general public watches them with interest—both their in-group and their out-group public.

At least three selective processes appear during this deliberately intensified period. They are, in a way, as selective as the processes in primitive puberty rituals which train a specific individual for whatever adult role he seems equipped, in that these begin to reveal the particular niche into which each débutante will fit. They are the processes of achieving (a) the individual's status in her group, (b) her placement in a sub-group, and (c) her status with the opposite sex.

(a) Once débutantehood is attained, the débutante must make her place in her group. Formerly adults were exceedingly influential in determining this place. Parents were direct and powerful in choosing and evaluating the companions of their daughters. They planned the parties and had final word on the guest list. This meant that a girl's popularity during the season depended a great deal on personality traits valued by the parent generation. And quite naturally it resulted in some deference on the part of the girls toward the behavior and qualities respected by the older generation. Emily Post writes "In Confidence to a Débutante" that a girl at her début should be very careful lest in her excitement at being with her young friends and in the limelight she neglect her duties as hostess toward the older guests. If she overlooks "Mr. and Mrs. Worldly" she may wonder why only she of all her crowd is not subsequently invited to "Great Estates." The number of times she is entertained, or a guest of honor, determines the frequency with which she is seen, the number of people who meet her, and how often her name appears upon the society pages. Therefore courtesy to, and the appearance of genuine interest in, the "Mr. and Mrs. Worldlys" was of great importance in seeking high rank among débutantes. The great survival value of this particular mode of behavior seems to be proved by the gracious bearing toward their elders that was usually visible in the popular girls of this particular set.

At the present time, however, the general opinion is that the parent generation has no direct influence at all in determining débutante status in her crowd. For the most part, the girls invite to their parties whomever they please (from a limited selection, of course), and in turn make their own decisions as to what parties they will and will not attend. There is suggestion, but little pressure, at home about who is a suitable companion and who is not. The result is that popularity is determined almost wholly by the young group itself and by their values. The elusive trait called "charm" still wins the day. But charm changes its meaning. The older generation is apt to stress background, conservatism, conformance, and the visible forms of gentle social etiquette. The younger generation values sportsmanship, energy, initiative, physical attractiveness, and independent spirit. A girl who is "good looking and good fun" is "charming" in the eyes of her peers. This makes for greater democracy of opportunity within the group, for the girl is on her own with her contemporaries. It also brings a rather general criticism from the elder public about bad manners and lack of consideration on the part of popular members of the young social set. In this situation, the role of the Director in advising an individual for or against entering the circle and in restricting the girl and boy lists with great care becomes increasingly important, for it is one remaining weight the parent generation holds to balance the freedom of youthful choice within the group.

(b) A second selective process appears with the extension of the débutante list. This is the individual's placement within a subgroup and is a development too recent to admit of rigid conclusions. However, during the season, the girls usually find their own social level. Again, it is based upon a financial, social-class, way-of-life status. Though they may entertain the whole set at a large party, the frequent activities during the season divide into groups of individuals who go to the same clubs, participate in the same kinds of sports, live in similar communities, go to the same resorts. There will be a Bar Harbor and a Newport set, and New Jersey resort sets. One débutante spoke of a Chestnut Hill set and a Main Line set (two adjacent Philadelphia suburban communities, but of separate tradition). Naturally the friendships formed in these smaller groups prove of greater influence and are more lasting. Time and further increase in number of débutantes will tell more concretely the bases of division and how free will be the mobility across these divisions.

(c) A third selective process grows out of establishing status with peers of the opposite sex. A minimum popularity with young men is still a practical necessity. There are times when a girl must have an escort. And a girl, though she may be admired by all her sister debs and held up as a model by her elders, if she must acquire her escorts from other girls and constantly be a wallflower at dances, carries a heartbreaking burden which can make her whole season a personal failure. She is, at least partially, a recognized social failure, too, because for full, ideal functioning in the group, she should have a status of marriageability within it.

All these factors and others go into making up the débutante hierarchy which begins to emerge as the season progresses. The outside observer can watch it being formed by following the local Sunday Society Section. There comes to be a group of "the season's most popular debs," and there are, too, the "also rans."

IV. Privileges and Responsibilities of Membership: Assimilation

The formal mark of the débutante's assimilation into the adult social group is the Junior Bal Masqué at the end of her seaeson. Just as the former Bal Masqué had been her separation ceremony, the second one denotes the end of her transition period of débutantehood. Her younger sisters now take the stage, and she becomes an incorporated member of society. This, however, is only a symbol. The change in her life is one of degree of participation and publicity. She is *less* separated, but assimilation has been proceeding gradually. When she becomes a débutante she takes on most of the privileges and responsibilities of her group.

One set of privileges which the débutante acquires is the relative lack of restriction which comes with formal emancipation from childhood. Another set is the kind of special treatment and admiration and concession which she gains from the general public by being a recognized member of her select set. Her group in society is a group set apart. Those of the group feel set apart and those not of the group recognize its exclusiveness. Quite generally, the débutante status and all that it stands for in terms of a future way of life is looked upon with a bit of interest, envy, or admiration—if not for the status itself, then for the hold it has upon the world of privilege and pleasant living—even by those who most sneeringly denounce it.

It is in this fact that the prime responsibility of débutantehood lies. The débutante is put glaringly in the spotlight of public notice, not only as an individual making her place in her set, but as a part of the reputation of her whole group. If a débutante becomes embroiled in a public fracas, it is not only headline news, but a reflection upon her whole social set, contemporaries and elders. Conservative leaders of the group go further than this in stressing responsibility. They know that the girl who is publicly proclaimed a "socialite" is a model for many girls who would like to be. If the débutante's manners, dress, behavior, and activities are worthy, they will be imitated. If they are not, they will be copied no less closely. There is, for instance, some feeling of consternation in the group at the present time toward the behavior of privileged members who do not take seriously their responsibilities as models of American family people. The habit of these members of drifting in and out of matrimony and shifting their children from home to home is decried, because it is felt that they glamorize family instability by the very height of their status. The group, then, feels that it should not indulge in certain kinds of obvious behavior out of responsibility to themselves individually, to their own group, and also to people outside their group. This is the negative aspect of the group duty.

On the positive side, the débutante has the obligation to perform useful service. The ideal is that this privileged girl will never have the physically hard and time-consuming tasks visited upon other women. If she leads a negatively useless and wasteful life she is cited as an example of what many people like to think is characteristic of a privileged class. Therefore, during the season, the débutante is already initiated into social services of many kinds as a beginning of what is firmly expected of her throughout her adult life in the group.

The Junior League. An organization which emphasizes the responsibility of the débutante is the Junior League. This is a select circle within a select circle and is a goal for débutante achievement. In primitive societies, it has been stated, "Where individuals are to occupy positions as leaders within a group, the length of the Rite of Passage is ordinarily greater, and its elaborateness in symbolic context and in the number of relationships involved increases markedly."[6] The Junior League is a contemporary extension of ritual to chosen, potential leaders.

A débutante can become a member of the Junior League by invitation only. She cannot here send in her name and take her chances. The purpose of the League is service, and the member must perform. The girls serve in many ways: at settlement houses, as distributors of food baskets, as models and performers at charity functions, as nurses' aides, etc. Each new season brings a new yield of workers, and older members become supervisors and officers.

Recently a provisional course in social service has been offered by the League to aspiring members. This, too, can be taken only by invitation. But it serves to widen membership, to further training, and to permit of closer scrutiny of prospective members. Those who show themselves of doubtful value to this very select group will not be able to pass the provisional course. But the gaining of membership in the Junior League is to the public a signal of assimilation. The girl who becomes a member of the Junior League has passed with a good grade her transition test in changing from a high school child to what is her group's ideal of a worthy functioning member of society.

HOW IMPORTANT ARE RITES OF PASSAGE?

A final suggestion which concerns the significance of rites of passage in the development of modern youth might be in order at this point. Such rites are largely absent in our society, and there are those who accept and approve this change as in keeping with the spirit of democracy. To many persons, lack of the ceremonial is interpreted as evidence of democracy. On the other hand, there are those who regard

[6] E. D. Chapple and C. S. Coon, *Principles of Anthropology.* New York: Henry Holt and Co., 1942, pp. 504-505.

such lack as but an index of a cheap and gaudy informality in our social life.

The age-old emphasis upon such rites raises at least a presumption in their favor, and suggests the desirability of a more serious study of the significance of those few that persist in modern culture and, possibly, a more careful consideration of the establishment of additional ones. For youth is a confused period in our society. At least some of its problems grow out of the relative abruptness of change from one age category to another. There is, for example, the change from a full-time school status at ages 16 to 18 to full-time employment in the world of industry. Millions of young people have the status of dependent children, living the sheltered life of the school, up to a given day, and then, without the benefit of a leave by your grace, are catapulted into the naked realities of the workaday world. Have past cultures which marked such changes with appropriate ceremonies of due formality been but idly playful, or are we today remiss in the casual indifference wherewith we regard such abrupt changes? Could the school commencement be made to serve in a more constructive and impressive capacity? Certainly the large-scale commencement exercises at which even the names of the graduates are considered too numerous to be read are a sorry substitute.

Another group of problems of modern youth grow out of the difference between the physical passage from childhood to maturity and the social transfer of the child to the status of adult. This problem does not arise in other societies which observe rites to signalize the outstanding landmarks in the life of the individual. In our society, the lack of such rites, combined with the high standards of compulsory school attendance and social protection, results in a situation in which grown young people retain the legal status of children long after they have become adults in other respects.

Consider, for example, the young man who lives at home while attending the nearby university. He may be treated as a child by his parents, then steps into an automobile where, as a responsible adult, he drives 160 horse power to the campus through hazardous traffic. He goes to class where he may be regarded as, and act like, a callow youth, only to serve later in the day as president of the student council. There are states where, although he has had two years of war service and a wound stripe, he may be under the jurisdiction of the juvenile court if he commits a criminal act. There are states where a girl may marry, have a child, be divorced, and yet, if she has sex relations with a man outside of the accepted social pattern and before a given age, the man will be guilty of contributing to the delinquency of a minor! When does the child become an adult? Have other cultures been wiser in commemorating the transfer with due solemnity? Rites of passage may be a more important subject for child development than has thus far been recognized.

SUMMARY

1. The contemporary American introduction into society conforms fundamentally to the concept "Rite of Passage" as described by Van Gennep. It is a framework of techniques, set up by the elders of a social group and handed down from generation to generation. Its purpose is the facilitating of the individual's passage from one life situation to another at a critical period of life and in a socially approved way. It adheres to the consecutive stages of separation, transition, and assimilation, with special ceremonies to mark each stage. It is a period of training and selection, and its goal is conservation of the best interests and values of the group.

2. A comparison of contemporary rite of passage with the more familiar primitive rites gives indications of the

effect of modern urban civilization on ritual itself. In stable, pre-civilized society, ritual is rigid and pervasive, changing slowly and often remaining to long outlive its first usefulness, sometimes retarding change or causing conflict and "cultural lag," but reinforcing individual stability. In this current rite of the début, it is seen that rapid social change has made alterations in the ritual within a generation or two, and has left the rites in a transitional stage at the present time. The fundamental structure remains as a felt need. But within that structure the signs of struggle between the "presiding elders" and the new generation for modification in forms more suitable to their present demands are clearly visible. Thus this ritual, which grows out of the way, values, and needs of social life, takes on flexibility as the social life changes rapidly. Specific studies of other contemporary rituals would help to answer the question whether, with ritual, adaptability means survival in a more adequate form, or whether, as is usually assumed, ritualism necessarily dies out with quick social change, and furthers a process of disorganization by its absence.

CHAPTER XV

The Family and the Child
Concluding Comments

Light—more light.—GOETHE

FOR more than the span of a generation, I have been concerned with the family and its relation to the personality development of its members. Surveying the work of the years, my own thinking, and that of other persons whose mental processes I respect, two fundamental problems persist to challenge me. One of these is the question of the relative importance of the family, both in degree and in point of time. How important is the family, and when is its role most effective? A second question is less specific but more comprehensive: what is the overall problem to which family research should devote itself? This concluding chapter presents some observations bearing on theses two points.

THE ROLE OF THE FAMILY

A Prevailing Theory. For a number of years, there has existed a group of students of human behavior who have insisted that the patterns of personality are formed in the first few years of life, and that the family is the chief architect in this process. Some of these students are psychiatrists who, on the basis of observations that many mental problems can be traced back to early child experiences, concluded that the entire personality took definite form during those years. Similarly, there have been anthropologists who, seeing the differences in child-rearing practices among cultural groups they studied, similarly concluded that the different behavior patterns of peoples were due to what happened during the first few years. Since most of the cultures they studied were primitive, with child rearing confined to the first few years, the conclusion seemed inevitable. Likewise, selected sociologists, studying personality differences in contemporary society, accounted for them on the basis of observable differences of child rearing in the home.

An old story, imputed to the Jesuit order, may be recalled as representative of this point of view: "Give me a child until he is seven, and it does not matter who has him after that." Or there is the oft-told story, probably apocryphal, of the great psychiatrist who was approached by a mother, to take in charge the education of her child. "And how old is your child?" asked the great man. "He is just six," beamed the mother. "Too bad, too bad," sighed the psychiatrist, "at six his education has been completed."

Unfortunately this notion has not been confined to academicians, but has become current coin in the parental realm, so that many parents believe that their important responsibilities are confined to the first five or six years of the child's life. As a result, some of these parents become so apprehensive lest they traumatize their children during these years that they develop neuroses themselves, and perhaps transfer them to their children; while other parents heave a sigh of relief when they come to the child's sixth birthday, believing that they have now done their full duty, and that nothing is of any real importance from then on.

Objections to the Theory. This theory, in spite of its widespread appeal and acceptance, is wholly untenable to me, and for a number of reasons. First of all, such a conclusion rests upon no organized body of reputable evidence. No systematic study has ever been made of the rates of personality development and changes at different periods or stages in the life cycle; it is merely an assumption which has been made or implied by students of behavior, some of whom have prestige in their respective fields. And this is perhaps the place to remind the lay, and scientific, reader that science operates often on the basis of prestige rather than of proof. Someone of prestige in a given field of science spins a theory; it is interesting and comes to be accepted. Quoting the source then becomes a mark of erudition. Lesser lights trim their wicks after the manner of greater lights, with the overall result that the theory, often erroneous, comes to be standardized. Standardized error is the plague of much textbook writing; theories that have been empirically refuted a decade ago continue to be cited because of the apparent prestige of the source.

Second, the theory of personality fixation during infancy is incompatible with the bases upon which it rests. One such basis is the plasticity of human nature. The first few years are so important, we are told, because human nature is so modifiable. Does this modifiability, then, stop at the age of six or seven? Does it not remain plastic, perhaps equally so, for a longer period? Perhaps for life? If what other people do to us molds us so completely before six, why does it not mold us even more at sixteen or twenty-six, when we can understand more completely what others are doing to us, and when we are more exposed to them? Is there any body of data to show that human nature is less plastic at twelve than at six?

Another basis upon which current personality studies rest is the role of the group in the determination of behavior patterns. If this is true, then obviously groups do not cease operating at age six, eight, ten, or even twelve. Group life continues for most of us throughout the life span—the play group of childhood becomes the recreational group of adolescence and adulthood, the school group gives way to the work group, the college fraternity is followed by the Masonic order or other fraternal group. Groups change in name, in size, in characteristics, in specific purpose, but group life as such continues throughout life. What groups do for children they do for adults, and it would be folly to say that one group is of exclusive importance, and in one given period of life.

Again, it is commonly agreed that culture is a determining factor in the development of personality. Why, then, assume that culture plays its primary role during those years when the child is least able to absorb the surrounding culture? Moreover, culture changes as the person ages. It changes because culture changes in course of time; often very rapidly. The child whose first six years were spent in the depression thirties found life different in many respects after World War II. Moreover, our cultural milieu changes because we change our habitat—from rural Tennessee to Nuremberg, Germany; from Muncie, Indiana, to Korea; from living among North Carolina Baptists to residence among Irish Catholics in South Philadelphia. As our cultural settings change, so must our adjustments, our behavior patterns, our values, all those things which we so glibly insist that culture determines. Culture is a highly changeable factor; to attribute any importance to its role in the determination of personality is to acknowledge the latter's corresponding changing nature.

Fourth, this theory denies the role of the learning and training process. The concept of behavior as the result of the learning process disposes once and for all of the idea that behavior is a finality at any stage, age, or phase of development. Just as one goes on learning all through life, so one's behavior patterns are in constant state of modification. To argue differently is to deny the possibility of all training programs for the young, in civil or in military life; to reject the pretenses of all curative work, as in the case of delinquents or neurotics; or to dismiss the reeducative treatments offered by psychiatrists to their patients. All of these are of no avail; they are too late, the die has been cast. The hopes of religious conversion, psychiatric treatment, psychoanalytic analysis, rehabilitative work in all its forms, are dismissed as pleasant fictions. Personality is not a process: it is the coalesced total of a series of infantile episodes.

One is tempted almost to think of this theory of the early fixation of personality formation as an illustration of the good old army game of passing the buck. Somewhere, from the dim past, I recall the following lincs, which seem to illustrate the point.

WHICH ONE?

THE COLLEGE PRESIDENT—
Such rawness in a student is a shame
But lack of preparation is to blame.

HIGH SCHOOL PRINCIPAL—
Good heavens, what crudity, the boy's a fool!
The fault of course is with the Grammar School.

GRAMMAR SCHOOL PRINCIPAL—
Oh, that from such a dunce I might be spared!
They send them up to me so unprepared.

PRIMARY PRINCIPAL—
Poor kindergarten block-head! And they call
That preparation! Worse than none at all.

KINDERGARTEN TEACHER—
Never such lack of training did I see!
What sort of person can the mother be?

MOTHER—
You stupid child—but then you're not to blame,
Your father's family are all the same.
Shall Father in his own defense be heard?
NO! let the mother have the final word.

A Suggested Revision. In rejecting the theory of the

childhood fixation of personality, I do not wish to minimize the role of family factors. The thesis I wish to present may well imply its even greater importance, for the heart of the contention is that the family, like a great many other determinants of behavior, operates throughout one's entire life. Family factors, like old soldiers, never die; unlike them, they do not even fade away.

To clarify my thesis, it seems necessary to emphasize that personality is never a fixed pattern, but a process which continues throughout life. In this never-ending process, early family influences are reappearing constantly, to be revalued in the light of an accumulating experience. Instead of an overwhelming emphasis upon childhood experiences per se, one needs to realize that subsequent experiences determine the importance of these early activities, and that the individual is the result of what adolescence, youth, and adulthood do to childhood experiences.[1]

It is my further contention that the influence of parents tends to reach its highest point, not in the child's first years, but when the child passes through the stages of development that the parent did when the child knew him. True, we come to know our parents when we are very young, but not really as persons: only as our need of them dictates. We think of them as providers, disciplinarians, counselors, comforters, protectors, but seldom, if ever, as persons with a life and problems of their own. It is later, when we marry and become parents, that we think of our parents as persons like ourselves. It is then that a whole series of new parental influences manifest themselves. Confronted with the tasks of parenthood ourselves, we think of our parents as parents; we may remember how they did thus and so; we decide perhaps that they were good and wise parents after all, to be emulated in turn; or that they were weak, or unjust, or

[1] Lawrence G. Brown, *Social Pathology*. New York: F. S. Crofts and Co., 1942, p. 11.

unreasonable, whose example is now to be eschewed. But even here we may understand a little more clearly the how and the why of the weakness or unfairness.

From then on we return home in memory, over and over again, with the full contriteness of the prodigal son. One's conversation reveals the return, and its spirit. "I remember what my father did when we were small." "My father always said to us children." "I'll never forget my father the day I played truant" (this on the day when your own son was truant). "My mother used to be so tired at night." "I didn't understand why my father was so opposed to—, but I do now." "I see now that my mother was right."

And thus it comes about that the adolescent boy, in constant rebellion against his father, accepts him as a model twenty years later; and the daughter, once so sure of her mother's unreasonableness, visits "grandmother" most every day, for comfort and counsel. Perhaps Santayana, the philosopher, has caught the full meaning of this when he writes:

> It is not only the open prodigal that returns repentant: daily and without acknowledgment, in a thousand small ways, the younger generation falls gradually back into the habits and views of the elder, ready to take the old man's place even before death has mercifully removed him. . . . Each member of a family is an exemplar, an indelible memory, a secret influence on all the rest; and in burying the father the children measure their own span, feel their own errors and insecurity, and see for the nonce how much they too are pilgrims and helpless strangers in this world.[2]

THE POINT OF HIGHEST RETURN

When I was a young instructor the social sciences were not as highly specialized as they now are, and I found myself a one-man department teaching Sociology, Economics, and Government. This presented its own difficulties, but

[2] George Santayana, *Dominations and Powers.* New York: Charles P. Scribner's Sons, 1951, pp. 69-70.

many of its effects were salutary because the experience kept me from walking prematurely the tight-rope of narrow specialization. One specific point in this early teaching experience was the instruction of the youth in the Law of Diminishing Returns in Economics. As then taught, this law held that, after a given point has been reached in the cultivation of an acre of land or the exploitation of a mine, increased applications of capital and labor yield less than proportionate returns, it being understood, of course, that no important change is made in the method of cultivation or exploitation.

Its application in various areas, chiefly economic, has shown its comprehensive application. Consider, for example, the development of large office buildings in downtown metropolitan areas. Buildings can be pushed higher almost without limit in these days of steel construction, yet at some time the stage is reached where the gain from additions to the structure begins to diminish, and where the construction of another building on a new site becomes a more profitable venture. This point may be at one place in an office building, at another in a mercantile establishment, and at still another in an apartment house, but in all cases there is eventually that given point. Similar application of the law is reported in cases of hospital and hotel administration.

This law has haunted me, in one way or another, for years. Far from being confined to the accountancy of economic production, I am convinced that it has universal application, and that in every aspect of life there is some optimum, or point of highest return. Gradually I have come to reject the phrase *law of diminishing returns* as being a negative concept, and re-thought it in positive terms of the problem of the point of highest returns. What is the point of highest returns in various aspects of human life? Of social relationships? Of community and national organization? Can these points be determined by human intelligence or must life forever be conceived of as an experiment performed upon man rather than by man?

Students of population have come to recognize the meaning of this in their concept of optimum population. By this concept is meant a population of the size best suited to achieve some end or purpose. Manifestly, this end or purpose may vary from one age to another and one society to another. In modern times it is concerned primarily in economic terms, so that the term *optimum population,* as currently used, means "that there is a certain size of population which is best fitted to secure the maximum economic returns per head from a given body of natural resources under a given system of production, or perhaps better, under a given type of social and economic organization."[3]

Quite recently, the President's Materials Policy Commission has made public a report called "Resources for Freedom." This report emphasizes the basic significance of natural resources in the national welfare and points out that sometime during the 1940's the United States passed this point of highest return in regard to its basic resources. This does not mean that we are facing absolute shortages of important materials, but that we do face "the more insidious prospect of remorselessly rising costs."[4]

This concept has equal applicability in the field of family life and child development. What is the optimum size for the family? Since the time of the ancient Greeks, man has been interested in the relationship between size of a group and the effective life of its members. The Greek concept of the city-state represented their judgment of the optimum compromise between the requirements of social order and individual liberty. Plato's ideal city was to be limited to 5,040 free citizens, plus their families and their slaves.

[3] Warren S. Thompson, *Population Problems.* New York: McGraw-Hill Book Co., 1930, p. 393.
[4] *Life,* editorial, "U. S. Ends an Economic Era," June 30, 1952, p. 18.

Aristotle agreed that there was an optimum size, believed that it was larger than Plato estimated, but thought the number should be fixed by experience.

Applying this same thought to the family, what is its size of highest return? For husband-wife relationships? For the optimum development of its child members? How does this size vary from one economic and/or social class to another? Does it vary from one occupation to another, and with variations in the working span at different occupational levels?

What is the maximum spatial area that is desirable for a family of this size? A preceding chapter has suggested a spatial index for family interaction. Is this measure satisfactory, or should some other one be devised? Should such measure, whatever it might be, vary on the basis of selected differences among families? Is the maximum at one place for persons doing mental work, and at another for those engaged in more arduous physical tasks?

What degree of cultural difference between parents is most desirable? For husband-wife relationships? For child development? What elements in the culture should differ? Are differences in religious background more important than educational ones? Or national origin ones? Are cultural differences involving the more intimate areas of life, such as patterns of sexual behavior, more important than those that are more overt and obvious?

What is the optimum age for marriage? Of men? Of women? What age combinations constitute the point of highest return? What age differentials between husband and wife make most for domestic happiness? For parental responsibility? What are the most desirable ages for parenthood? Studies of infant mortality have identified the age of mother making for the lowest death rate among children. Can similarly inspired studies determine the ages for most effective motherhood? For optimum exercise of fatherhood?

These are very basic questions. They are of the most fundamental importance. Perhaps they surpass in importance any problems to which research in the family field has devoted itself. Personally, I am inclined to believe this. At any rate, they pose problems which can be dealt with by modern techniques of research. Once sociologists will cease to make laws and seek to discover them; once large foundations will cease to finance projects designed to save mankind in six easy lessons, and support efforts to understand the processes of human development—advances will be possible in answering the questions that have been raised. To one who sees the appropriation of billions of dollars to develop the maximum in methods to destroy the human race, is it too idle to dream of what efforts of lesser scope might do in determining the points of highest return in family living?

Subject Index

Index of Authors